THE TYNE BRIDGE

PAUL BROWN

The Tyne Bridge

Icon of North-East England

HURST & COMPANY, LONDON

First published in the United Kingdom in 2022 by
C. Hurst & Co. (Publishers) Ltd.,
New Wing, Somerset House, Strand,
London, WC2R 1LA
© Paul Brown, 2022
All rights reserved.
Printed in Great Britain by Bell and Bain Ltd, Glasgow

The right of Paul Brown to be identified as the author of
this publication is asserted by him in accordance with the
Copyright, Designs and Patents Act, 1988.

A Cataloguing-in-Publication data record for this book
is available from the British Library.

ISBN: 9781787387935

This book is printed using paper from registered sustainable
and managed sources.

www.hurstpublishers.com

CONTENTS

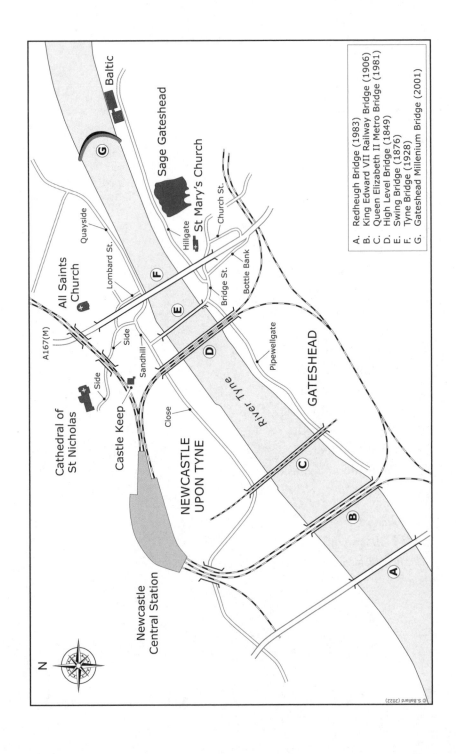

N

Newcastle
Central Station

Cathedral of
St Nicholas

NEWCASTLE
UPON TYNE

Castle Keep

A167(M)

Side

Side

Sandhill

Close

All Saints
Church

Lombard St.

Quayside

Baltic

Sage Gateshead

St Mary's Church

Hillgate

Church St.

Bridge St.

Bottle Bank

River Tyne

Pipewellgate

GATESHEAD

A. Redheugh Bridge (1983)
B. King Edward VII Railway Bridge (1906)
C. Queen Elizabeth II Metro Bridge (1981)
D. High Level Bridge (1849)
E. Swing Bridge (1876)
F. Tyne Bridge (1928)
G. Gateshead Millenium Bridge (2001)

© S.Ballard (2022)

"It's cold up there in summer,
It's like sittin' inside a fridge,
But I wish I was on the Quayside,
Lookin' at the owld Tyne Bridge."

Home Newcastle by Busker (Ronnie Lambert, 1981).[1]

CHRONOLOGY

c122   Roman Pons Aelius Bridge built
c1250   Medieval Old Tyne Bridge built
1771   Old Tyne Bridge destroyed in Great Flood
1781   Georgian Tyne Bridge opens
1849   High Level Bridge opens
1871   First Redheugh Bridge opens
1876   Swing Bridge opens
1901   Second Redheugh Bridge opens
1906   King Edward VII Railway Bridge opens
1922   Thomas Webster proposes new Tyne Bridge
1923   Stephen Easten appointed Lord Mayor of Newcastle
1924   Bridge Committee forms and Dorman Long wins contract
1925   Surveys conducted and work officially begins on 1 July
1926   Caissons sunk and foundations built
1927   Approach spans built and arch takes shape
1928   Arch closed on 25 February, official opening on 10 October
1929   Tyne Bridge completed on 27 March
1981   Queen Elizabeth II Metro Bridge opens
1983   Third Redheugh Bridge opens
2001   Gateshead Millennium Bridge opens

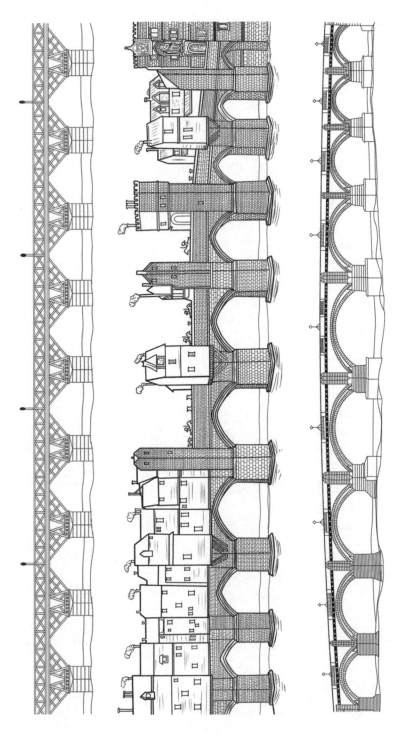

A: Old Tyne Bridges: Roman Pons Aelius Bridge; Medieval Old Tyne Bridge; Georgian Tyne Bridge

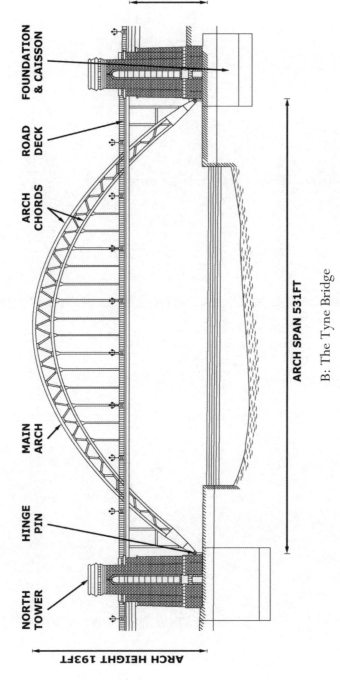

B: The Tyne Bridge

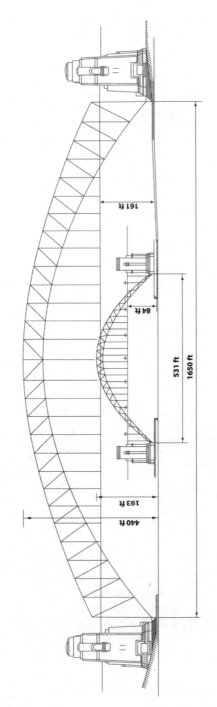

C: Comparison of Tyne Bridge and Sydney Harbour Bridge

INTRODUCTION

"Ladies and gentlemen, we are now approaching Newcastle."

The train rattles along the tracks through a warren of concrete underpasses, signal lights and overhead lines. Passengers snap shut laptops, disentangle from headphones, and scrunch discarded crisp packets into empty coffee cups.

"Change here for Sunderland, Hexham, Carlisle, Morpeth, Berwick-upon-Tweed, and connections on the Tyne and Wear Metro."

Three hours and 280 miles after leaving King's Cross, the train slows to a trundle through Gateshead, passes the Sage, the Central Bar and the Hilton Hotel, then bears north onto the High Level Bridge. We stand and stretch, put on our coats, and grab our backpacks and briefcases.

"Before you leave the train, please make sure you have all your luggage and belongings with you."

Then the train crosses the great river Tyne. Ahead are Newcastle Central Station, the Castle Keep, the Cathedral of St Nicholas. But it is to our right that attention is drawn. Heads turn, necks crane over seatbacks, and a few cameraphones are readied. And there it is, framed perfectly in the grimy widescreen of the train window: that hulking bottle-green arch.

"Please retain your tickets for the exit barriers and mind the gap between the train and the platform."

It straddles the river like its great protector, bold and strong, and a century old. It's a symbol of the ingenuity, industry and soot-blackened graft that has made Tyneside great, and it's familiar even to those who have never properly seen it. "Oh, Mum!" says a young woman on the train. "Look at the bridge!"

"Thank you for travelling with us. Our next stop is Newcastle upon Tyne."

For visitors, the first glimpse of the famous arch represents a heartening welcome to Tyneside. For locals—for Geordies—the

1

familiar sight of the Tyne Bridge, like warm and reassuring open arms, means we are home.

* * *

The Tyne Bridge is one of Britain's most iconic structures. Linking Newcastle upon Tyne and Gateshead, it has become a symbol of Tyneside, an emblem of the region's cultural identity, and a monument to the Tyne's industrial past.[1] The striking steel arch bridge is a Grade II*-listed building designated for its architectural and historical interest and its group value alongside the Tyne's other bridges, which together form a dramatic river scene. From its silhouette on bottles of Newcastle Brown Ale and its use in numerous films and TV shows to the backdrop it provides for the opening stages of the Great North Run, the Tyne Bridge is recognised around the world.[2]

This 1920s engineering marvel is what is known as a two-hinged through-arch bridge. A grand arch rises from hinges on each bank, and a suspended deck runs through the arch to span the river. Its foundations are sunk 90 feet deep into the riverbanks. The bridge's total length is 1,276 feet, meaning the Tyne Bridge is slightly longer than the Empire State Building is tall. At the time of its construction, the bridge's arch span was the longest in Britain at 531 feet— around one and a half times the length of the football pitch at nearby St James' Park. The arch rises 193 feet above the high-water level, which means it could easily accommodate Nelson's Column, even if Admiral Horatio was wearing a much taller hat.[3]

The bridge structure contains 7,122 tons of steel, equivalent in weight to around 1,500 adult male African elephants. The steel was originally painted with three coats of special paint supplied by J Dampney and Co of Gateshead. The original outer coat was Dampney's Superlative Middle Green. In more recent years, the bridge has been repainted with a British Standard green known as "Hollybush". But the Tyne Bridge has not always been green. For a couple of decades, it was blue. It requires repainting every decade— although funding issues have not always allowed that to happen.

The structure also contains more than 400,000 cubic feet of concrete, enough to fill four and a half Olympic-sized swimming pools, should that unlikely task ever be required. The bridge's concrete and steel towers rise 125 feet above the water level and are faced with Cornish granite. The towers were intended as warehouses but were never used and have remained empty for a century. They are now home to a colony of more than a thousand pairs of nesting kittiwakes—the largest inland colony in the world.

The bridge was built by Middlesbrough contractors Dorman, Long & Co and designed by engineer Ralph Freeman and the firm of Mott, Hay & Anderson. When Dorman Long won the contract to build the Tyne Bridge, they were already preparing to build the Sydney Harbour Bridge. Although the two share similar features, neither the Tyne Bridge nor the Sydney Harbour Bridge is a copy of the other. They were built concurrently, and the smaller Tyne Bridge was the first to be completed. The designs for both were inspired by an entirely different bridge—the Hell Gate Bridge in New York.

The current structure is not the first Tyne bridge. The earliest-known bridge across the Tyne gave the settlement of Newcastle its original name—*Pons Aelius*, or the Bridge of Hadrian, built by the Romans in around the year 122. From its inception, Newcastle's purpose was as a river crossing. The longest-lasting crossing was the medieval Old Tyne Bridge, a ramshackle pile of stone arches crowded with buildings, which stood for five centuries before being washed away by the Great Flood of 1771. A replacement stone arch bridge was completed in 1781, but this Georgian Tyne bridge was soon made obsolete by the relentless advance of the industrial age. The first part of this book tells the story of the Tyne Bridge's predecessors, from the Roman to Victorian eras, and the people who built and used them.

When work began on the current Tyne Bridge in 1925, there were already four bridges linking Newcastle and Gateshead—including the engineering triumphs that are Robert Stephenson's High Level Bridge and William Armstrong's Swing Bridge. However, by the 1920s, they were unsuitable for the increasing volume of traffic crossing the Tyne. But there was another reason for building the Tyne Bridge. The global recession had ravaged the industries that had made Tyneside great. Coal production had slowed, and shipbuilding orders were down. More than a third of the Tyne's shipyards had closed, and the unemployment rate on Tyneside had hit 40 per cent. The Tyne Bridge was conceived as a partial solution to this problem, acting as an employment scheme for out-of-work shipbuilders, steelworkers and coal miners to keep their families out of poverty and retain their skills in the hope that their industries would bounce back after the recession.

The bridge was a uniquely tricky project. Due to the importance of the Tyne to local industry, the construction could not interfere with river traffic. This meant no river piers, no navigational obstructions, and no construction materials raised from the river. The Tyne had to be kept completely clear. So, rather than being built up from the river, in an inventive and bold undertaking, it was built out from each bank in two halves, the weight of its arch supported by steel cables until the halves eventually met in the middle. It was a remarkable technical feat but also a great physical one. Hundreds of skilled grafters—many of them former shipbuilders—spent months climbing the growing structure, in many cases risking their lives in a remarkable high-wire balancing act that attracted crowds of awestruck spectators. The second part of the book focuses on the building of the bridge, the importance of the project, the unique difficulties it presented, and the ingenious manner in which those difficulties were overcome.

The Tyne Bridge was officially opened by King George V on 10 October 1928, although it wasn't quite finished, and work continued until March 1929. The total cost was more than £1m (equivalent to more than £64m in 2022).[4] The new bridge was hailed locally and around the globe as a great masterpiece of civil engineering, and one critic called it "a thing of beauty whose like Keats did not dream of, its splendid curve as satisfying as the dome of St Paul's".[5]

During the four years that it took for the bridge to be built, John Logie Baird transmitted the first television pictures; Charles Lindbergh flew solo over the Atlantic; and Alexander Fleming discovered penicillin. F. Scott Fitzgerald published *The Great Gatsby*; Al Jolson talked and sang in *The Jazz Singer*; and *Steamboat Willie* introduced Mickey (and Minnie) Mouse. Claude Monet, Wyatt Earp and Harry Houdini died. And Margaret Thatcher, David Attenborough and Elizabeth Alexandra Mary Windsor—later Queen Elizabeth

II—were born. On Tyneside, Newcastle Breweries launched Newcastle Brown Ale; General Strikers derailed the Flying Scotsman; and Newcastle United won the Football League. (That last achievement, in particular, seems an eon ago.)

While it was a triumph of industrial engineering, the new bridge did not bring the Tyne back to life. Work continued to disappear, shipyards continued to close, and many bridge workers went back on the dole. Within a year of the bridge's opening, much of the world slid into the Great Depression. The third part of the book looks at the bridge's century of life on the Tyne, from the aftermath of its arrival through to modern regeneration.

Today, the Tyne Bridge has become a symbol of Tyneside while the region has changed, almost unrecognisably, around it. Shipbuilding and heavy industry have disappeared, the Tyne has been dredged and cleansed. New industries—arts, technology, tourism—have arrived on the quaysides. The former Baltic Flour Mill has become a leading modern art gallery. The curved glass and steel Sage Gateshead concert venue is an eye-catching addition to the riverscape. New bars and restaurants have transformed the quaysides into leisure destinations.

New bridges now span the Tyne. The latest, the Gateshead Millennium Bridge with its "blinking eye" design, is a spectacular and popular addition to the riverscape. Gateshead also has another new icon, the Angel of the North. But neither have eclipsed the Tyne Bridge in the hearts of locals or visitors. Tyneside has become a tourist destination, and the bridge has become a selfie-friendly photo backdrop for the Instagram age. Each year, as more than 50,000 Great North Runners make their way across it on their way from Newcastle to South Shields and the Red Arrows display team swoops in formation overhead, the Tyne Bridge reminds viewers worldwide of the proud achievements of Tyneside.

This book is a celebration of the Tyne Bridge and everything that makes it special. It is not an architectural or engineering study. The story of a bridge is really the story of the people who build it and use it. Who walk across it, drive across it, ride across it. Who gaze upon it, photograph it, write about it, draw or paint it, sing about it. The people who give it life. So this book is a tribute to the ingenuity and skill of the men and women who built an engineering marvel. It reclaims the forgotten history of the bridge and its pre-decessors that crossed the Tyne and explores what the Tyne Bridge means to the people of the North East and why it has such a deep connection with those who live here.

For Geordies, the Tyne Bridge is "Wor Bridge". It symbolises who we are. All great bridges are icons of their towns or cities: the Brooklyn Bridge in New York, the Golden Gate Bridge in San Francisco, Tower Bridge in London... and of course the Sydney Harbour Bridge. The Tyne Bridge stands among them as one of the world's great bridges, and as the indisputable symbol of North-East England.

1

PONS AELIUS

The Reverend Doctor John Collingwood Bruce was standing by the remnants of a dismantled bridge pier midstream in the River Tyne, which flowed by like a never-ending pour from a bottomless bottle of Newcastle Brown Ale. On the steep north bank was the grand industrial town of Newcastle upon Tyne, its splendid buildings and sweeping streets soot-blackened by centuries of tough graft. To the south was Gateshead, another hardy and historic Tyneside town, its bulging population driven by the advance of industry. Dr Bruce (as he was commonly known) was here to uncover the secrets of a long-forgotten bridge across the Tyne—a crossing that could be considered the first Tyne Bridge. What he found would tell us much about the origins of Tyneside and how it came to be defined by its bridges. But Bruce's Tyneside was not the place we know today. Our Tyne Bridge did not yet exist. To place ourselves alongside him, we need to strip away much of what we know about Newcastle and Gateshead's famous modern riverscape and return to a Victorian era of coal, ships and steam power.

It was March 1872, more than fifty years before the construction of the current Tyne Bridge. Work was underway to build the hydraulic Swing Bridge. It was being built on the site of the Georgian Tyne Bridge, the previous crossing, which was demolished to improve passage for the increasing volume of traffic using the Tyne. Improvement works to deepen the great river in preparation for the Swing Bridge allowed Dr Bruce the rare opportunity to stand "high and dry" on what previously would have been the natural riverbed.[1] Looming a hundred feet above him in the spring sky was the cast-iron High Level Bridge. Built a couple of decades earlier, the High

Level was, in 1872, the only permanent bridge between Newcastle and Gateshead over the Tyne. Nearer to Bruce, down at quayside level, was the Temporary Tyne Bridge. This 660-foot-long timber structure spanned the river during the dismantling of the Georgian bridge and the construction of the Swing Bridge.

On the Newcastle bank, towering above the river, Bruce could see the familiar Newcastle landmarks of the Castle Keep, the Church of St Nicholas (not yet bestowed with cathedral status) and All Saints Church. Up high on the Gateshead bank was the bell tower of St Mary's Church. All along both quaysides, butted right against the river, were ramshackle rows of stone and timber buildings—warehouses, factories and slum housing. Tall-masted sailing ships and smoke-stacked steamboats were moored along the quays. Around him, the Coaly Tyne rolled past on its long journey from two separate sources near the Scottish border and in the North Pennines, via its confluence in Northumberland, out to the North Sea.[2]

Dr Bruce was a tall, spare man with a cumulus cloud of white hair and a pair of large, bushy mutton-chops. He was a non-denominational minister, a schoolmaster, a folk musician, and a dedicated historian. In 1872, Bruce was sixty-seven years old. According to his son, he lived a life "occupied in scholastic duties, in quiet and unostentatious literary and antiquarian research".[3] His primary interest was Roman Britain. He was a leading expert on Hadrian's Wall, the seventy-three-mile-long defensive fortification built in the second century to separate Emperor Hadrian's Britannia from northern barbarians.[4] Bruce knew every inch of the wall and invented the numbering system still in use today for its milecastles and other structures. He led tours along the Wall and travelled along it with his pilgrim band, which played ancient and previously-lost Northern folk songs. He had been summoned to the river to view a remarkable set of finds connected to the first Tyne Bridge, built by the Romans almost two thousand years ago.

During the removal of the Georgian Tyne Bridge, workers found several ancient Roman coins in the river, including a fine large brass example depicting the bearded and laureled head of Hadrian. Newcastle was long-known as having been a Roman settlement, and Bruce was very familiar with Roman coins. But the coin of Hadrian, found in "almost mint condition", was particularly significant because it linked the great emperor and his reign to the first crossing over the Tyne—the first Tyne bridge. Its findspot at the bridge site and its depiction of Hadrian made it "the most evocative relic of Roman Newcastle".[5] Now, from his privileged viewpoint, Bruce could see something of what the Romans might have seen when that coin was dropped into the river.

The works had revealed the apparent foundations of three separate Tyne bridges: the Georgian Tyne Bridge; the medieval "Old Tyne Bridge"; and the (at the time) seventeen-centuries-old Roman bridge. Bruce observed three different types of timber in these exposed foundations. The wood from the foundations of the Georgian bridge was described as being "quite fresh"; that from the medieval bridge was a brown and slimy oak "with a greenish tint of decay"; while the third type was jet back and crumbling on the outside, but had a "strong but fibrous" heart. This, Bruce decided, was Roman oak, which "must have been used for the foundations of the Bridge of Hadrian".[6]

This Roman Tyne Bridge was the first crossing over the river and the oldest ancestor of the modern steel arch we know today. More than that, it was the first significant structure on Tyneside. The settlements of Newcastle and Gateshead were initially established on either side of the bridge to build and defend it. Both towns expanded and flourished due to the trade and traffic the bridge attracted. Bruce, the leading expert on the Romans' influence on Tyneside history, knew it had all started with the Bridge of Hadrian. Everything that would follow—including the medieval bridge, the Georgian bridge and (long after Bruce's death) the twentieth-century Tyne Bridge—arrived because the Romans had established Tyneside as a river crossing. The crumbling timber foundations Bruce witnessed were the very foundations of Tyneside as a city of bridges.

* * *

Emperor Hadrian was born Publius Aelius Hadrianus. Keen to visit the extremes of his Empire, he spent more than half of his twenty-year reign away from Rome. He arrived in Britannia or Roman

Britain in, or just before, AD 122. It had been under Roman rule for almost eighty years yet was facing an existential crisis in the wake of several uprisings, particularly in the North. After Hadrian arrived from Germania, across the "German Ocean", or North Sea, he ordered the construction of a vast frontier wall "to separate Romans from barbarians".[7] It would eventually extend from Bowness on the Solway Firth to Segedunum at present-day Wallsend and is known as Hadrian's Wall.

Hadrian left Britannia a few months later and never got to see his wall. But he left an indelible mark on Northern Britain—and present-day Newcastle. He was honoured with the naming of the bridge his army built across the Tyne. *Pons* means bridge and *Aelius* was Hadrian's family or clan name. The fort, constructed to build and protect the bridge, took the same name. So the original Tyne Bridge and the first substantial settlement at Newcastle upon Tyne were both named *Pons Aelius*.

The Tyne's Pons Aelius bridge was the only known bridge outside of Rome named for an emperor, which indicates its considerable importance.[8] An arrow-straight Roman road (the precursor of the Great North Road, or A1) ran north from the key settlement of Eboracum at present-day York up to the River Tyne. The bridge was an extension of the road, built in order to carry it across the river and connect the southern settlements with the wall forts around Newcastle. (Although Hadrian's Wall is most often associated with the wild hill country of Northumberland, its course ran through what is now Newcastle city centre.)

On his departure in 122 Hadrian appointed his close friend Aulus Platorius Nepos as governor of Britannia and tasked him with building the wall. To accomplish that objective and transport his army and logistical supplies, Nepos needed to bridge the river. Several Roman Legions carried out the work, including the Sixth, *Legio VI Victrix*: a particularly celebrated Legion designated *Victrix*, or victorious, due to its successful military record, including a famous victory over Mark Antony and Cleopatra at the Battle of Actium. It's the Sixth Legion that is most evidently associated with the Roman Tyne Bridge, as Dr Bruce would soon discover.

But who were the men of the Sixth Legion? The Sixth sailed to Britannia from Germania, perhaps with Emperor Hadrian. Germania encompassed parts of the Netherlands, Belgium, Luxembourg and the North Rhine-Westphalia of Germany. The Legion recruited natives from across that area. The Sixth had previously served across the Mediterranean—in Spain, Sicily, Greece, and as far west as Syria—so its membership was diverse. A Roman legion consisted of between 5,000 and 6,000 well-trained legionaries, who were Roman citizens, plus around the same number of auxiliaries, who were subjects from across the Empire. Each legion was divided into cohorts of around 500 soldiers. The main body of the Sixth Legion was stationed at York, one cohort of which built the Pons Aelius.

When the Sixth arrived on Tyneside, which was then nothing more than a steep and rocky gorge, they set up an encampment—or perhaps two encampments. It's known the Romans occupied the site on the Newcastle side of the river that would become the fort of Pons Aelius. But excavations during the building of a Hilton hotel in the 1990s at Bottle Bank on the Gateshead side revealed evidence of a Roman settlement that might have pre-dated the Newcastle encampment. It's possible the Legion set up camp on the south bank of the Tyne before crossing to the north, or had camps on each side of the river to assist with the bridge's construction and defence.

The encampment on the north was the more formal settlement that would eventually become Newcastle and initially it housed the cohort of men that built the bridge. Military engineers were on site for many months, and the legion's soldiers protected the workers and their bridge. We can imagine that the settlement began as a temporary camp with goatskin tents surrounded by a defensive ditch or rampart which then grew into a permanent garrison station with wooden buildings and stone fortifications.

The Romans were not the first settlers on Tyneside, and—although archaeological evidence is scarce—there would have been sporadic native settlements in the Newcastle and Gateshead areas. These were self-sufficient agricultural communities, dwelling in small farmsteads with little round huts. The Romans had no great interest in these farmers and hunters, and the lives of the Iron Age leftovers were probably largely unaffected by the conquering army. But the proto-Geordies would have been amazed by the foreign newcomers' sophisticated bridge-building techniques. As Bruce noted, "The native inhabitants must have viewed the operation with astonishment."[9]

Of much more interest to the Romans than the farmsteaders were the dominant Celtic tribes of the *Hen Ogledd* or Old North, which were a constant threat throughout Hadrian's reign—as they had a right to be in the face of an unwanted invasion. (These tribes might have given the Tyne its name, from their Celtic-language word "tain", meaning "river".)[10]

According to Bruce, the building of the first Tyne Bridge, "if we take into account the comparative barbarism which at the time pervaded the district", was a "bold and adventurous undertaking". It was also a remarkable feat of engineering. Huge stone blocks and tall oak trunks were extracted, felled, and then transported to the building site. Stonemasons, carpenters and labourers toiled away, while the Imperial engineers used their remarkable ingenuity to tame the river. "Vast would be the efforts required to shape the various materials and drag them to the spot," wrote Bruce, "and great the skill put forth by the military architects."[11]

The Romans liked to use local materials. They built Hadrian's Wall from stone that was easily quarried in the Northumbrian hills. Elsewhere in the Empire, they built fortifications from earth and timber. By the Tyne, the Romans had access to stone and timber, and they likely constructed the bridge using both. Improvements and repairs over the 250 years or so of the Roman settlement probably saw initial timber constructions evolve into more permanent stone structures. The bridge, subject to the constant traffic of marching sandal boots and loaded supply carts—plus the unpredictable rushes and surges of the Tyne—must have required regular maintenance.

The Pons Aelius bridge likely consisted of a horizontal timber superstructure laid across several support pillars or piers. The road deck was perhaps 12 or 15 feet above the river's surface. According to the Georgian-era bridge workmen who first uncovered the ancient pier foundations, the old piers were built without springs for arches, indicating that the bridge was not arched. The pillars were likely made from stone blocks, or faced with stone blocks and filled with concrete. (Roman concrete was a widely-used mixture of rubble aggregate and mortar bound with volcanic ash so it could be set underwater.) Each pillar was built up from a foundation of wooden piles, which were driven deep into the river bed and topped with pile caps. At the time, without quays or other developments, the Tyne was thought to be wider than it is in the present day. So the Pons Aelius bridge was likely substantially longer than the present-day Swing Bridge.

As for the Pons Aelius fort, it occupied the same lofty site as the original Norman "New Castle" and subsequent medieval castle. Newcastle has long provided a natural advantage for fortification builders, given its location on the high ground above the Tyne Gorge—a strong defensive position. For the Romans, it offered a solution to the "necessity of defending the bridge and commanding the Tyne". Bruce said it was no wonder the fort should take its name from the bridge, and it was "a striking indication of the importance of the place, even in the days of Hadrian".[12]

There is no surviving account of the Roman settlement at Newcastle, and limited excavations undertaken between such historically significant buildings as the Castle Keep and the Cathedral have found few visible remains.[13] But there seems little doubt the settlement was important, initially for its role in building and maintaining the bridge and later due to the benefits the bridge and river provided. Pons Aelius was a vital trading and transport hub. The Tyne provided access to and from the North Sea and to the European ports of the Roman Empire. And the bridge and the Roman road were the line of communication to York and beyond. "No place in the north of England was so well fitted as Newcastle to be the emporium of the commerce of the North," wrote Bruce.[14]

From his unique viewpoint on the river, with the exposed pier foundations in front of him, Bruce was certain the Roman bridge must have occupied the same site as the Georgian and medieval bridges—at the location of the Swing Bridge. He produced a plan of an uncovered Tyne Bridge pier showing Roman, medieval, and "modern" (meaning Georgian) work. "The lower framework shown in this plan is undoubtedly Roman," he wrote. "The oak trees which supplied the timber must have been growing on the banks of the Tyne when our blessed saviour was walking the streets of Jerusalem."[15]

Subsequent historians have argued Bruce was mistaken and had wrongly identified an outer protective piling as the medieval pier work and the medieval work as Roman work.[16] However, during the 1770s, workers demolishing the ruined medieval bridge observed "the distinguishing characteristics of Roman masonry" (and found numerous other Roman coins).[17] They concluded the piers of the medieval bridge must have been laid upon the foundations of the Roman bridge. This suggests, while his plan may have been wrong, Bruce was likely correct in his claim that the Roman bridge occupied the same site as the medieval, Georgian and Swing Bridges. And, in subsequent decades, further discoveries would support his theory.

In 1872, Bruce obtained several piles of "fine black oak" from the remains of what he believed to be the foundations of the Roman bridge.[18] They were found to be in "a state of excellent preservation" and were left to dry, naturally and gradually, for twelve months. Several souvenirs and pieces of furniture, including a large bookcase, were crafted using this "primaeval oak". Bruce used the bookcase to keep his most-prized books, including a folio copy of his own *The Roman Wall*, which he had bound in carved black oak cover boards. He also had two chairs, a letter opener, and a walking staff made from the ancient wood, which he proudly used when leading his pilgrim band along Hadrian's Wall.

* * *

In 1875, three years after Bruce stood on the bed of the Tyne, there was another remarkable find. During the ongoing works to build the Swing Bridge, a dredger brought up three pieces of a broken stone slab that, when put together, were revealed to form a complete Roman altar. Dr Bruce hurried to examine it and declared it "exceedingly interesting" and unlike anything he had ever seen.[19] Around 50 inches tall and 20 inches wide, it was remarkably well-preserved. On the face of the altar was a bold carving of a trident with a dolphin wrapped around its handle. Across the capital was a carved dedication to *Neptuno* or Neptune, the god of rivers and fresh water, from the *p(ia) f(idelis) Legio VI Victix* or the pious and faithful Sixth Legion. This was strong evidence that the Sixth Legion had built the bridge.

More than a quarter of a century later, in 1903, during dredging to improve passage through the Swing Bridge's north channel, workers found a second altar—this one complete. It was of the same dimensions and style as the first altar, suggesting they were made as a pair by the same craftsman. The second altar bore the image of an anchor, and a dedication from the Sixth Legion to *Ociano* or Oceanus, the god of the oceans and seas. This altar with its inscription to Oceanus was considered to be extremely rare, "almost unique" according to one historian.[20]

Workers also found an altar base, which fitted the Neptune altar. Both altars were found in the north channel, suggesting they had entered the water from the Newcastle section of the bridge. It seems likely they were part of a shrine designed to bestow divine protection upon the bridge from the river and ocean gods. Today, both altars can be viewed in the Hadrian's Wall Gallery at Newcastle's Great North Museum.[21] They are two of the city's oldest and most extraordinary relics.

Dr Bruce did not get to see the second altar. He died in 1892 and was buried in Jesmond Cemetery, after a funeral procession lined with local people paying their last respects. In his eulogy, the minister said, "Newcastle today is burying her best known and perhaps most distinguished citizen."[22] The strength of Bruce's reputation and his importance to the people of the city is evident at the Cathedral of St Nicholas. There, alongside monuments to such local heroes as Admiral Lord Cuthbert Collingwood, is an alabaster memorial to the Reverend Doctor John Collingwood Bruce, depicting him lying at peace with his feet resting on a copy of his book about the Roman Wall.[23]

Bruce had established the importance of the Roman Tyne Bridge to Britannia and the wider Empire, and he must often have considered what the bridge meant to individual Roman Britons beyond its functional value as a river crossing. It was important enough to warrant military and divine protection. But was that only due to the need to keep the trading and transport routes open, or did the bridge assume a greater cultural or emotional significance? Did the Romans and their Romanised citizens develop an attachment to it, as so many modern Tynesiders have to the present-day Tyne Bridge? Did the bridge become a symbol of Roman Tyneside?

Certainly, the Roman Tyne Bridge was an important ancestor of the present Tyne Bridge. Tyneside's rich, full, colourful history can all be traced back to the Pons Aelius bridge. The Romans recognised the value of the Tyne and began the trades that turned it into one of the world's great rivers. Newcastle and Gateshead came into existence because the Romans decided this spot—the site of the present Swing Bridge—would be a good place to cross the river. It all goes back to the Bridge of Hadrian.

The Pons Aelius bridge seems to have served the Romans to the end of their occupation in around AD 410. Several coins retrieved from the foundations were dated later than Hadrian's reign and might have been deposited during repairs and alterations. After that, it was used, damaged, repaired, destroyed, and rebuilt over several centuries by the Angles and Saxons, the Danes and Normans. Bruce reasoned that only the ancient piers survived the various reconstructions.[24]

After the Romans left, the Pons Aelius settlement fell into disuse. During the Viking invasions in the early Middle Ages, the abandoned Roman fort at Newcastle was thought to have become a refuge for a community of monks, leading to the settlement being known as Monkchester. By the time of the Norman Conquest in the eleventh century, the place was, according to Bruce, "utterly ruinous and deserted". With the settlement unoccupied, the bridge was similarly abandoned. After many centuries of renovation, it was no longer known as the Pons Aelius and no longer the Roman Bridge. It was now simply the Bridge over the Tyne, or the first crossing known as the Tyne Bridge.

There is a reference to the bridge in the *Life of St Oswin*, written by a monk at Tynemouth Priory around 1111.[25] Although the bridge was in use at the time of his writing, the monk wrote that it had not been useable in 1072, when William the Conqueror returned with his army following his victorious invasion of Scotland. This was due to substantial flooding that had either overrun the bridge or swept parts away. Alternatively, Bruce suggested the people of Newcastle might have deliberately damaged the bridge to prevent the hated William's return. William had waged a brutal campaign to subjugate the North that would have negative consequences for many centuries to come.

In 1080, William sent his eldest son, Robert Curthose or Robert II of Normandy, to the settlement then known as Monkchester to defend the kingdom against the Scots. To protect his northern base,

Robert built a wooden motte-and-bailey (mound-and-stockade) fort—the New Castle. A century later, between 1172 and 1177, Henry II had his master mason, named Maurice, replace the wooden castle with a stone one. The Castle Keep still exists in restored form today and offers some of the best views of the present riverscape and the current Tyne Bridge from high up on its battlement roof.[26]

The revival of Newcastle as a settlement demanded the revival of its bridge. Some texts suggest the bridge was properly restored by Stephen, grandson of William the Conqueror, who reigned as King of England from 1135 to 1154. So perhaps the Roman bridge became a Norman bridge around then. By the time Henry II built the stone castle, the bridge had reclaimed its status as an important crossing point between north and south.

The Roman bridge—at least in its reconstructed form—survived until 1248. In that year, according to another monk, Matthew of Paris, "the greatest part of the borough of Newcastle upon Tyne, together with its bridge, was consumed by a raging fire".[27] After 1,100 years, what remained of the original Tyne Bridge was damaged beyond repair. Newcastle and Gateshead would need to build a replacement. This medieval crossing—a distinctive and characterful structure—would have a long and celebrated life and be fondly remembered by Tynesiders as the Old Tyne Bridge.

2

THE OLD TYNE BRIDGE

Early on a Sunday morning, 17 November 1771, the residents of Newcastle and Gateshead were startled by a thunderous crash. Most were already awake, unable to sleep due to the constant barrage of rainfall on their rooftops and the almighty roar of the swollen river as it rushed between their towns. Ceilings sprung leaks, and streets became streams. In the darkness, through bucketing rain, it wasn't easy to see. But that booming, doom-laden crash must have conjured terrifying images in the mind. This was no ordinary rainstorm. North-East England was being drenched by a cataclysmic deluge of water, leading to the worst natural disaster the region had ever seen. It would become known as the Great Flood, one of the most significant events in the history of Tyneside, and it led to the destruction of one of the Tyne's most famous and beloved structures. The terrible sound that so alarmed residents on that dreadful Sunday morning was that of the collapse of the remarkable medieval stone arch crossing, the Old Tyne Bridge.

By the time of the Great Flood, this medieval Tyne Bridge was five centuries old and had a storied history. It was a fantastical structure that looked like something out of a storybook—perhaps a crossing between magical lands in Tolkien's Middle Earth. The bridge was full of life because many people lived on it. It was lined with buildings—stone towers, timber houses, shops, chapels, and defensive gates. To an observer on the banks of the Tyne, it must have looked as if a crowded street had been ripped from the centre of town and thrown across the river. It was one of Tyneside's busiest and most important streets, heavy with traffic because it was part of the main thoroughfare between England and Scotland—the Old North Road.

The rambling multi-storey timber-frame buildings were piled like stacking blocks along each edge of the bridge, with their jettied upper floors projecting out over the river—to maximise the space allowed by their cramped footprints. Locals and travellers squeezed along the narrow street on foot, on horseback, in carriages and with carts. Boats lowered their sails to pass under the arches or stopped to unload at the cellars that hung under the bridge's buildings, skirting the surface of the river. Smoke billowed from chimneys and twirled into the sky. It was a lively, bustling, vibrant street, and it was suspended—rather precariously, it would turn out—above the fast-flowing currents of the River Tyne. But long before the flood, the Old Tyne Bridge had built a colourful reputation as one of the most impressive and interesting structures in the country. In its time—and for a big chunk of history—it was every bit as iconic as the current Tyne Bridge.

* * *

The Old Tyne Bridge was built as a replacement to the burnt-out Roman bridge following the fire of 1248. At this time, royal charters allowed the burgesses (or citizens) of Newcastle to form their own local government, known as the Corporation, led by the town mayor. Gateshead was part of the County Palatine of Durham and was governed by the Bishopric of Durham. The Newcastle Corporation and the Bishop of Durham joined together to rebuild the Tyne Bridge, and work started around 1250. Newcastle, then as now considered the senior partner of the Tyneside towns, was responsible for two thirds of the bridge, and Durham for the remaining third. Both Newcastle and Durham made appeals for money, manpower and materials to rebuild and then maintain the new bridge, which would be built out of stone.

In 1256, the then-Bishop of Durham, Walter of Kirkham, offered an indulgence (remission of punishment for sins) to anyone who contributed towards the renovation of the bridge. The Archbishop of York, along with bishops in Scotland and Ireland, also offered indulgences for the same purpose, indicating the significance of the Tyne Bridge beyond Tyneside. "Its national importance was recognised throughout the kingdom," wrote one old historian. "Its restoration was of much more than a local moment."[1]

The bridge was originally constructed with twelve Gothic arches founded on substantial piers, which were built around piles that were driven into the river bed—likely based upon the foundations of the original Roman bridge. Each arch was supported by several parallel ribs. In subsequent centuries, two of the bridge's arches were subsumed by the expanding quays on either side of the river. This meant, by the 1700s, the bridge had only ten arches. Of the two hidden arches, one is under Bridge Street at the Gateshead end of the Swing Bridge, and the other is still visible in the cellar of the Watergate Buildings on Sandhill at the north end of the bridge. Because parts still survive, the Old Tyne Bridge is listed today as a scheduled ancient monument (alongside the Castle Keep, the Black Gate and the Town Walls).

The most substantial structures on the bridge were three stone towers—the Magazine Gate at the Newcastle end, the Tower on the Bridge in the middle of the Newcastle section, and the Drawbridge Tower at the Durham (or Gateshead) end. Newcastle's two-thirds of the bridge had several timber houses and shops on each side of its street, but were less densely packed than Gateshead's third, which was loaded with wooden buildings that were jammed up against each other with barely a gap between them. Each of the bridge's arches had a name—the Great Arch, the White Arch, the Magazine Arch, the Keelman's Arch. The arch nearest to the Gateshead side of the river was the Drawbridge Arch. By the 1700s, the drawbridge had been removed, and the resulting gap in the stone bridge was filled with "roughly-executed" timberwork.[2]

The Old Tyne Bridge was a patchwork affair in a near-constant state of renovation. According to the pioneering civil engineer John Smeaton, who was asked to survey it several times towards the end of its life, the bridge was "originally very ill-built, and in general of too small stones, and not of the best kind".[3] Smeaton said the bridge's many inconveniences were well known to any person who had ever passed over it. The bridge was narrow—15 feet wide between its parapets and reduced in places to 9 feet wide by buildings and other obstructions. The confined street and the steep ascent from the southern approach rendered the bridge "extremely dangerous to every passenger, whether in a carriage, on horseback, or on foot" and frequently caused "great interruptions and confusion when carriages or a number of passengers happen to meet upon it". As the bridge carried the main road between north and south, many travellers were exposed to its hazards.

The bridge also proved dangerous to river traffic. The very wide piers were significant obstructions, and cellars and basements that were built under the bridge's houses and shops—often down to the river's high-tide level—partially or completely blocked several of the arches, making passage under the bridge difficult and risky. These obstructions also funnelled the flow of water and caused the river to rush between the piers and "gull away" the riverbed under the arches.

Yet as dilapidated and downright dangerous as it appeared, the bridge was a coveted spot for Tyneside's merchants and residents. For the former, the shops were located on a busy thoroughfare with a constant passing trade. For the latter, the houses enjoyed a precious flow of fresh air that blew up and down the river. Also, residents could chuck their waste straight out of the window and into the river, which was a great benefit to anyone reliant upon medieval sewerage systems.

During its long life, the Old Tyne Bridge underwent many changes, and the bridge of the 1200s was likely barely comparable to that of the 1700s. In 1339, a flood destroyed part of the bridge—and part of the town walls. 120 people were killed in this huge inundation (yet "the Great Flood" was still to come). In 1342, the bridge was reported to be in ruinous condition. Funds were collected and some repairs were made. By 1370, a huge sum of £1,000 was required to return the bridge to an acceptable state. By the end of the century, a royal grant had been issued to restore it.

More floods and fires and other tests of time followed, but the bridge withstood them and became a source of pride for locals and a notable attraction for visitors. Henry VIII's chaplain and antiquary John Leland, writing around 1535, said the Tyne Bridge "hathe ten arches and a stronge warde [fort] and towre on it" and "a gate at the bridge ende".[4] In 1603, when James VI of Scotland travelled through Newcastle on his way to London to be crowned James I of England, he "bestowed in viewing the towne, the manner and beautie of the bridge and keye, being one of the best in the North parts".[5]

There was no greater test of time for Newcastle and the Old Tyne Bridge than the Civil War Siege of Newcastle in 1644, when the Royalist town courageously held out for eight months against Scottish Covenanter forces. Many of Newcastle's defences were damaged or destroyed, including swathes of the Town Walls. Parts of the Quayside were ruined, but the bridge, although requiring some repairs, stood firm.

After the Civil War, clearer descriptions of the bridge emerged. The Newcastle topographer William Grey wrote in 1649 that the Old Tyne Bridge "consisteth of arches high and broad, having many houses and shops upon the bridge, and three towers upon it".[6] When trailblazing travel writer Celia Fiennes visited the Tyne in 1698, she described "a fine bridge over the Tyne river with nine arches [sic], all built on as London Bridge is", reminding readers that the medieval London Bridge was also crowded with buildings.[7] In 1736, Newcastle historian Henry Bourne described the bridge as "a pretty street, beset with houses on each side for a great part of it."[8]

The bridge's Magazine Gate was a large, fortified stone entrance tower that was used to store the town's armaments and had once been fitted with a portcullis. It was built in 1636 to replace an earlier entrance gate. Set into the south-facing wall of the Magazine Gate was a statue of Charles II wearing a Roman tunic, which was installed following the King's restoration in 1660. Underneath was engraved the motto: *Adventus Regis Solamen Gregis* (The Coming of the King is the Comfort of his People).[9] Above Charles II, at the apex of the Magazine Gate, was a carving of the town's coat of arms, depicting a heraldic lion and a shield of castles supported by two seahorses, with the motto *Fortiter Defendit Triumphans* (Triumphing by Brave Defence), which was bestowed on the town following its stubborn resistance to the siege of 1644. The carving was dated for 1646—just two years after the siege.[10]

The Magazine Gate—or at least its predecessor—also had a rather gruesome purpose. According to local law, high criminals were to be exposed to the public gaze after they had felt the executioner's axe across the back of their necks. So, the severed heads—and sometimes the quartered bodies—of treasonous and faithless miscreants were displayed on spikes above the battlements of the Magazine Gate, in full view of the townsfolk and within spitting distances of the upper floor windows of the Quayside merchant's houses (including the two surviving buildings now known as the Bettie Surtees House, dating from the 16th and 17th centuries). Often, these were the heads of moss-troopers—cross-border brigands captured during their raids of Northumberland—but there were also several more famous exhibits.

After William "Braveheart" Wallace was hanged, drawn and quartered (and emasculated, eviscerated and beheaded) in London in 1305, one of his quarters—thought to have been the upper right—was sent to Newcastle to be displayed on the Tyne Bridge. (It was also said an "unmentionable part" was displayed in the Castle Keep.)[11] In the first decade of the 1400s, during the Percy Rebellion against Henry IV, quarters of both Henry Percy (the 1st Earl of Northumberland) and his son Harry "Hotspur" Percy (Shakespeare's tragic hero) were displayed on the bridge. And in 1593, the head of Catholic martyr Edward Waterson, who was executed in Newcastle, was stuck on a spike at the top of the Magazine Gate for all around to see.

Part of the Old Tyne Bridge between the Magazine Gate and the Tower on the Bridge was free from buildings and open on both sides. This was the setting for an extraordinary (and perhaps apocryphal) story from the mid-sixteenth century. It was a tale that became known as "The Fish and the Ring". The protagonist was Francis Anderson, a prominent public servant who was listed in a Newcastle muster-roll as being available to provide armed support to the town's Aldermen with a helmet, bow and halberd (a long-handled pick-axe). He was subsequently appointed as the Sheriff of Newcastle. He lived in "the house at the Bridge-end".[12]

One day in or before the year 1559, Anderson was looking out over the side of the bridge and talking to a friend when his precious and ancient gold signet ring slipped from his finger and fell into the murky river, surely never to be seen again. A few days later, so the story goes, one of Anderson's servants bought a salmon at the market and, on gutting the fish, found in its belly his master's ring. So, Francis Anderson was reunited with his lost ring over a tasty fish supper. Almost two centuries later, Henry Bourne wrote that he had seen the ring, which was in the possession of one of Anderson's descendants. The ring, bearing the figures of Spes (representing hope) and Abundantia (abundance), was thought to be a Roman antique dating from the second century—around the time of the building of the Pons Aelius bridge. It had subsequently been embossed on the underside with Francis Anderson's initials and an engraving of a fish.

About 60 feet south of the Magazine Gate was the Tower on the Bridge, which stood on the Great Arch. It was built by George Bird during one of his five reigns as Mayor of Newcastle between 1494 and 1511, and was adorned with the Bird Mayoral Coat of Arms. One of the Tower's purposes was to house "lewd and disorderly" persons until they were dealt with by the mayor and perhaps removed to the nearby gaol at Newgate in the Town Walls. One of their number was Harry Wallis, a master shipwright, who was incarcerated in the tower during the late-seventeenth century after drunkenly abusing the puritanical Newcastle Alderman Ambrose Barnes. The Tower was also used as a warehouse, and Wallis was detained in a room containing a large quantity of malt—no doubt used to make intoxicating liquor. Noting the irony, the "drunken beast" Wallis began to shovel the malt out of a window and into the river while chanting: *O base malt! Thou didst the fault; and into the Tyne thou shalt.*[13]

Beyond the Tower were a handful of other buildings owned by Newcastle, supported on what was known as the White Arch. Then, set into the pavement at the two-thirds mark, was the *Blew Stone* or Blue Stone, marking the boundary between Newcastle and Gateshead—or, more accurately, between the town of Newcastle and the county of Durham. Originally, there were thought to have been two Blue Stones, known as the St Cuthbert Stones. These were removed in the late fourteenth century when Newcastle made a claim to the full length of the bridge. This dispute rumbled on for several decades before Durham reclaimed its section of the bridge and a new Blue Stone was laid. The surviving one, a long, narrow and smooth slate-coloured slab that must have appeared blue next to the sooty grey stone of the bridge, has been preserved and can be found on display at the Castle Keep in Newcastle.

At around the time of this dispute, records from 1429 show a hermit lived on the bridge in a hermitage. The will of wealthy Newcastle merchant and mayor Roger Thornton requested the hermit to sing for Thornton's soul for an annual bequest of six marks (or four pounds). According to several Newcastle historians, the hermit was still there in 1562—and in 1643, suggesting religious solitude rewarded the hermit with an unnaturally long life, or more likely it was a position filled by a succession of different individuals. What happened to the hermit in the following year, during the Siege of 1644, isn't recorded, but he does not seem to be heard of again.

South of the Blue Stone, the Gateshead and Durham third of the bridge was much more densely packed with buildings than the Newcastle portion, with barely a gap between them. The author of a 1751 book of bridges could recall only two other crossings in England that had been "converted into a street"—the Old London Bridge and the Old Bristol Bridge. The unknown author suggested "impartial persons" believed it to be the third-best bridge in England, after the Old London Bridge and the medieval bridge at Rochester.[14]

The author Daniel Defoe, who lived for several years on Tyneside, wrote in 1727 that the Tyne Bridge was "a very strong and stately stone bridge of seven [sic] very great arches, rather larger than the arches of London Bridge; and the bridge is built into a street of houses also, as London Bridge is". Defoe said Newcastle was "a spacious, extended, infinitely populous place" seated on "a noble, large and deep river".[15] He did not mention Gateshead in his writings, despite having called the town home. Defoe lived at Hillgate on the Gateshead quays while seeking refuge from debtors from around 1706 to 1710, shortly before he wrote *The Life and Strange Surprizing Adventures of Robinson Crusoe*.[16]

One of Defoe's friends in Gateshead was Joseph Button, known as "the bookseller on the bridge". The Old Tyne Bridge was a hive of pioneering booksellers. During the 1700s, Button, Martin Bryson, William Charnley, Richard Randall, John Linn, Robert Akenhead, and James Fleming were all recorded as selling books, bibles and stationery—plus miscellanea such as Indian ink, elixirs, and fiddle strings—on the bridge.[17] (According to the Georgian-era Newcastle author and publisher Eneas Mackenzie, the first book catalogue was printed on the Tyne Bridge in April 1693 by a bookseller named Joseph Hall.)[18]

However, the Tyne's main commodity was not books but coal. During the reign of Henry III, the townsfolk of Newcastle were granted a royal licence to dig for coal on the banks of the river.

Tyneside was particularly rich with coal seams, and the Tyne allowed that coal to be transported to the coast and around the country. Within a century, Newcastle was exporting coal to London and Europe and was one of the richest towns in England. The rise of the coal trade encouraged the growth of other industries, particularly shipbuilding—initially connected to the transport of coal. Other Tyneside industries fuelled by coal included glass, pottery and iron, all of which thrived. As Henry Bourne wrote in 1736: "It is observable in this place when the coal trade is brisk, that all other business is so too."[19]

When Welsh travel writer Thomas Pennant visited what he called the "Coaly Tyne" in 1769, he described both banks of the river as very steep, with the lower parts "very dirty and disagreeable".[20] Tyneside, he said, was remarkably populous, with Newcastle and Gateshead having almost 30,000 inhabitants, plus at least "400 sails of ships". Pennant said the vast commerce of Tyneside, chiefly from the coal trade, was very apparent, particularly in several of Newcastle's "handsome, well-built streets". This was some fifty years before Richard Grainger began to build Newcastle's celebrated classical Georgian and Victorian streets. Pennant crossed the Old Tyne Bridge on his way to visit Scotland in 1769, but he was unable to do so on his return journey in 1772, because the bridge was no longer there.

* * *

Toward the end of its life, there were twenty-one houses on the Gateshead section of the Old Tyne Bridge—eleven on the east side of the road and ten on the west. The last house on the west at the Gateshead end of the bridge was the home of Scottish-born surgeon Dr James Oliphant. One of the grandest houses on the bridge, it had four floors, including a cellar built into the bridge arch below. There was a surgery on the ground floor, a kitchen and parlour on the second floor, and living quarters on the top floor. The cellar had a door that allowed loading from the river, just above the usual high tide mark.

In July 1764, a few months after the newspaper's launch, the Newcastle *Chronicle* reported that the body of a young woman named

Dinah Armstrong had been found floating in the Tyne near Dunston Staiths. It was reported she had been both "hang'd and drown'd", and the coroner offered a verdict of wilful murder.[21] Dinah was the youngest servant of Dr James and Mrs Margaret Oliphant, and had last been seen in the cellar of their house on the Old Tyne Bridge. According to witnesses who saw her body when it was pulled from the water, "her master and mistress were her murderers".

The Oliphants had appointed Dinah in May 1764 and soon came to trust her to work alongside their other servant, Mary Shittleton. However, in July of that year, Dinah was accused of stealing some napkins from a local merchant's wife. Margaret Oliphant was advised to dismiss Dinah, but she refused, saying she wanted to save her from "public shame and ruin". Dinah continued to work for the family, taking the children to school, bringing water up from the cellar, and fetching ale for dinner from the nearby Queen's Head pub.

On 17 July, Mrs Oliphant realised Dinah was missing and asked Mary Shittleton to find her. Mary went down through the shop and into the cellar where, she said, she saw Dinah leap from the cellar door into the river. Mary raised the alarm and neighbours began a search, but there was no trace of Dinah—until she was found floating at Dunston several days later.

During a chaotic coroner's inquest, a surgeon who examined the body explained that Dinah had a white circle around her neck. According to the surgeon, and the keelman who first found the body, the girl had been strangled to death. But Dinah often wore a black ribbon around her neck, and was wearing one when last seen alive. Was it possible the ribbon had caused the white circle? It was then claimed that Dinah had been confined by the Oliphants in their cellar for five days before her disappearance. When Dr Oliphant tried to refute this story, Dinah's sister, Tamar Armstrong, exploded with anger and called the surgeon a "murderous dog".

Despite an apparent lack of evidence, the inquest decided James Oliphant, Margaret Oliphant and their servant Mary Shittleton had strangled Dinah Armstrong with a cord, and they were each charged with murder. On the following day, the Oliphants and Shittleton were conveyed to Durham Gaol. After a month in the primitive confines of the old medieval prison, they faced trial at

Durham Assizes. With no evidence against them, and with witnesses confirming Mary Shittleton's original story, all three defendants were acquitted. But Dr Oliphant described the devastating effects the case had on his family: "My business greatly reduced, my reputation sullied, my peace of mind deeply wounded, my wife's health much impaired."[22]

Oliphant said he was unable to pursue action for damages due to the expense and his reduced circumstances. He attempted to rectify matters by writing his own account of the affair. This was published by one of Oliphant's Tyne Bridge neighbours, Benjamin Fleming, "bookseller and stationer under the Magazine Gate on the bridge". Writing three years after the affair, Oliphant said the events were "ruinous in the highest degree". If the pamphlet did anything to restore Oliphant's standing, more suffering was to come.

* * *

The final chapter in the story of the Old Tyne Bridge was told on that fateful Sunday, 17 November 1771, when Tyneside was overwhelmed by "the most dreadful inundation that ever befell that part of the country"—the Great Flood.[23] Rain had fallen heavily and incessantly since Saturday morning. The river rose to dangerous levels—in some places 12 feet higher than the usual high tide mark. At the Tyne Bridge, the water level was higher "than the memory of man or tradition had ever taken notice of", and seven of the bridge's ten arches were "totally filled up with water above their crowns or keystones".[24] The cellars and warehouses underneath those arches were completely submerged. Throughout the night, the floodwaters rushed fast and heavy against the bridge, putting immense pressure on the ancient structure. At a little after five on Sunday morning, the bridge collapsed.

One unidentified citizen of Newcastle provided a contemporary account. On the Saturday, he said, "I could never remember so dark and dull a day."[25] However, he went to bed as usual and heard the night watchman "call the hour" without any warning of a high tide. He was woken at 4 am by a loud knock on his door. Outside, a gentleman named Joseph Robinson was yelling: "Pray arise, sir, for the river is swell'd prodigiously and increasing very fast!" Relieved it was not a fire, the witness lit a candle and went downstairs, where he found the water level was up to his knees. After moving his violin and family bible upstairs, he hurried along the riverside street known as the Close to warn some friends. As he passed the Magazine Gate, he saw the water level was so high that passage onto the bridge was impossible. He was concerned to see very few citizens were awake, but he roused his friends, then returned home. It was between 5 and 6 am, he said, when "my ears were alarmed with the falling of the bridge, which gave me the most shocking sensations imaginable".

"The idea of the sleeping inhabitants rushing in a moment into eternity, the rending of the houses, with the crush and noise made by their falling, added to the dreadful gloom and darkness of the night, created most terrible reflections, and brought to my mind all the horrors…"

Peter Weatherly was a shoemaker who lived in a house on the Newcastle section of the bridge with his wife, two young children, and their maid. He was woken early in the morning by the roar of the flooded river. He opened a window and saw his neighbours, Mr and Mrs Fiddas, hurrying with their two children and maid towards the south end of the bridge. The Fiddas family crossed the Blue Stone and reached solid ground. But, once there, the maid realised she had forgotten a bundle of supplies and needed to go back. Mr Fiddas accompanied the maid and hurried back to their house, leaving Mrs Fiddas and the children in relative safety. As Mr Fiddas and the maid attempted their return, one of the bridge arches gave way beneath them, and they tumbled into the river.

Weatherly, horrified by the scene, immediately roused his family and rushed to the door, where they saw the swollen river crashing past and the pavement cracking and buckling under its force. First, they headed towards Newcastle, but the rupturing pavement was impassable. And there was no way south to Gateshead due to the collapsed arches. The family were trapped on a crumbling section of the bridge, about 20 feet square. By daybreak, as they huddled on their precipice, there were thousands of spectators watching them from the flooded quaysides. It was hopeless to send a boat to them, and "escape seemed impossible". Then up stepped a Gateshead bricklayer named George Woodward.

Daring and selfless, Woodward laid planks of timber across the surviving sections of piers to reach a row of shops that were clinging to the east edge of the bridge. He smashed through the wall of the first shop, then smashed through into the second, gradually making his way towards the trapped family. Eventually, he was able to reach them and guide them back through the shop walls and over the timber planks to safety. The family had been trapped on their crumbling platform for six hours. The Weatherly children were thought to be "past all recovery", but they did survive, thanks to Woodward's bravery.[26] And he was not the only hero that day. Other Tynesiders waded along flooded streets, plunged into submerged houses and leapt into the angry river to save their friends and neighbours. As a result, the death toll was miraculously low.

Mr Fiddas and his maid did not survive. Nor did Christopher "Kit" Bryerley and his son, who were killed when Bryerley's home and hardware shop was swept into the river. Anne Tinkler, recorded as a "dealer in stuffs and checks" (materials for clothing and household linen), died when her house on the bridge was destroyed in the flood. An unnamed apprentice to cheesemaker John James also perished when Mr James's building fell into the Tyne. Remarkably, these were the only six confirmed fatalities at the collapse of the Old Tyne Bridge. However, reports said a tradesman's wife named Mrs Mabane and a maid who worked for mercer Thomas Patten died later "from the fright and shock of the calamity". The Rector of Gateshead's St Mary's Church, Andrew Wood, died three months after the flood, apparently of "a fever which he contracted by exerting himself, with the utmost humanity, to save his parishioners on the fatal night when the bridge of Newcastle fell".[27]

The immediate aftermath of the Great Flood revealed "a scene of horror and devastation too dreadful for words to express or humanity to behold without shuddering".[28] The street by Newcastle's Quayside known as Sandhill was flooded, in some parts 6 feet deep, and residents had to be rescued with rowing boats. "All the cellars, warehouses, shops and lower apartments of those dwelling houses, from the west end of the Close to near Ouseburn were under water," noted one account.[29] Boats, timber and merchants' goods were floating around the quaysides. Ships had been torn from their moorings and carried down the Tyne.

Most notably, the Old Tyne Bridge was in pieces. Much of the Gateshead section was gone, the stumps of its broken arches barely visible above the swollen river. The shell of a ruined house clung to the end of the Keelman's Arch. The White Arch at the centre of the bridge was gone. The Tower on the Bridge had somehow survived, its Great Arch enduring the pressures of the floodwater. But the bridge was fatally damaged, and its remains were in imminent danger of collapse. Only four of its arches had escaped destruction, and they were standing "upon the edge of a precipice".[30] All around was debris—heaps of fallen stone, stacks of broken timber, and floating clothes, cooking pots and furnishings from destroyed homes.

The mercer Thomas Patten's house on the bridge was swept down the river for seven or eight miles as far as Jarrow Slake. When it was found, the house was empty except for a dog and a cat—both alive. According to another incredible survival story, a baby that was swept from its home and out to sea during the Great Flood was recovered alive floating in its wooden cot off the coast of North Shields. All but one of the nine bridges along the full length of the River Tyne were destroyed. The only surviving crossing was at Corbridge, some twenty miles to the west. There was great devastation along the rivers Wear and Tees, too.

In addition to those belonging to Bryerley, Tinkler, James and Patten, the houses of Mr Hills and Edward Wilson, both shoemakers, and Mrs Haswell, a milliner, were also destroyed when the bridge collapsed that night. During the following day, four more houses collapsed into the Tyne. Shortly afterwards, the whole row of shops at the Gateshead section of the bridge—those George Woodward had broken through to rescue the Weatherlys—also fell from the bridge. Within a few weeks, all of the houses on the southern part of the bridge had fallen, with the exception of one—belonging to Dr James Oliphant.

His house clung obstinately to the edge of the bridge, propped up with wooden stays. But it was on borrowed time. During a hearing in the mayor's chamber, the stays were said to be insufficient, and the house was declared to be in imminent danger of falling into the river. It was demolished along with the other ruined remains. Dr Oliphant and his family had already abandoned the house, left Tyneside, and moved to Scotland. Oliphant became Professor of Medicine at the University of St Andrews before settling at Irvine on the coast of the Firth of Clyde. He died in 1791, twenty years after the Great Flood.

When the stalwart Tower of the Bridge was taken down during the demolition, a coffin containing a skeleton was found 5 feet below the pavement. Who the skeleton belonged to and why it was buried in the foundations of the bridge were unknown. Workmen demolishing the remains of the bridge with mauls and hammers also found a "mystic scroll"—a piece of inscribed parchment of unknown age—cemented between two stones. "There, visible and clear, were the characters traced by the scribe in some bygone age," wrote historian James Clephan. "'And in a moment all was *dumb*.' The letters vanished; the parchment crumbled to ashes, and the story of the unknown writer, so carefully written down for posterity was lost in dust!"[31]

The Medieval Tyne Bridge needed to be replaced, but the removal of the old crossing and the building of a new one was a long and difficult process. In the meantime, within a week of the bridge's collapse, the Newcastle *Chronicle* carried an advertisement for a new ferry service, which would operate from six in the morning until eight at night and would carry pedestrians, carts and carriages. The ferry was drawn from each quayside by ropes and horsepower. When Thomas Pennant returned to Tyneside following his visit to Scotland, he crossed the Tyne via the ferry.

Over the next few months, the citizens of Newcastle and Gateshead began to rebuild their lives without their bridge. Peter Weatherly, the rescued shoemaker, opened a new shop in Newcastle. "I hope the old customers will continue," he wrote in a newspaper advertisement. "I and my family were left upon the Bridge six hours in a melancholy condition and have suffered much by the water." The Great Flood, he said, was "a stroke of providence which no human prudence could prevent". He hoped his debtors would consider this and "come and pay me what they owe". But he added he was very grateful "for the charitable contribution that I have received by being a sufferer upon the bridge".[32]

The Old Tyne Bridge was afforded a special place in Tyneside history and became an almost legendary part of local folklore. Geordies who had never set eyes on the bridge were drawn to its image, captured for posterity in a handful of etchings and sketches. Even today, when pictures of the Old Tyne Bridge appear on social media, they generate comments of wonder and amazement. Back in 1883, James Clephan—who had never seen it—conjured an image of the bridge as a picturesque "fantasy in stone" of "imperishable fame".[33]

Remarkably, the Old Tyne Bridge did rise again, more than a century after it fell. In 1887, during the Royal Mining, Engineering and Industrial Exhibition in celebration of Queen Victoria's Golden Jubilee, a two-thirds scale replica of the Old Tyne Bridge was built over the lake on the part of Newcastle's Town Moor now known as Exhibition Park. Alongside mechanical demonstrations, military band concerts, fine art displays, theatrical performances, sculptured gardens, a 360-foot-long toboggan slide and a working model coal mine, the bridge was the main attraction of what became known as the Newcastle Jubilee Exhibition.

The replica bridge was remarkably detailed, with all three towers and various shops and houses stacked along its length. The shops sold confectionary and "attractive novelties" to visitors and hosted various museum exhibits.[34] Of particular interest to the public was the "famous old Blue Stone", recovered from the old bridge and set into the pavement of the replica, although the *Chronicle* noted it was "only a blue flagstone" and "quite an ordinary-looking object".[35] The replica bridge, though, was a "pleasing memento of Old Newcastle".[36]

The exhibition version of the Old Tyne Bridge could not have survived a Great Flood—nor a particularly heavy downpour. Despite its substantial appearance, it was largely constructed from paper. It was built on a wooden framework, then covered with a large quantity of Willesden's brand 4-ply. It had a substantially shorter life than the real bridge. At the end of the exhibition, the replica bridge was demolished and its materials auctioned off. The Old Tyne Bridge would not be forgotten, but by then, Tyneside had built several new crossings to connect Newcastle and Gateshead across the mighty river.

* * *

3

A PLACE OF BRIDGES

Thomas Ferens was born in the riverside slums of Oakwellgate in Gateshead in 1841 and was orphaned before the age of five. Visual impairment and a nerve palsy in his hands prevented him from finding employment. There was little support on Victorian Tyneside for a disadvantaged youth. So, from the age of about 15, he stood on the Tyne Bridge asking passers-by for small change, constantly swinging his arms and waggling his head to attract their attention. He stood on the bridge between 11 am and 4 pm every day except Sundays and Christmas Day and viewed it as his occupation. He earned on average between four pence and a shilling each day. Over subsequent years and decades, he became a familiar and popular character on Tyneside known as "Blind Tommy" or, more commonly, "Tommy on the Bridge".[1]

Tommy's first pitch was on the Georgian Tyne Bridge, which had replaced the medieval Old Tyne Bridge. The new bridge was a low, stone-block crossing with nine arches. It had none of the stacked buildings and tall towers of its predecessor. It was built with local stone, from quarries at Elswick and St Anthony's on the Newcastle side and a quarry near Tommy's Oakwellgate on the Gateshead side. Above each arch, the parapet walls were interrupted by ornamental balustrades, designed to give the structure "an air of greater lightness".[2] It was a handsome and elegant structure, even if it had little of the fantastical appeal of the Old Tyne Bridge.

Tommy stood very deliberately on the Blue Stone marking the boundary between Newcastle and Gateshead, which was removed from the remains of the Old Tyne Bridge and inserted into its replacement. Then, when a constable approached him from either side, he would step over the boundary into the opposite jurisdiction to avoid being apprehended for soliciting. Although he hadn't received an education, Tommy chatted to passers-by very intelligently on various subjects, including politics, which he discussed "with a considerable amount of ardour". He often drew a crowd— which occasionally caused obstructions on the bridge.

Although he generally wore a smile on his face, Tommy also had a bad temper and responded with indecent language when he didn't get enough "coppers". Constant teasing from young and old passers-by hardly helped. One observer said Tommy "always secured more abuse than halfpence".[3] Kids would throw pebbles and buttons instead of coins into his collecting tin, although it was said Tommy could identify any donation—button, penny or shilling—by the sound it made when it rattled into the tin. (He would chuck the buttons—and minimal value coins that weren't worth his attention—over his shoulder into the Tyne.) Despite his efforts to avoid the authorities, Tommy was occasionally arrested for using abusive language and causing disruption on the bridge and spent several short periods in jail.

Tommy on the Bridge became famous across Tyneside and beyond. He was sketched for newspaper profiles and snapped for early photography exhibitions. These images showed a short, squat man with his hat attached to his jacket via a piece of string to prevent it from being blown off into the river. He was the subject of poems and songs. Racehorses and homing pigeons were named after him. Tommy was famous enough that a waxwork model stood alongside more widely-known characters in a waxworks exhibition on Newcastle Quayside. According to one story, a pitman who visited the exhibition while "a little foggy with the drink" mistook the waxwork model for the real Tommy on the Bridge. Placing a coin into the model's waxy hand, the pitman told it, "Wey Tommy, aa's weel pleased te see thoo's getten an inside job."[4]

* * *

The Georgian Tyne Bridge opened in 1781, a decade after the collapse of the medieval Old Tyne Bridge. The delay in building the new bridge was due to disagreements about its location and difficulties removing its predecessor. During this delay, Tyneside relied on ferries—and a somewhat makeshift temporary bridge. This came up at the site of the Old Tyne Bridge using timber platforms laid in a crooked course across the remains of the old piers and a series of floating booms.[5]

Workmen began driving the first piles for the permanent bridge into the riverbed in July 1774. Again, responsibility for building the bridge was divided between the Newcastle Corporation and the Bishopric of Durham. Local surveyor John Wooler oversaw the work on the new bridge for Newcastle, and Scottish civil engineer Robert Mylne supervised for Durham. Tyneside's newspapers published advertisements calling for labourers, carpenters and masons. The first stone of the Durham or Gateshead section of the bridge was laid on 14 October 1774, while the Newcastle section's was laid on 25 April 1775 by the town's mayor Sir Matthew Ridley "amidst a great concourse of people who ardently wished prosperity and permanency to the undertaking".[6]

In July 1776, workers installed a commemorative medal into one of the new piers at the boundary between the Newcastle and Gateshead sections, below the location of the restored Blue Stone. The copper medal was about 4 inches in diameter and enclosed in a thick glass case. It bore an image of Newcastle's Guildhall and the motto: *"Quod Felix Faustumque Sit"* ("May It Be Fortunate and Prosperous").

The last arch of the Newcastle section of the new bridge was closed on the morning of 13 September 1779. There was a celebratory procession for the workmen to the Wilkes' Head pub in Newcastle's Flesh Market, where they received "a plentiful dinner and a hearty regale".[7] The bridge was still some way from completion. However, the work impressed the Newcastle *Chronicle*, which commented: "The whole structure, for strength, elegance, and good workmanship, reflect much credit on the architect and builders."[8] Already, the bridge was a source of local pride. Another Newcastle paper, the *Courant*, said the "noble structure" was "beyond example" and should cause the Newcastle Corporation to be "exalted above every other in the kingdom".[9]

The new bridge was officially opened on 13 May 1781, without ceremony. Unfortunately, it was almost immediately found to be unfit for purpose. This was because Britain was entering the era of the mail coach. Introduced by the Post Office in 1784, mail coaches ran letters, packages and handfuls of passengers across Britain at great speeds, powered by relay teams of horses. In 1786, the Post Office added a service between London and Edinburgh. The quickest route was across the Tyne Bridge. (It was this mail coach traffic that turned the old Roman road into the Great North Road.) Other businesses, adopting the speedy, heavy-load Post Office model, also sent big coaches and powerful horse teams across the bridge, and soon these bulky vehicles were crossing the bridge from different directions at the same time.

The new Tyne Bridge was too narrow at just 21 feet and 6 inches wide to accommodate the free passage of these coaches. In 1801, work began to widen the bridge by 12 feet. Unfortunately, the jointing work between the old and new parts of the bridge was found to be defective, and the whole thing had to be clamped together with unsightly iron bars. Previously regarded as "rich and picturesque" in appearance, the bridge had now assumed a more utilitarian aesthetic.[10] Nevertheless, it was strong and stable and would serve the people of Newcastle and Gateshead well—until the unstoppable march of progress again rendered it obsolete.

* * *

In 1810, a seven-year-old boy named William Pearson was playing with pals at the end of the Georgian Tyne Bridge when he toppled backwards into the river. The boy rose to the surface once, then sank out of sight. The accident was witnessed by James Pollock, a dyer on the Close on the Newcastle riverbank. Pollock jumped into a boat and pushed off from the shore, then leapt into the river and grabbed Pearson by the collar. Heaving him into the boat, Pollock rowed the unconscious boy back to shore. Then, "using means to restore suspended animation", Pollock attempted to revive Pearson—eventually with success. Pearson survived, and Pollock was a hero. The boy's parents were described as being in humble circumstances and, although they were surely grateful, Pollock never saw or heard from them.[11]

Fifteen years later, in June 1825, Pollock, who lived at Windmill Hills in Gateshead, was visited by a stranger named Mr Freeman.

Freeman told Pollock he was acting on behalf of a young man who was employed by a highly respectable merchant banker, and he handed Pollock a letter and a silver medal. The letter begged Pollock to accept the medal "as a small token of gratitude from one who, through the blessing of providence, owes his life to your humanity". The sender explained he had never forgotten Pollock's selfless act and had always wanted to show his thanks but was unable to do so due to his young age and unfortunate circumstances. "I cannot find words to express the fullness of my heart," wrote the sender, who, of course, signed his name as William Pearson.

Pearson was fortunate. Although it may seem unlikely today, the Gateshead end of the bridge was a popular bathing (and fishing) spot, particularly for residents of the poverty-stricken tenements on the Gateshead quays. There were many tales of people drowning after falling from or swimming off the Georgian Tyne Bridge and reports of others taking their lives by deliberately throwing themselves from the bridge. It was not particularly high, but a fall—or jump—into the cold, dark Tyne was considered likely to be fatal.

Late one night in January 1828, a young passer-by named Thomas Matthewson noticed a man walking backwards and forwards on the Tyne Bridge "apparently in great distress of mind".[12] The man, who had recently lost his job, placed one foot on the balustrades and another on the top of the bridge wall, evidently preparing to make a leap that would have "hurried him instantaneously into the presence of his Maker". Matthewson hurried to the man, spoke to him at some length about his circumstances, and eventually managed to talk him down from the balustrades and walk him away from the bridge. The story prompted discussion in the local press about how best to help others in similar situations banish their "gloomy ideas".

* * *

The era of the Georgian Tyne Bridge coincided with the rise of Tyneside's most popular pre-football sport—rowing. It's no surprise that a district defined by its river should take to a river sport, and rowing was a way of life on the Tyne. Keelmen and wherrymen (piloting coal-carrying keels and cargo-ferrying wherries) rowed up and down the river every day, and it was from their ranks that

Tyneside's first professional competitive rowers emerged. The most famous of these was Harry Clasper, a former wherryman who became a genuine sporting legend and was very much the Alan Shearer of his day.[13] If Clasper was the Shearer of nineteenth-century Tyneside, the bridge was his Gallowgate End, often acting as the start or finish line for his challenges. Ahead of each race, huge crowds gathered on the bridge, thronging its balustrades and climbing its lamp poles.

In November 1845, Clasper beat leading Thames rower William Pocock over a five-mile course from the Tyne Bridge to Lemington to become "the unrivalled champion of aquatic sports". The bridge and quaysides were packed with spectators, who also crammed into fleets of boats—and steam trains that followed the race's progress from riverside rails. "The result of this contest, it is almost unnecessary to say, excited the most lively feelings of joyous satisfaction in the town and neighbourhood," said the Newcastle *Journal*. The victory of the Tyne over the Thames "appeared to afford an unusual degree of pleasure to the sporting circles of our 'canny' town".[14]

In the previous January, thousands of spectators had gathered on the Tyne Bridge to watch a very different kind of spectacle on the river. A famous actor named Mr Wood (one half of the Mr and Mrs Wood theatrical duo) was floating down the Tyne in a bathtub drawn by four geese to promote a pantomime at Newcastle's recently-opened Theatre Royal. Dressed in a clown's outfit, Wood's stunt "excited considerable attention". Sadly, one of the geese "paid the debt of nature" before the bathtub reached the bridge. It was subsequently revealed that, although the tub was harnessed to the geese, it was actually being pulled by a small steamboat with the tow rope hidden under the water. On the following day, two of the surviving geese were served up with sage and onion stuffing at a slap-up supper.[15]

Even when there were no rowing races or clowns in bathtubs being towed by geese, the Georgian Tyne Bridge was a popular vantage point for strollers and ship-spotters. Like the Old Tyne Bridge, it could be a busy marketplace, with street traders selling fruit, flowers, cheese and bacon from baskets and carts. The bridge really came alive on "Barge Day", an annual regatta on the Tyne to mark Ascension Day. When boats flying flags and banners approached the bridge, spectators crowded against the balustrades to watch. Big crowds were always a boon for street hawkers, pickpockets, and beggars like Tommy on the Bridge, who kept police constables unduly busy. Tommy called the Georgian Tyne Bridge "the Low Bridge" because, by the time he pitched up, it was dominated by a new high-level crossing.

* * *

Both Newcastle and Gateshead were transformed during the era of the Georgian Tyne Bridge. By the mid-1800s, much of central Newcastle had been handsomely renovated by builder Richard Grainger, architects John Dobson and Thomas Oliver, and town clerk John Clayton. At its centre, Grey's Monument stood tall at the head of the outstanding sweep of Grey Street—Grainger's masterpiece and the best street in Britain.[16] Gateshead, previously little more than a tumble of buildings running down Bottle Bank to the bridge, had "extended itself eastward, westward and southward". It was now a populous and independent borough, free from the whims of the Bishop of Durham.[17] Much redevelopment had occurred on the quaysides due to the importance of the River Tyne's thriving industries. The cramped and overcrowded Georgian Tyne Bridge was becoming a barrier to progress. Tyneside needed new crossings, and the first to arrive was the High Level Bridge.

There was another reason to build a new bridge—the arrival of a new form of transport and a boom known as "Railway Mania". Tyneside engineer George Stephenson, born up the river from the Tyne Bridge at Wylam, developed his first steam locomotive in 1814. With his son Robert, he ran the first locomotive to carry passengers, *Locomotion No 1* on the Stockton and Darlington Railway, in 1825. During the 1840s, northern railway companies began to build what would become known as the East Coast Main Line between London and Edinburgh. There was no possible way for a steam train to cross the Georgian Tyne Bridge, so—if the new line was not to bypass Newcastle—a new bridge was required. And it was George's son Robert Stephenson who would build it.

Robert Stephenson, born at Willington Quay on the north bank of the Tyne in 1803, is best known for Stephenson's *Rocket*, the most advanced steam locomotive of its time. His High Level Bridge remains a masterpiece of engineering. It is the oldest surviving bridge between Newcastle and Gateshead. Today, it is a Grade I listed building, described by Historic England as "one of the finest pieces of architectural ironwork in the world".[18] The High Level was so widely admired that it was studied by a young American engineer named Washington Roebling, who visited Newcastle in 1867, shortly before being appointed as the chief engineer of the Brooklyn Bridge.[19]

The High Level is a six-span tied-arch bridge constructed mainly of cast iron. It sits upon five ashlar stone piers. Strikingly, it has a double-deck design, with a rail deck running above a road and pedestrian deck. The rail deck is 120 feet above the high water level, and the road deck is 96 feet above the Tyne. The overall length of the High Level Bridge, from Castle Garth in Newcastle to Wellington Street in Gateshead, is 1,338 feet.

More than 1,300 workmen were involved in constructing the High Level Bridge. One of those was John Smith, a shipwright who lived on Tyne Street in Newcastle. While removing the wooden scaffolding from the High Level Bridge one Saturday morning in July 1849, Smith experienced "one of the most won-derful escapes from impending death that was ever heard".[20] He went to cross from the scaffolding to the rail deck when he stepped on a loose plank, which spun him into the air, 120 feet above the river and the protruding cornice of the stone pier. Smith's imme-diate thought was, "I'm gone!" However, as he toppled, the hem of one of the legs of his fustian trousers caught on a projecting nail. "He hung suspended, swinging to and fro in the wind, and gazing downward upon the cornice and the flood, which threat-ened him with a double death," reported the *Daily News*. A painter named Edward Ward rushed over and grabbed Smith's leg but could not pull him up. Eventually, after Ward repeatedly shouted for help, a group of workmen on the road deck below used a lad-der to bring Smith to safety.

Smith's propitious pants, or "lucky bags", were praised for their remarkable toughness and strength, and a Newcastle clothier placed an ad in the local press claiming to have supplied them. However, a few days later, Smith wrote to the newspapers to contradict that claim: "Sir—Observing in your paper that Messrs Joseph and Co. in their advertisement take to themselves the credit of having made the clothes I wore on the occasion of my falling from the High Level Bridge, I beg to state that I bought the trowsers which saved my life from Messrs Spence and Son, No 1 Sandhill, and I think it is due to them publicly to correct the statement."[21]

When the High Level Bridge was first opened to railway traffic in September 1848 it was still a temporary structure heavily framed in timber scaffolding. Nevertheless, thousands of spectators gathered on the quaysides and on the prime viewing platform of the Georgian Tyne Bridge—the Low Bridge—to watch the ceremonial crossing. The first train to cross the bridge was greeted with the sound of cannons from the Castle Keep, the peal of bells from St Nicholas's and "the most deafening cheers" from proud Tyne-siders.[22] There was more work to done, and the High Level was officially opened a year later with a fleeting visit from Queen Victoria, who paused briefly while crossing the bridge but never got off the royal train.

The High Level Bridge proved to be a challenging ground for several foolhardy men. One Saturday morning in 1850, a man named Williamson, an iron striker from Gateshead, climbed onto the road deck railing of the High Level and leapt 90 feet or so into the Tyne. Williamson survived the jump and swam under one of the arches of the Tyne Bridge, where he was picked up by some companions in a boat. According to the *Tyne Mercury*, the motive for his "mad act" was a wager for a pint of beer. "It is said," the newspaper needlessly added, "this foolish man was at the time in a state of intoxication."[23] Several others attempted to emulate Williamson, including famous high divers Llewellyn Gascoigne, Stephen "the Diver" Jeffrey, and "Professor" Charles Peart, who claimed to be "the World's Champion Diver" and could have bought several pints of beer with his winning wager of £50.

* * *

At around half past midnight on the morning of 6 October 1854, a devastating fire started at the J Wilson and Sons worsted mill on the Gateshead quays. The conflagration quickly destroyed the six-storey building and spread to adjoining warehouses, gaining intensity as it moved. One of those warehouses stored a large quantity of combustible materials. "No sooner had the flame reached the compound," wrote one reporter, "than an explosion took place which no pen can describe, and which made Newcastle and Gateshead shake to their foundations." The Georgian Tyne Bridge shook "as if it would fall to pieces" and the High Level Bridge vibrated "like a thin piece of wire". The river surged and swelled like it was being driven by a great storm.[24]

The explosion was felt as far north as Blyth and as far south as Seaham, both around twelve miles away. Residents of North and South Shields thought they were experiencing an earthquake, and ship's captain heading toward the Tyne felt the shockwaves ten miles out to sea. In Gateshead and Newcastle, terrified residents rushed from their homes in their nightdresses. Burning beams and rafters were flung clear across the Tyne onto the Newcastle Quayside, and buildings on both sides of the river began to combust, the fire passing quickly from house to house. Wooden ships moored to the quaysides also caught fire. Many people in close proximity headed to the safest place they could see—the Tyne Bridge. Unlike its predecessor, this stone structure had no wooden buildings to catch alight. Many hundreds of people stood in shock on the bridge as the fire roared around them. Hundreds more went up onto the High Level Bridge and watched from its elevated vantage point, silhouetted against the enormous flames that filled the night sky.

At least 53 people were killed in the Great Fire of Newcastle and Gateshead. More than 500 were injured. Many buildings—and entire streets—were destroyed on both sides of the river. St Mary's Church was badly damaged. Today, boulders that fell as debris from the explosion can be seen next to the rebuilt St Mary's. There is a blue plaque on the south tower of the current Tyne Bridge marking the site of Wilson's worsted factory, where the devastating fire started.

* * *

The High Level was a toll bridge, and there were toll gates at each end of the road deck. The toll on opening was a penny for pedestrians or threepence for a horse and cart. Few ordinary citizens of

Gateshead and Newcastle were inclined to spend a penny every time they crossed the river, so the Georgian Tyne Bridge—the Low Bridge—remained the regular crossing for most foot passengers. The Tyne Bridge was generally busier and more bustling than the High Level, thus benefiting the likes of Tommy on the Bridge.

In August 1859, the recently-created Tyne Improvement Commission calculated that, on average, more than 28,000 pedestrians, 1,200 carts, 100 carriages, 60 wagons, 120 horsemen, and 580 livestock crossed the Tyne Bridge each day. (By comparison, around 4,500 pedestrians and 400 carts crossed the High Level.) Of particular concern, though, was the increasing amount of traffic that was passing under the bridge. Two hundred and fifty keels and thirteen steamboats negotiated the Tyne Bridge carrying 800 tons of goods every day.[25] Only low-slung boats (and those that lowered their masts) could pass under the Low Bridge, which was an increasingly bothersome problem.

"The trade of the Tyne has gone on increasing from year to year," said an editorial in the *Chronicle*. "The few masts of the last century have become a forest. The banks which confine our river are covered with houses and workshops and docks from the bar to the bridge, and the sound of industry is heard with louder and louder note." The "strong and stately" Georgian Tyne Bridge had "resisted the accidents and shocks" of more than eighty years. However, its time had passed. "The very river itself has had to submit to change and reformation, and the bridge, with its numerous pillars, stout and sturdy, blocking up the waterway and hindering navigation, must give place to a structure more suitable to the times."[26]

So, in its eighth decade, the Georgian Tyne Bridge was to become a victim of Victorian progress. It would be demolished and replaced. The *Gateshead Observer* was delighted, remarking, "The greatest obstacle—the greatest nuisance—to the tidal integrity of the Tyne has at last been condemned."[27] But the Newcastle *Chronicle* expressed sadness at the demise of the bridge that had been "a good and faithful servant". "It has served its purpose well, and thousands who have been in the habit of crossing it daily for many years will feel a pang of regret when the time has arrived for them to pass for the last time over 'the Blue Stone'. But the Tyne Bridge, like everything else, must make way for improvements."[28]

The Georgian Tyne Bridge was never as fondly remembered as the Old Tyne Bridge. It was not as distinctive nor as long-lasting. It was not afforded such a prominent position in the annals of Tyneside. Yet, during its lifetime, it was an essential part of life in Newcastle and Gateshead. Despite the fact it survived into the era of photography, images of the Georgian bridge are rarely seen today in pictures on Newcastle pub walls or in posts on Facebook local history groups. One place the bridge has been recalled, however, is on the cover of one of Tyneside's most famous rock albums. When local heroes Lindisfarne released their chart-topping 1971 album *Fog on The Tyne*—featuring the beloved Tyneside anthem of the same name—its cover featured the stone-arched great nuisance that was the Georgian Tyne Bridge, ensuring, at least among fans of Geordie folk-rock, it would never be entirely forgotten.

Back in the 1860s, it was decided the replacement would occupy the same site as the Georgian bridge (and the previous Old Tyne Bridge and Roman Bridge) but would have a revolutionary design. It was a swing bridge that would pivot on a central pier, allowing river traffic to pass freely through two open channels. Although initially referred to as the New Tyne Bridge, it soon became known as the Swing Bridge. It was constructed from cast and wrought iron by WG Armstrong and Co, the Elswick-based company founded by the great Tyneside engineer and industrialist Lord William Armstrong.

Armstrong was born in Shieldfield in Newcastle in 1810. His father was a former corn merchant who had ascended through the Corporation to become Mayor of Newcastle. Armstrong studied law and worked as a solicitor for more than a decade before his engineering genius prompted a change of career. He went on to become—alongside Robert Stephenson—one of the great engineers of the Industrial Age.

The Swing Bridge mechanism was operated using steam-powered hydraulics, one of Armstrong's specialities. Armstrong also had a vested interest in the construction of the new bridge. When open, it would allow free passage for boats carrying materials and goods to and from his Elswick factory and would enable warships to travel up the Tyne to have fitted another of Armstrong's specialities— naval guns.

The removal of the Georgian Tyne Bridge and the construction of the Swing Bridge took a considerable length of time (longer even than the removal of the medieval bridge and the construction of the Georgian bridge). In the meantime, Tyneside required another temporary bridge. The Temporary Tyne Bridge—as it was creatively called—was a rather more substantial structure than its name might suggest. It was located just a few feet to the west of the Georgian Tyne Bridge, between it and the High Level. It was almost within touching distance of the Georgian bridge and was of similar dimensions, except its arches were wider to allow a freer flow of river traffic. Built from plans prepared by Tyne Improvement Commission engineer John Ure, the Temporary Bridge was constructed from timber instead of stone. The first pile of the Temporary Bridge was driven on 7 September 1865, and the bridge was officially opened—without ceremony—on 17 September 1866. For two days, both the Georgian Tyne Bridge and the Temporary Tyne Bridge were open side-by-side and "passers to and fro between Newcastle and Gateshead had their choice of viaducts".[29]

On 24 June 1866, three months before the Temporary Bridge opened, there was another huge fire, this time at Mr Brown's steam flour mill on the Newcastle side of the river between the Temporary Bridge and the High Level Bridge. Thousands of spectators gathered on the Tyne Bridge despite fears of another explosion—like that of 1845. Many citizens also gathered on the still-under-construction Temporary Bridge, despite it being timber-built and in close proximity to the flames. The Temporary Bridge escaped, but the High Level Bridge caught fire. Its asphalt-covered decking seethed and boiled, and it was feared the great structure might be destroyed. However, teams of firemen, railway workers and navy reserves ripped up long sections of the burning decking and were lowered in bosun's chairs onto the parapet of the bridge to direct hoses at the flames. The flour mill was destroyed, but the bridges remained intact.

The bridges also survived another major flood in January 1871, a century after the Great Flood, when an "immense" rush of water accompanied by large quantities of ice crashed down the Tyne. "The Temporary Tyne Bridge at Newcastle was watched with great anxiety as the water rushed through the arches like a maelstrom," reported one newspaper, "but it stood the test bravely and was not injured in the slightest degree."[30] By December of that year, how-

47

ever, the bridge was beginning to subside, and there were complaints about its unsafe condition.

At the time of that flood, another crossing was being constructed over the Tyne between Newcastle and Gateshead. The first Redheugh Bridge was located a little over half a mile west of the old Tyne Bridges, between the Redheugh area of Gateshead and the railway district of Newcastle, near to Central Station. It was a slender iron girder bridge with four spans supported by three piers, each 152 feet tall. During the icy flood of January 1871, the temporary supports for the bridge were swept away downriver, under the High Level and through the Temporary Bridge, all the way down to Shields and out to sea. Work continued, and the Redheugh Bridge opened in the spring of 1871. (In 1895, after less than a quarter of a century of use, the bridge was found to be in a perilous condition due to cracks, corrosion, and poor workmanship. Repair costs were prohibitive, so it was decided to build a new bridge. The second Redheugh Bridge would open in 1901.)

Before the Swing Bridge could be built, the Georgian Tyne Bridge had to be dismantled. In March 1872, workers discovered the copper medal enclosed in glass that had been inserted into the foundations almost a century earlier. One of the workmen's picks grazed the glass, but it was not broken. (Workers also removed the Blue Stone, which would subsequently be presented to Newcastle's Society of Antiquaries for display among their "collection of curiosities" in the Castle Keep.)[31] In the same month, Dr Bruce was called to the site to view the foundations of the Georgian, medieval and Roman bridges. In May, Bruce presented his findings to the Society of Antiquaries. He also offered his thoughts on the new Swing Bridge. "When it is constructed," he said, "the inhabitants of Tyneside will have to boast of the greatest work of its kind in the world."[32]

The Swing Bridge survives today as a Grade II listed building. A distinctive red and white iron superstructure with granite abutments, the bridge is 561 feet long and 32 feet wide. The arched swinging section is 281 feet long.[33] The bridge was opened to road traffic on 13 June 1876 and first swung open for river traffic on 17 July 1876. The Temporary Bridge had to be demolished before the Swing Bridge could swing, and this was done very quickly.

Thousands of people crossed the Swing Bridge on its opening day, gawping at the "new and curious fabric with its massive iron swing". It was, said one newspaper, "more the object of curiosity than a means of crossing the river".[34]

The first boat to pass through the Swing Bridge was the Italian *Europa*, which sailed up to the Elswick works to collect a hundred-ton Armstrong gun—then the largest gun in the world. The bridge took around 90 seconds to swing open (and another 90 seconds to swing closed). There was no official ceremony, but workers climbed all over the bridge, waving and cheering, and thousands of spectators watched from the quaysides, from rowing boats, and from both decks of the High Level Bridge. One spectator, an old woman, was heard to remark, "Ah, hinnies, the warks of god is wunnerful, but the warks of man is far mair se!"[35] The *Chronicle* said the completion of the Swing Bridge marked "an epoch in the history of operations which have transformed the Tyne... from a sluggish, narrow, ill-navigable stream into a river which may become the Thames of the North".[36]

The replacement of the Georgian Tyne Bridge with the Swing Bridge led to the decline of professional rowing on Tyneside. Most professional rowers had started as keelmen or wherrymen—like Harry Clasper. But the arrival of the Swing Bridge allowed coal and cargo ships to travel further up the river and made keels and wherries and their rowers redundant. The glory days of Clasper and co would never return.

After the Georgian Tyne Bridge was dismantled, Tommy Ferens, who was considered "a living relic of that last bridge", moved his pitch to the Temporary Bridge and then to the Swing Bridge.[37] One local correspondent, who had returned to a much-changed Newcastle after several years away, was pleased to see the familiar "living pendulum still swinging in mid-river". "The Swing Bridge has succeeded the Stone Bridge, the smiling-faced, light-haired lad has aged and grown grey," wrote the correspondent in a letter to the *Chronicle*, "but there he was still with one hand stretched partly out... and that singular wag of the head going perpetually on."[38]

Unfortunately, Tommy on the Bridge was operating in increasingly reduced circumstances. He found it more difficult to earn a living and was more regularly in trouble with the police. A vintage photograph of an older Tommy in a flat cap and winter coat shows a weary and weather-beaten man with no hint of a smile. He told one acquaintance he was doing "very badly" and, despite having stood there all day, had made only "tuppince-hapny oot ov awl the hundrids of folks thit's gyen ower the bridge".[39] Supporters wrote to local newspapers asking passers-by to offer him charity rather than "insulting jokes" and suggesting some form of public subscription might be collected for his upkeep. "It is very sad to see this poor impatient soul," wrote one correspondent. "He has impressed me at times as being in abject want. I have seen him convulsed with sobbing, the tears running down his poor, thin, weather-beaten face, whilst a jerky motion of the hand to his stomach suggested he was suffering the pangs of hunger."[40]

One of the reasons Tommy was struggling—in his own opinion—was the replacement of the Georgian Tyne Bridge with the Swing Bridge. The new bridge would swing open several times a day for up to fifteen minutes at a time. Whenever the advance warning whistle blew, Tommy would vacate his pitch and wait while the bridge slowly swung open then closed again, a bell ringing continuously as it moved. Infuriated by his lost trade, Tommy threatened to "pitishun the Corporation te get the bridge altor'd" and to claim compensation for being prevented from "myekin a livin".[41]

Because the Swing Bridge had no Blue Stone, it was more difficult for Tommy to step over the boundary to avoid apprehension by police constables. Regularly appearing in court at either Newcastle or Gateshead, he would argue he had been in the opposite jurisdiction, and maps would be produced to show he was wrong. Unable to pay his fines, he would be sent to prison. On one occasion at Gateshead Police Court, Chief Constable Trotter told Tommy— despite it being his seventh appearance in the court, and despite having failed to pay previous fines—he would not be sent to prison and would be let off from paying his fines if he promised to behave himself. Tommy promptly launched into a lengthy proclamation, which was cut short by the clerk of the court, who told him he was wasting the court's time. He would now have to pay the fines and costs or serve fourteen days in prison for each fine. "I will go the fourteen days," said Tommy, to which Chief Constable Trotter replied, "*Two* fourteen days, Tommy."[42]

During the later years of his life, Tommy witnessed the construction of another two bridges over the Tyne—the second Redheugh Bridge and the King Edward VII Bridge. The King Edward—which still survives—is a lattice steel girder railway bridge with four spans supported by five sandstone piers, three of which are in the river. It was designed by Charles Augustus Harrison, the Chief Civil Engineer of the North Eastern Railway, and built by the Cleveland Bridge & Engineering Company of Darlington. Construction began in 1902, and the bridge was opened by the titular Edward VII on 10 July 1906. Although often overlooked in deference to its more celebrated neighbours, the 1,150-foot-long and 112-foot-high Grade II Listed structure continues to carry heavy railway traffic more than a century after its construction and has been described as "Britain's last great railway bridge".[43]

There were now four bridges between Newcastle and Gateshead—the Redheugh, the King Edward, the High Level, and the Swing. The now-familiar riverscape was taking shape. Tyneside was now a place of bridges. It would be another couple of decades before work began on the Tyne Bridge, but the canvas on which it would be painted had been set on its easel. Part of what makes the Tyne Bridge such a magnificent spectacle today is its setting among the complementary suite of other bridges. The Tyne Bridge would not have the same visual impact without its companions, particularly its nearest neighbours, the High Level and the Swing.

Tommy Ferens died on the Swing Bridge on New Year's Day 1907, aged 66, after collapsing during a snowstorm. He had suffered a stroke, his condition worsened by exposure to the severe cold weather. For his funeral in Gateshead, hundreds of mourners lined the streets. Despite this public show of support, a subscription for funeral expenses gained only two donations totalling one pound and eight shillings. The coroner, commenting to the press, said there was "no other man of his class so well known to the public" and he would be greatly missed.[44] The man who spanned the eras of the Georgian Tyne Bridge and the Victorian Swing Bridge—and witnessed Tyneside's extraordinary bridge-building transformation—was gone.

4

A NEW TYNE BRIDGE

In 1922, a young engineer named Thomas Webster wrote to both the Newcastle *Journal* and *Chronicle* to propose a new Tyne Bridge between Newcastle and Gateshead.[1] Webster was born in Newburn, right by the Tyne. He was a former student of the Elswick Mechanics Institute founded by Sir William Armstrong. Webster was an engineering draughtsman in the ordnance department at Armstrong Whitworth's Elswick Works and lived with his widowed mother in a terraced house on Ladykirk Road, just off Elswick Road.[2]

Webster, an associate member of the Institution of Civil Engineers, had previously written to the local press concerning a scheme to reduce the dangers to public health (and to laundry on washing lines) of belching chimneys in "excessively smoky districts" such as Tyneside. The idea was to use a series of current-carrying electric wires to remove the smoke's "solid matter" and leave only transparent gas.[3] But it was the idea of a new bridge that really inspired him, as a potential solution to what newspapers called the "Trans-Tyne Traffic Problem."[4]

The motor car had arrived on Tyneside's roads in a great cloud of exhaust fumes, and the road bridges between Newcastle and Gateshead—the Swing Bridge, the High Level and the Redheugh—were struggling to cope. In a few years' time, Webster said, as the number of tram cars, motor cars, omnibuses and lorries increased, traffic on Tyneside's roads would be "as bad as Oxford Street, London". Webster viewed a new Tyne Bridge built at high level as the solution to the traffic congestion and other pressing problems of the 1920s.

The idea for a new high-level Tyne Bridge had actually been proposed almost half a century earlier, in 1883, by Newcastle councillor

Sir Charles Hamond, who felt the tolls for passengers on the existing High Level Bridge were as high as the crossing.[5] The proposal was forgotten, then remembered in 1892, when another Newcastle councillor, William Cowell, said if the new bridge had been necessary in 1883, it was "very much more so now".[6] Committees were formed, meetings were held, and plans were made. The new bridge would run between Pilgrim Street in Newcastle and Gateshead High Street, in the same location as the current Tyne Bridge. In 1899, the Newcastle *Chronicle* published a sketch of the proposed bridge, depicting an alternate reality vision of the Tyne's familiar riverscape. The proposed new bridge was of similar scale and size to the current Tyne Bridge and sat in exactly the same position, but it was a suspension bridge rather than an arch bridge.[7] Unfortunately, the proposal was considered too expensive at around £560,000.

Gateshead Council favoured a longstanding proposal by Benjamin Plummer, the secretary of the Chamber of Commerce, which would only cost £200,000. Plummer's proposal, however, which had originated as far back as 1860 and pre-dated even the Swing Bridge, was dismissed as "too previous".[8] More broadly, detractors suggested the last thing this famous place of bridges needed was another one. At a meeting of Gateshead Council, one attendee commented there were "too many bridges altogether".[9] Discussions rumbled on for a few years, but by 1908, the decision was made not to proceed.

By the 1920s, though, a new Tyne Bridge was back on the agenda. Tyneside was bursting at the seams. The combined population of Newcastle and Gateshead had more than doubled since the building of the Swing Bridge in the 1870s to more than 550,000 at the time of the 1921 census.[10] Although still very separate conurbations, the city of Newcastle and the county borough of Gateshead were perpetually connected via the river and its bridges. The people of Tyneside were continually crossing the bridges for work, for shopping, and to watch football at St James' Park. (Newcastle United, entering a brief period of success, were attracting record crowds of more than 60,000.) So, there was a considerable amount of local traffic, plus a constant flow of vehicles following the main route between Scotland and the south.

Tramcars now criss-crossed Tyneside and motor cars were becoming mainstream. The pioneering Ford Model T and models from Austin, Rover, Mercedes-Benz, Bentley, Rolls Royce—and Thomas Webster's Armstrong Whitworth—were all chugging around Tyneside's roads. Motorcycles were also an increasingly common sight. And, of course, the horse and cart was still a relied-upon mode of transport. (Newcastle City Council's fleet of seventeen municipal vehicles were all horse-drawn carts until replaced with motor vehicles in 1923.) Tramlines were being strung across the road deck of the High Level Bridge, and the congestion caused by those works and the anticipated heavy flow of tramcars made that toll bridge even less attractive.

Tolls for motor cars were considered disproportionately high (at fourpence for a light motor car). This expense diverted drivers away from the High Level down the steep and winding approaches to the toll-free Swing Bridge. The Redheugh Bridge was also a toll bridge, which deterred many passengers from using it. So most of this traffic crossed between Newcastle and Gateshead via the Swing Bridge, which was always jammed. And when the bridge swung open, traffic came to a complete stop. Lines of cars, vans and carts snaked around Sandhill up into Newcastle and over Bridge Street and up Bottle Bank into Gateshead, bringing the centres of both metropolises to a standstill. Pedestrians, too, had to stand and queue to cross the river.

Tyneside in the 1920s was a place of faded glamour, the facades of its grand Georgian and Victorian buildings made soot-black by decades of smoke-spewing industry. That industry had served Tyneside well, but hard times were underway. The world was dealing with the aftermath of the Great War, in which more than a million British lives were lost. Hundreds of thousands more were injured—gassed, wounded, blinded, physically disabled—and many more were dealing with mental traumas. Almost every family, street and workplace lost relatives, neighbours and colleagues, and Tyneside was full of veterans who could not easily return to their old lives.

For those who could still work, jobs were hard to find. After a brief post-war boom, industry declined and unemployment rose. Falling demand meant Tyneside's leading industries—coal mining and shipbuilding—were particularly badly hit. Visitors to the Coaly Tyne saw a great river waning, with vacant shipyard berths and empty dry docks making clear the severity of the situation. Every idle shipyard meant hundreds of unemployed men. Support was slow to arrive. In August 1920, when Newcastle North MP Sir Nicholas Grattan-Doyle asked government minister Sir Eric Geddes in the House of Commons if he was aware of the increase in unemployment in Newcastle and the high number of workers being made redundant by large firms on Tyneside, Geddes admitted he was not.[11]

In 1922, Yorkshire MP William Pringle described unemployment on Tyneside as "abnormal compared with anything we have ever experienced in this country". Speaking in the House of Commons, Pringle said unemployment had hit 40 per cent in shipbuilding and similar levels in the iron and steel industries.[12] A proposed solution was the provision of grants to fund projects that might provide employment and keep workers and their families out of poverty—projects such as building a new bridge.

Thomas Webster said his idea for a new Tyne Bridge had first come to him in 1919, following the end of the war. His bridge would run from Pilgrim Street in Newcastle to Gateshead High Street, just like the 1880s proposal (which he said had been "practically forgotten").[13] He had noticed that Pilgrim Street and High Street were almost in a straight line at almost the same height above the river. "I saw it just as though I could leap from one street to another," he recalled.[14] So he decided to make some surveys and draw up a design for a bridge. Webster went down to the riverbanks to make his surveys with a home-made theodolite by the first gleams of sunrise on summer mornings to avoid attracting attention. By 1922, he said, "I felt the time was ripe to postulate the proposition of a new Tyne Bridge." Webster considered his proposal to be "the natural solution to the traffic problem".[15]

Webster submitted a sketch of his bridge with his proposal and—although it occupied the same position—it didn't look much like the eventual Tyne Bridge. It was a steel lattice crossing similar in appearance to the King Edward railway bridge but supported by piers on either riverbank and a single pier in the middle of the Tyne. Webster's bridge was 1,600 feet in length, and the roadway was 80 feet above the high water level. Because its only river pier was in line with the central pier of the Swing Bridge, it should not hinder river traffic. And because of its great height, nor should it interfere with any buildings of importance. It was wide enough to carry separate lanes of tramcars and toll-free traffic. "It is surely better to spend money on a thing which is needed," wrote Webster, "and not to overcrowd or overload an existing bridge."

The proposal quickly gained support. Newspaper correspondents commended the idea and reasoned the benefits would justify the costs. But there were doubts the councils would sanction it. "The authorities of the neighbouring towns apparently have neither the vision nor the courage to undertake such a beneficent or responsible piece of work," wrote one correspondent. "I suppose we will have to wait and see what happens."[16]

The tramway service between Newcastle and Gateshead over the High Level Bridge opened in January 1923. As predicted, this considerably worsened traffic congestion. One tram car crossed the bridge in each direction every 60 seconds during regular hours and every 45 seconds during rush hours. This meant almost every motor car, omnibus, delivery van, or horse and cart encountered a tramcar on the narrow two-lane road deck of the bridge, and everything was held up by the trams. Much of this traffic inevitably diverted to the already-congested Swing Bridge.

In a speech at a celebratory luncheon to mark the launch of the tram service, Newcastle MP and shipowner Sir George Renwick said it would not be long before Tyneside would need to seriously consider building a new bridge.[17] The Lord Mayor of Newcastle, William Bramble (a self-made entrepreneur known as "the Dick Whittington of Newcastle"), said the "teeming multitude" of people using the trams proved another bridge was necessary. "It is only a question of time before the two authorities are in a position to bear the financial responsibility of making another bridge so both towns can develop."[18] Sir John McCoy, the Mayor of Gateshead (and another wealthy Tyneside shipowner), agreed, and said it was time for a new bridge.

In McCoy's Gateshead, unemployment was the pressing issue. At a meeting of Gateshead Council, local unemployed workers were invited to present their views. They were unhappy with the inadequate provision of so-called "relief work" and the increasingly high number of men being turned away from the Labour Exchange each week. Those who could not find work were advised to go into the Workhouse (also known in Gateshead as the Poorhouse), a Dickensian institution that would not be fully abolished until after the Second World War. The unemployed workers suggested the council apply for government grants to fund projects that would create work for the unemployed and keep them out of the Poorhouse. Gateshead, they recommended, should build a new market, baths and washhouses, and—most importantly—a new Tyne Bridge.[19]

Meanwhile, a joint council of Tyneside planning committees discussed alternative proposals for crossing the Tyne—three bridges and a tunnel. Newcastle Council's favoured proposal was a crossing known as the Pelaw Bridge, some two miles downstream of the city centre. However, there was another proposal on the table for a new bridge "in the vicinity of the High Level" between Pilgrim Street and High Street.[20] That proposal might have seemed familiar.

Thomas Webster was still taking his idea to various council members in the hope of convincing them to make a start on his Tyne Bridge. In October 1923, Sir George Renwick invited Webster to present his proposal to the Newcastle Chamber of Commerce. Webster reported the estimated cost of his bridge to be £400,000, and he expected financial assistance could be obtained from central government.[21] He had noticed several new government schemes aimed at creating employment. Webster left his plans with the secretary of the Chamber of Commerce for members to consult. He had undoubtedly opened ears and minds, and his proposal would have a lasting legacy, but Webster would no longer be involved in planning the new Tyne Bridge. It would take the promotion of a particularly determined new local official to finally get the project underway.

* * *

Stephen Easten was chairing a special meeting of Newcastle City Council in the council chambers at Newcastle's old Town Hall. It was January 1924, and Easten had in November been appointed in a unanimous decision as the city's Lord Mayor. Easten was a building contractor by trade. He was born in Lowick, near Berwick-upon-Tweed, and served a building apprenticeship before moving to Newcastle in 1887 at the age of 21. Despite his youth, he had the confidence and determination to win several big contracts and soon established himself as one of the most prominent builders in the expanding city. One of his constructions was Milburn House, a grand red-brick building down by the Castle on the Side. Easten had served as a councillor since 1906, so he knew much about local politics, although he was not necessarily a natural politician.

Nor was he an eloquent speaker, and he could be blunt and impatient. But he was a practical thinker with a knack for wrapping his head around problems and getting them solved. He did not bully his way to a consensus; rather, he was described as "rather modest and retiring" and had developed a reputation for solving disputes through good humour.[22] He would listen to others' points of view, "however lop-sided or distorted", try to make sense of them, then assuredly bring them around to his way of thinking.[23] It worked because of his energy and enthusiasm and the strength of his reputation. According to one local paper, "Men trusted his word and respected his capacity and foresight, his ability to grapple with facts."[24]

In 1924, Easten was 57 years old and a widower. (His "charming and graceful" 19-year-old daughter May acted as lady mayoress.)[25] He had a round face, close-cropped grey hair and a white goatee-style beard. He lived in a house named "Esperance" on Akenside Terrace in Newcastle's leafy suburb of Jesmond. Easten had gained a national reputation in the building and allied trades, serving as the president of the Master Builders' Association, the chairman of the National Wages and Conditions Council, and as an advisor to the government on post-war reconstruction schemes. More than anything, he had a reputation for getting things done. And what he wanted to get done in 1924, before the end of his short twelve-month term as mayor, was to finally jumpstart the scheme to build the new Tyne Bridge.

Newcastle's old Town Hall was a huge, grandly neoclassical building situated on St Nicholas Square, between the Bigg Market and the Cathedral. The ground floor contained a corn exchange and shops, and the upper floors housed the council chambers and an enormous music hall. It was built during the great regeneration of the city in the 1850s. Unfortunately, it had not been properly maintained and by the 1920s, it was shabby and run-down. (An ornate clock tower that stood over the Bigg Market entrance was so dangerously decrepit that it was demolished in the 1930s. The entire building—then derelict—was demolished in the 1970s.)

Easten considered the Town Hall to be "more or less a joke" and was embarrassed to invite visitors to meet there.[26] Happily, he said, if visitors turned their backs on the southern facade of the hall, they would see the Cathedral spire, "one of the finest examples of architecture or engineering to be found in this or any country". Looking beyond the Cathedral and past the Black Gate and Castle Keep, visitors would see the High Level Bridge, another engineering triumph of which locals should be proud. But, he said, Tyneside needed a new bridge, a structure that—unlike the Town Hall—would not become a liability. Instead, although its full value might not be apparent for several years, it would be a distinct asset to the city and the region. This was only the beginning of a new era on Tyneside, and time would show the value of a new Tyne Bridge.

Easten was aware efforts to get previous proposals moving had hit roadblocks as frustrating as the traffic jams that snaked up from the river into Newcastle and Gateshead. Now he was in a hurry to get on with the project, relieve the traffic problems, and provide work for the growing number of unemployed tradespeople on the Tyne. And there was little time to spare. According to figures published in January 1924, there were 50,000 men out of work on the banks of the river.[27]

At the special meeting in the "joke" of a Town Hall, Mayor Easten, wearing his newly-bestowed chain of office, put forward a resolution to create a New Bridge Committee. The committee's purpose was to formulate a scheme to construct a new toll-free Tyne Bridge to carry traffic and a tramway. Easten dismissed the proposed Pelaw Bridge, and said the new bridge would cross near to the High Level and Swing bridges. The committee would have the authority to enter into negotiations with Gateshead Council, the Ministry of Transport and other relevant parties, and to obtain a preliminary report from a bridge engineer. The ultimate aim was to get the go-ahead for the bridge via an act of Parliament. The resolution was carried unanimously.

Within days, Easten was in London, along with Newcastle's long-standing town clerk Arthur Oliver and city engineer W.J. Steele, to meet Ministry of Transport officials and discuss Parliamentary approval for the work and allocation of funds. Newcastle's Bridge Committee also interviewed and appointed two of the country's leading civil engineers—Sir Maurice Fitzmaurice (of the Goode, Fitzmaurice, Wilson & Mitchell firm) and Sir Basil Mott (of Mott, Hay & Anderson)—to make a joint report on the bridge scheme. The engineers were paid a fee of £900 to determine the best site for the crossing, the most suitable type of bridge, the estimated cost of construction, and the estimated length of time it would take to build. This report was used to prepare a Parliamentary Bill.

A new Tyne Bridge between Newcastle and Gateshead could only be built with the cooperation of both councils. At the beginning of February, Gateshead Council, led by Mayor Sir John McCoy, agreed the new bridge was necessary and appointed its own committee to liaise with the Newcastle committee and get the scheme moving. Then, on Monday 11 February 1924, both the Newcastle and Gateshead committees met at Newcastle Town Hall, where they formed a Joint Bridge Committee, headed up—of course—by the Lord Mayor of Newcastle, Stephen Easten. There were many more meetings to come involving various committees of bearded men in dilapidated chambers, but the project was now firmly kicking into gear.

At the beginning of March, Newcastle councillor Sir George Lunn (Sir John McCoy's partner in the Lunn & McCoy shipping company) outlined the preliminary report prepared for the Parliamentary Bill. As suggested in previous proposals (not least by Thomas Webster), the bridge would occupy the site between Pilgrim Street and High Street because this presented the fewest engineering difficulties. It was a single span bridge with a clearance of 84 feet above the Tyne—subject to negotiations with the Tyne Improvement Commission, which was responsible for the maintenance and usage of the river. The estimated cost to build the bridge and its approaches was £580,000. Land purchases and other expenses would push the total bill to £888,000—although it was noted that, with all eventualities, this could creep nearer to £1m. The cost would be split between Newcastle and Gateshead in proportion to rateable values—meaning the larger Newcastle with a richer public purse would pay a bigger share. Interest on the payments would be covered by receipts from the tramways, which would be re-routed over the new bridge. However, this was all dependent on receiving a sizeable grant towards the cost from the Ministry of Transport. Mayor Easten, responding to the report, said he did not know how much the grant might be for, but he would not want to proceed with the scheme unless it was a "substantial amount".[28]

One dissenting voice, Newcastle councillor and former engineer David Adams, suggested the committee was acting in too great haste and might have to repent at leisure. Adams argued the proposed bridge would create further congestion in Newcastle city centre, and another site should have been selected. And he made a significant point in stating that, in addition to commercial and utilitarian considerations, the bridge should be built with aesthetic considerations. It was important to consider what the bridge would look like.[29] He wanted the bridge to be beautiful so it would be properly appreciated and Tyneside could be proud of it.

Despite Adams' misgivings about the location, the report was adopted. The next step was to seek the approval of the citizens of Newcastle and Gateshead via town meetings and secure the go-ahead and funding from the government via the Parliamentary Bill. There was also the possibility of an objection from LNER (the London and North-Eastern Railway), which was concerned that the arrival of the new Tyne Bridge would divert traffic away from the High Level Bridge, where it drew income from tolls. Also, Newcastle Council paid LNER one halfpenny for every passenger that travelled over the High Level in a tram. If the trams were removed to the new Tyne Bridge, this revenue would be lost. Lloyds Bank was also expected to object, because the proposal would require the demolition of several buildings, including one of its branches.

Mayor Easten led a delegation at a special meeting to head off the concerns of the Tyne Improvement Commission, which comprised representatives of local councils and businesses that relied on the river for their trade. Its chief engineer was Newcastle-born R.F. Hindmarsh, who had worked for the Commission since the 1890s and had overseen the addition of numerous docks, quays and engineering yards on the Tyne. The Commission's chairman was Sir Alfred Palmer, the son of the founder of the Palmers Shipbuilding and Iron Company, which owned Palmer's shipyard at Jarrow. Palmer said the Commission's main concern was that the proposed height of the bridge, at 84 feet above high water during ordinary spring tides, might prevent taller ships in the future from travelling up the Tyne. It would be preferable, he said, if the height was raised to 100 feet. In response, Easten said he was very mindful of the influence the new bridge might have on the river and had enormous respect for the work of the Tyne Commission. (Between 1850 and 1923, the Commission had excavated 146m tons of material from the river bed—more than was excavated to build the Suez Canal—to improve its passage.)[30] But, Easten said, raising the height to 100 feet would seriously devalue the scheme and was "wholly incompatible" with their aims.[31]

Easten pointed out that both the High Level Bridge and the King Edward Bridge were lower than the proposed new bridge. So any obstacle the new bridge might create would be no greater than those that already existed. In any case, Easten claimed the number of vessels affected by such a height restriction was "so infinitesimal as to be scarcely worthy of consideration". But what was worth considering was the additional disruption and cost—around an extra 15 per cent on the total bill—to the residents of Newcastle and Gateshead if the bridge had to be raised by an additional 16 feet. "Your duty," Mayor Easten concluded, "while giving every consideration to the interests of the river, is to consider the interests of the communities adjoining the river." The meeting adjourned and, after a brief discussion, the Commission agreed they would have no objection to the bridge being built at the height of 84 feet—and with no obstructions to the river such as piers or pillars. The Commission would later make further demands on the bridge builders, but for now, Easten and his colleagues could move on to gain the approval of their public.

First, though, the Lord Mayor had another important civic duty to perform. On 26 April 1924, Easten was at the British Empire Stadium at Wembley to see Newcastle United win the FA Cup. Newcastle beat Aston Villa 2–0 with goals from Stan Seymour and Neil Harris. Two days later, Easten and immense crowds of jubilant supporters were at Newcastle Central Station to greet the victorious team on their return from London. The train arrived just after 7 pm—after clocking-off time in the shipyards and factories. Despite rain, hundreds of thousands of flat-capped fans filled the streets. "No Cup winners have ever had a more rousing reception," said the *Daily Mirror*.[32] The crowds were so great that Easten had to delay his official welcome until the players were ferried through the thronged streets in motor cars to a reception at the Empire Theatre—a journey of a few hundred yards that took two hours. Once there, Easten congratulated the team on behalf of the city in his full civic regalia, and a band played "For They Are Jolly Good Fellows". Newcastle's Tyneside-born captain Frank Hudspeth told the reception audience, rather straightforwardly, they had set out to win and they had won, and as a local lad he was very proud to have captained such a fine team.[33] Mayor Easten and Hudspeth were photographed together with the gleaming English Cup.

On the following day, as Tyneside basked in the warm afterglow of the cup win, Easten and his committee set out to gain approval from the public for the bridge. Two separate public meetings were held in Newcastle and Gateshead on Tuesday, 29 April. Both were sparsely attended, and newspapers suggested interest was lacking. (Tyneside might have been nursing a pronounced hangover following the football homecoming.) In Newcastle, Easten outlined the proposal. He stated that the existing three traffic bridges carried 36 million passengers each year, and the High Level alone carried 13.5 million motor cars. And he reiterated he was in a hurry to get things moving to put unemployed men back to work. But the project would only go ahead on the condition it received a substantial grant of at least 50 per cent of the cost from the government. Easten moved a resolution to approve the Newcastle upon Tyne and Gateshead Corporations (Bridge) Bill. At the end of a very short meeting, the bill was unanimously approved with a vote of 56 to nil. Over in Gateshead, a similar meeting saw the same bill approved by "an overwhelming majority".[34]

When the bill came before Parliament, LNER initially opposed it but later withdrew the objection after the parties came to an amicable agreement. Lloyds Bank also retracted its objection. The bill went through the House of Commons and the House of Lords and was given royal assent on 7 August 1924 to become the Newcastle-upon-Tyne and Gateshead Corporations (Bridge) Act. At a meeting of Newcastle and Gateshead's Joint Bridge Committee, Mayor

Easten said the committee had achieved its aim, which had been to "get the Act". Now, he said, it was up to the two councils to go forward and "get the bridge".[35]

A few days later, Mayor Easten announced he had received a telegram confirming the Ministry of Transport and the Treasury had agreed to make a grant of 65 per cent of the estimated cost of the bridge. Now placing the estimated cost including land purchases at around £970,000, Easten said this meant the grant would be worth more than £600,000, and no one would argue that was anything but generous. "We can safely say now that all the difficulties are out of the way," he said, "although there is still a good deal of work to do."[36]

In response, Sir Arthur Munro Sutherland, another local shipping tycoon and the owner of the Newcastle *Chronicle* newspaper (and the Aston Martin car manufacturer), said this result—achieved in such a short time—was a feather in the cap of the Lord Mayor. When Easten first mooted the idea of a new bridge, everyone thought it might be "a hardy annual for several years". But, before his year of office expired, the Lord Mayor had got his bill through Parliament and persuaded the government to contribute 65 per cent of the cost. This, said Sutherland, "augured well for the success of the bridge".

In November, Stephen Easten passed his chain of office to the new Lord Mayor, Walter Lee. By then, preliminary borings for the new bridge were being sunk on the Gateshead side of the river by William Coulson Ltd. (This Durham-based firm of boring contractors or "master sinkers" was one of the oldest companies in the North East, founded in 1764, while the Old Tyne Bridge was still standing.)[37] Thomas Webster submitted a new design—this one inspired by the Forth Bridge—hoping the design contract would be put up for open competition.[38] That didn't happen, and it was decided Mott, Hay & Anderson, whose Basil Mott had worked on the preliminary report, would design the bridge. But the contract to build the bridge was up for competition. The Joint Bridge Committee invited tenders from the beginning of November and expected to make a decision within a few weeks. As for Stephen Easten, he was not yet finished with the bridge, or perhaps the bridge was not yet finished with him.

5

AN INGENIOUS PLAN

The vast steel arch curves into the air above the river. The ends of the arch are anchored with massive hinges on each bank. A horizontal deck runs through the arch, flanked by two giant stone towers. It's what is known as a two-hinge through-arch bridge. At the time of its construction, it was the longest arch bridge in the world. This remarkable piece of engineering will look very familiar to anyone from Tyneside. But this is not the Tyne Bridge (nor the visually-similar Sydney Harbour Bridge). This bridge sits more than 3,000 miles away from the Tyne, over a tidal strait of the East River in New York. It was built a decade before the Tyneside crossing and is painted red, not green. This is the Hell Gate Bridge, and it was the engineering inspiration for the men who designed the Tyne Bridge.

The Hell Gate Bridge crosses the Hell Gate strait between Astoria in Queens and the conjoined Randalls and Wards Islands in Manhattan. It was built between 1912 and 1916 by the American Bridge Company and designed by a remarkable engineer named Gustav Lindenthal. The Austrian-born Lindenthal was entirely self-taught and clambered up the city's ranks to become New York's Commissioner of Bridges. He had previously designed the Queensboro Bridge, which also crosses the East River between Queens and Manhattan. He was modest, plain-speaking, and a bridge-building genius. "To an engineer, one bridge differs from another only in magnitude, much as one egg is bigger than another egg," said Lindenthal during the construction of the Hell Gate Bridge. "All such structures have basic principles that persist no matter what may be their proportions."[1] Despite its difficulties, Lindenthal considered the Hell Gate project to be "all in a day's work, although it represents a lifetime's experience in bridge construction."[2]

One of the men inspired by Lindenthal's Hell Gate Bridge was British civil engineer Ralph Freeman. Freeman was born in West Hackney in London in 1880. The son of a cigar manufacturer, he won a scholarship from the Siemens telegraph and electric company to attend the Central Technical College in Kensington. He emerged as an outstanding and prize-winning student. After leaving school, he joined the London firm of consulting engineers Sir Douglas Fox & Partners. Freeman was heavily involved with the design of the Victoria Falls Bridge over the Zambezi, which was completed in 1905, and he worked on other bridges and railways in Africa and South America. He became a partner in the firm in 1912 and began to travel regularly to the United States to supervise engineering projects. It's not known when exactly Freeman visited the Hell Gate Bridge, but he did sail to New York for a month at the end of October 1913, while the bridge was being constructed.

A few days after Ralph Freeman arrived in New York for that visit, Gustav Lindenthal led a group of 200 engineers on a tour of the bridge. The group enjoyed boat rides, cigars and refreshments on a "perfect afternoon" in late fall New York.[3] During the tour, Lindenthal and his engineers explained the unique difficulties they had faced, and how those difficulties were overcome. As the Hell Gate was a busy shipping channel, there could be no interference with the river traffic. This meant the bridge could not stand on piers in the river, so it had to be constructed with a huge single span— 978 feet long (about the length of three American football fields). Lindenthal determined an arch bridge on a scale that had never been built was most suitable for this crossing. He could not raise the bridge from the river, so he built it out from the banks in two halves, each supported by anchors until they met in the middle. As well as being the world's longest arch bridge, it would also be the heaviest, containing 19,000 tons of steel alone. The tour group was left with no doubt the Hell Gate Bridge was "one of the wonders of the engineering world".[4]

Ralph Freeman—a dashing, clean-shaven fellow with a side-parted executive haircut—understood the engineering principles behind the Hell Gate Bridge. In 1906, while a student, Freeman won the Institution of Civil Engineers' Miller Prize for a paper on two-hinged steel arch bridges, in which he proposed that this type of arch bridge was more rigid and less costly than an equivalent girder bridge and more pleasing to the eye. "The steel arch is a form of bridge which possesses, in addition to the advantages of economy and simplicity of erection, that of artistic merit," wrote Freeman, "and it is surprising, especially in view of the importance attached in recent years to aesthetic treatment in the design of engineering structures, that this type of bridge has been so seldom adopted by British engineers."[5]

By 1922, Freeman—then forty-one years old—had become the senior partner at Douglas Fox following the death of Sir Douglas.[6] Douglas Fox were the consulting engineers for the Cleveland Bridge & Engineering Company, which had built the Victoria Falls Bridge as well as the King Edward VII Bridge on Tyneside (and the Tees Transporter Bridge on Teesside). Cleveland Bridge was planning to tender for a contract with the government of New South Wales in Australia to build a bridge over Sydney Harbour. The company asked Freeman to prepare a design for this Sydney Harbour Bridge, which was intended to be a cantilever bridge—essentially a purely horizontal structure. "I agreed to do so provided I was also allowed to design an arch," Freeman recalled, "for I was convinced that an arch was the right bridge for the site."[7]

Freeman based his arch design on that of the Hell Gate Bridge, modifying and enlarging it to suit Sydney's much wider body of water with a massive span of 1,650 feet. But Freeman's work came to a halt in September 1923 with the sudden death of Charles Frederick Dixon, the chairman of the Cleveland Bridge company. Following Dixon's death, Cleveland Bridge decided not to tender for the Sydney contract. "I believed that my designs were good," said Freeman, "and it would have been a great disappointment to have lost the work done."[8]

A few days later, Freeman was called to a meeting with Sir Arthur Dorman, Sir Hugh Bell and Lawrence Ennis, the chairman, vice-chairman and general manager of Dorman, Long & Co, the Middlesbrough-based steel producer. The company was diversifying into bridge-building and, following the withdrawal of Cleveland Bridge, Dorman Long was keen to tender for the Sydney contract. But time was running short to submit a proposal for one of the biggest and most expensive bridges ever built. As Freeman had already prepared his designs for the Cleveland Bridge company proposal, would he now act as consulting engineer for Dorman Long? "In the special circumstances in which this decision had to be reached, the utmost promptitude was essential, and our interview was concluded within an hour or so," recalled Freeman.[9]

In February 1924, with Freeman's preferred arch design, Dorman Long won the contract to build the Sydney Harbour Bridge. Construction work would not begin until December 1926. In the meantime, Dorman Long submitted a tender to build the Tyne Bridge. This would be somewhat smaller than the Sydney bridge, but it represented a similar—and in some ways more complicated—challenge. Once again, the proposal relied on a design by Freeman. Inspired by Hell Gate and informed by Sydney, Freeman's Tyne Bridge would be another extraordinary steel arch bridge.

* * *

Back on Tyneside, having secured the Parliamentary Act and the generous grant, the Newcastle and Gateshead Joint Bridge Committee invited tenders for the construction of the New Tyne Bridge in October 1924. Alongside Dorman Long, other interested parties included Cleveland Bridge (back in business without Ralph Freeman) and Tyneside's Armstrong Whitworth (the builders of the Swing Bridge). Within a month, the committee had received five tenders of varying cost:

Motherwell Bridge Co, £743,938;

Sir WG Armstrong, Whitworth & Co, £743,229;

Sir William Arrol & Co, £606,454;

Cleveland Bridge & Engineering Company, £604,421;

Dorman, Long & Co, £571,225.[10]

The tenders were discussed at a meeting chaired by the former mayor—now councillor—Stephen Easten. Councillor Easten said the committee's estimated cost was £580,000, and all but one of the tenders were in excess of that figure. Local favour was with Tyneside's Armstrong Whitworth. Sir George Lunn said he would like to see the contract go to a North-Eastern firm, but Armstrong Whitworth's tender was 30 per cent higher than Dorman Long's, and "local patriotism would not stand that strain".[11] So Easten proposed that the committee accept the lowest-priced tender—from Dorman Long—subject to the approval of their firm of engineers, Mott, Hay & Anderson. A week later, the engineers approved the tender. And a week after that, on 17 December 1924, Newcastle City Council, on behalf of the Joint Bridge Committee, agreed to award the contract for the new Tyne Bridge to Dorman Long.

If the announcement did not quite satisfy local patriotism on Tyneside, it caused celebration on Teesside. Dorman Long already had the Sydney Harbour Bridge in the bag. They would manufacture and ship steel from Teesside to New South Wales to be shaped into sections for the Sydney bridge in Australian workshops. The Tyne Bridge contract meant more work and more jobs, and in this case, the steel—more than 7,000 tons of it—would be manufactured and the sections fabricated entirely on Teesside. And Dorman Long had a longstanding connection to Tyneside, as the company's roots could in part be traced back to the banks of the Tyne.

It began with Newcastle-born Isaac Lowthian Bell and his brothers Thomas and John—trading as Bell Brothers—who, in the 1840s, started to manufacture pig iron (crude iron made by smelting iron ore) at Walker on the north bank of the Tyne. In the following decade, the brothers founded the Clarence Ironworks at Port Clarence on the north bank of the Tees (near to the Transporter Bridge at a site today located opposite Middlesbrough FC's Riverside Stadium). Meanwhile, metal broker Arthur Dorman, from Ashford in Kent, was working at a steel mill in nearby Stockton. In 1876, Dorman went into partnership with engineer Albert de Lande Long to form Dorman, Long & Co.

In the 1890s, Dorman Long formed a joint venture with Bell Brothers to make steel from pig iron on Teesside. By then Isaac's son, Walker-born Hugh Bell, was the chairman of Bell Brothers. Dorman Long gradually absorbed Bell Brothers, took over the Clarence Ironworks and expanded to become one of the world's leading steel manufacturers. The last strands of the takeover came together in 1923. (Dorman Long's headquarters was the grand former Bell Brothers building on Zetland Road in Middlesbrough.) Now—having both been knighted in 1918—Sir Arthur Dorman was the company chairman and Sir Hugh Bell was the vice-chairman of Dorman, Long & Co.

According to Sir Hugh, the company's success was down to its control of the entire process of turning raw materials into finished products. By the time they came to build the Tyne Bridge, said Sir Hugh, Dorman Long were "not only owners of mines, collieries, blast furnaces, rolling mills, and other constructional works... but stand among the leading bridge builders of the world".[12] Both Arthur Dorman and Hugh Bell were older men. Both peered through spectacles; Sir Arthur had a drooping moustache, and Sir Hugh had a Santa Claus beard (and a cheerfully festive personality). When they won the Tyne Bridge contract, Sir Arthur was 76, and Sir Hugh was 80. Yet Ralph Freeman noted their youthful enthusiasm and their hands-on direction. Their great wish was to live to see both the Tyne Bridge and the Sydney Harbour Bridge completed.[13]

* * *

Within days of the Tyne Bridge contract award, in January 1925, Dorman Long's surveyors were at work on the banks of the Tyne. Their new bridge needed to navigate both the big river and a tricky set of restrictions. The river was like a two-lane highway, busy with traffic that passed up and down between the mouth of the Tyne, the shipyards, the coal staiths, and Armstrong Whitworth's Elswick Works. It was the vein through which Tyneside's industry flowed. That industry might have been treading water, but Tyneside's trade relied on the river to survive, so the boats kept chugging along, puffing clouds of steam into the air. The Tyne was so important to the local economy that there could be no interruption to river traffic. Armstrong Whitworth in particular, having lost out on the contract to build the Tyne Bridge, was not about to have its business affected by Dorman Long.

The restrictions were imposed by the body responsible for the stewardship of the river and its traffic. The Tyne Improvement Commission, having set the new bridge's clearance height at 84 feet above the high tide level, stipulated the full width of the river should be kept entirely clear during and after construction. This meant no support piers in the water and required the bridge to cross the river in a single span. There could be no construction activity in the river, no staging platforms, no boats fetching supplies, and no materials raised from the water. The bridge could not be built up from the river, so it would have to be built out from the riverbanks. All of this made the Tyne Bridge an extremely challenging project.

A bridge is perhaps the most easily appreciable of all engineering solutions. It solves a straightforward problem—how to cross a body of water without getting wet. It's easy to appreciate a bridge for its usefulness in getting users from one side of a river to another and, sometimes, for its striking visual appeal. But it's often not so easy to appreciate the ingenuity that has gone into building it. "The layman and the engineer naturally look at such an undertaking from totally different points of view," noted Gustav Lindenthal. "The average man considers the work as a spectacle or as a means to an immediate end. At best, he grasps the structure as a visible whole. He realises but little if anything of the difficulties overcome."[14]

The key difficulties on the Tyne were the long span and the requirement to keep the river completely clear. Also, the bridge needed to be particularly strong to bear the "exceptionally heavy load" of local industrial traffic.[15] As there could be no staging in the river, it was initially proposed that temporary falsework could be erected on the quaysides, but this plan was abandoned as the costs of taking over the existing dock sheds on the Gateshead quays, in particular, were prohibitive. So the Tyne Bridge required a clever structural design and an inventive erection scheme. Although both were unique, Freeman said he used "much of the investigation made for the design of the Sydney Harbour Bridge". And that design, he acknowledged, was based on the Hell Gate Bridge—although he retained nothing from it where he thought it could be improved.[16]

Dorman Long set up a bridge design department in London for Freeman and his team of engineers to produce their calculations and drawings. This involved complicated mathematics—equations, geometry, conversions, analysis—done with chalk on blackboards using reference tables, slide rules and mental agility. Then the plans were drawn up with pencils at drafting tables, using compasses, T-squares and steady hands. And these were not just plans for the overall structure and shape of the bridge, but plans for every component—every girder, every plate, every bracket—showing how they should be positioned and fitted together, down to a fraction of an inch and the placement of each individual rivet. Freeman and his colleagues worked for many months on the plans for the Tyne Bridge, adapting and refining the design and carefully preparing hundreds of drawings—many of which were swiftly discarded and superseded by new versions. But from the very earliest drawings, Freeman's vision was clear.

Like the Hell Gate and Sydney Harbour bridges, the Tyne Bridge was a two-hinged through-arch bridge. A main arch would rise from hinges on each bank (hence "two-hinged"), and a suspended road deck would run through the arch to span the river ("through-arch"). The arch was comprised of two identical ribs connected together with diagonal beams. And the road deck was suspended from the arch with vertical tie-rods and horizontal cross-girders. The bridge would be built from steel and flanked with tall granite-faced abutment towers. The foundations for the towers and the abutments that housed the hinges—the crux of the structure—would be sunk deep into each riverbank.

The Tyne Bridge's arch was parabolic—a symmetrical plane curve. An arch bridge bears its load by carrying the forces it is subjected to outward from the crown of its arch to its ends, in this case to its hinge pin bearing points. An arch is an efficient structure for bearing load, and a parabolic arch is a super-efficient form of arch, so it's well suited to spanning long distances. The secret to the shape of a parabolic arch lies in complex mathematical equations, but a simple example can be found in nature. Take a banana and hold it like an inverted "U" and you will be looking at a good approximation of a parabolic arch.

So far, the Tyne Bridge closely resembled the Hell Gate and Sydney Harbour bridges. But Freeman's plans also showed some significant differences. The Tyne Bridge's arch ribs adopted a crescent shape comprised of two chords, upper and lower, that met at the ends, where they were fixed to the hinges. (Draw an outline around that banana and you will see an approximation of the crescent and the two chords.)

So the Tyne Bridge was a crescent arch bridge. This made it a striking rarity, as there were (and are) very few similar examples. On both the Hell Gate and Sydney Harbour bridges, the arch ribs were also comprised of two chords, but these chords did not meet at the ends, and only the lower chords were fixed to the hinges. The ends of the upper chords flattened out into spandrels (sections between the outer edge of the arch and its rectangular frame), so the Hell Gate and Sydney were known as spandrel arch bridges.

When planning the Hell Gate Bridge, Gustav Lindenthal produced both crescent arch and spandrel arch designs. A drawing he made in 1905 of the crescent arch design appears almost identical to that of the Tyne Bridge. The drawing was reproduced in a 1918 report on the Hell Gate Bridge that the Tyne Bridge engineers used as a reference.[17] So Ralph Freeman and his colleagues had in their possession a crescent arch design prepared two decades earlier. Lindenthal discarded that design, but it surely inspired the design of the Tyne Bridge.

The civil engineer Sir Harley Dalrymple-Hay, who did much work on the London Underground, later told Ralph Freeman his crescent-shaped Tyne Bridge was "a most beautiful design". He wondered why Freeman had not used a similar design for the Sydney Harbour Bridge, which he considered a less elegant structure. The answer, he assumed, might have been that a crescent arch was more expensive than a spandrel arch, and the cost of building a crescent arch over the much larger span of Sydney Harbour might have been prohibitive.[18] Freeman did not provide a clear answer, but his choice of a crescent arch was unusual, and few crescent arch bridges have ever been built.[19]

When we look at the Tyne Bridge today, we might appreciate its elegance without necessarily appreciating the role played by that crescent-shaped arch. It's a shape drawn from nature (see also the waxing and waning crescent moon), and it's naturally pleasing to the eye. Along with the horizontal road deck and flanking towers, the crescent arch gives the Tyne Bridge its characteristic silhouette. Despite other similarities, the crescent arch makes the Tyne Bridge's silhouette distinct from that of the Sydney Harbour Bridge. Sir Harley Dalrymple-Hay was not alone in thinking the crescent arch makes the Tyne Bridge more attractive than its Australian mate.

Freeman's arch erection scheme was another unique feature of the Tyne Bridge. The arch would be built out over the river in two halves, each anchored to the bank with heavy-duty cables—as was done at Hell Gate. What was new here was that the arch would be assembled using mobile derrick cranes, which were fitted to the arch ribs and moved out along those ribs as the structure grew over the river. Each time the 20-ton derrick cranes were moved, they were disassembled and reassembled using smaller 5-ton cranes. The larger and smaller cranes would move out along the growing arch in a "leap-frog" fashion. This manner of erection was perhaps the most innovative part of Freeman's design and had no precedent in the plans for Hell Gate or Sydney.[20]

* * *

The plans that came out of Dorman Long's bridge design department were stamped with the names of Ralph Freeman and his colleague, G.C. Imbault. Georges Camille Imbault was a highly experienced French engineer who led the project to build the Victoria Falls Bridge and designed the Tees Transporter Bridge. He was closely associated with Freeman as chief engineer of the Cleveland Bridge & Construction Company. When Freeman went over to join Dorman Long, Imbault went with him to work for the bridge department on the crossings at Sydney Harbour and over the Tyne—and ended up going out to Sydney to represent the firm. (The consulting engineers' office was for a time named as "Sir Douglas Fox & Partners & G.C. Imbault".) Freeman later said he was "delighted to recognise Mr Imbault's valuable cooperation... my primary business being 'design' and his [being] 'erection'".[21] This suggests Imbault had a hand in the innovative "leap-frog" crane scheme. While his name appears in black and white on the plans, Imbault is something of a forgotten figure among the men who built the Tyne Bridge.

Another overlooked person involved in the construction of the Tyne Bridge was a pioneering female engineer named Dorothy Donaldson Buchanan. "Dot" Buchanan was the daughter of a church minister from Langholm, Dumfriesshire, in Scotland. Her childhood interest in engineering might have been inspired by Georgian engineer Thomas Telford, the first president of the Institution of Civil Engineers, who was a famous son of Dumfriesshire. Buchanan studied civil engineering at Edinburgh University and was awarded her degree in 1924.[22] Armed with strong references from her tutors, she went to London to look for a trainee position at an engineering firm, initially without success. Then she heard Ralph Freeman was setting up an office in London as the bridge-building consultant for Dorman Long. Chancing her luck a little, Donaldson went to see Freeman, and impressed him. He recruited her to join his staff as a trainee on £4 plus overtime per week—the same as the male employees—from April 1924. Freeman acted as a mentor, and Buchanan soon proved her worth, although it was said she was regarded as a curiosity by her male colleagues, who "came to gawp".[23] She stated her profession as "designer and draughtsman"[24] and worked on "intricate mathematical calculations and drawings" for the steelwork on the Sydney Harbour and Tyne bridges.[25]

In 1927, after completing her training and during her work on the Tyne Bridge, Buchanan applied to become the first woman among almost ten thousand men to be granted membership of the Institution of Civil Engineers. Ralph Freeman and Basil Mott of Mott, Hay & Anderson recommended Buchanan based on their personal knowledge of her work. In January 1928, she was formally accepted as a member. "I felt that I represented all the women in the world," she later said. "It was my hope that I would be followed by many others."[26]

Dot Buchanan's time in engineering was short-lived. In 1930, she married electrical engineer William Fleming and gave up her career to become an "industrious housewife" in a South London flat. Her old colleagues rarely saw her, and her loss to the profession was described as "a big blow" by the secretary of the Women's Engineering Society, who noted her "important part in preparing the drawings and calculations" for the Tyne Bridge.[27] But Buchanan—now Mrs Fleming—was optimistic about her lifestyle change. "Housekeeping is quite as interesting as bridge building," she said. "I have taught myself to cook and control the household. I knew nothing about it before… I still keep in touch with the profession and watch new tenders but only as an onlooker. When I was a child, my hobby was engineering. Now I have made work my hobby. I think that is the right way to look at life."[28] One newspaper wrote about Buchanan's change of career under the headline: "Engineer Girl Can Cook!"[29]

* * *

THE TYNE BRIDGE

While Ralph Freeman was the consulting engineer for Dorman Long, each bridge also had its engineers for the works appointed by the local authorities. Freeman and his team prepared the detailed designs for the structure and erection process, and the works engineers oversaw the design and building process. For the Sydney Harbour Bridge, the engineer representing the government of New South Wales was Dr J.J.C. Bradfield. For the Tyne Bridge, the engineers representing the Joint Bridge Committee of Newcastle and Gateshead were Mott, Hay & Anderson, whose Basil Mott had prepared the preliminary report for the Parliamentary Bill. Freeman worked in collaboration with these engineers, and there was input and involvement from both sides. In Sydney, there would be a heated dispute between Freeman and Bradfield over who exactly designed the bridge. On Tyneside, things were apparently more congenial—although there were disagreements. Freeman certainly considered himself the bridge's designer and later offered a definition of what he meant: "The word 'design' applied to a bridge has a clear meaning. It means the selection of quality of steel to be used and the preparation of calculations and drawings required by the builder in order to build the bridge."[30]

The plans produced for the Tyne Bridge demonstrate the extent of the cooperation involved. Plans from 1925 (showing the project as the "Newcastle Gateshead Bridge") are numbered and labelled for Dorman, Long & Co. They are marked with a stamp that says: "Ralph Freeman & G.C. Imbault; Approved by Messrs Mott, Hay & Anderson." This stamp gives an indication of the partnership and hierarchy at work. Freeman and Imbault produced the designs, but they had to be approved by Mott, Hay & Anderson. That firm, like Freeman's Douglas Fox, was based in London, yet they had a constant presence on Tyneside during the building of the Tyne Bridge.

So who were Mott, Hay & Anderson? The firm was formed back in 1902 by experienced railway, bridge and tunnel engineers Basil Mott and David Hay. Mott, from Leicester, and Hay, from Casterton in Westmorland (now Cumbria), worked together on the London Underground, and later on bridge projects alongside a younger engineer named David Anderson. Anderson was born in Leven, Fife, and studied at Dundee and St Andrews. He became a partner in 1923. "When people come up against a river, they usually

78

call us in either to get them over it or under it," Anderson once explained, adding that he preferred going over rather than under. "Tunnelling is a blindfold job—you never know what you are to meet," he said. "I do not think it is nearly such interesting work as bridge building."[31]

Basil Mott was the president of the Institution of Civil Engineers from 1924 to 1925 (as George Stephenson had been from 1875 to 1877) and was an esteemed figure in the world of engineering. Speaking at a meeting of the Institution in Newcastle during the early stages of the building of the Tyne Bridge, Mott said the great city was an important centre of the engineering industry, and they were living in an "astounding epoch" for engineering.[32] Another speaker called the River Tyne "a standing monument to the engineers of the past" (including George and Robert Stephenson, William Armstrong, Charles Parsons, Charles Merz and more). In spanning the river, Mott's Tyne Bridge would itself become a monument to engineering.

Mott, who was in his mid-sixties, was often the representative face of the firm. But David Anderson, then in his forties, was the bridge expert and he took a lead role on the Tyne Bridge. Like Ralph Freeman, he produced scores of plans for the ongoing work, and later wrote and spoke in detail about the technical aspects of the project. And, like Freeman, Anderson was inspired by the Hell Gate Bridge. He used calculations based on a formula used at Hell Gate in his work on the Tyne Bridge. This formula was published in the same report that contained Gustav Lindenthal's unused crescent arch design for Hell Gate.[33] Due to the restrictions placed on the project, Anderson regarded the Tyne Bridge as "an engineering feat of considerable magnitude".[34]

So David Anderson emerged, alongside Ralph Freeman, as a key design engineer on the Tyne Bridge. In a subsequent discussion at the Institution of Civil Engineers involving Anderson and Freeman, Anderson stated the Tyne Bridge was designed by his firm, and it was referred to as "his bridge". (Freeman responded that he had designed "the structural details and the erection scheme".)[35]

Like Freeman, Anderson worked mainly from London, at the firm's Westminster offices. The resident engineers on Tyneside were Mark Mott, Basil Mott's son, and his assistant Jack Hamilton, a Scot who lived in Fenham in Newcastle. William Haldane was the assistant to David Anderson in the London office. Anderson credited Haldane with producing the calculations for the Tyne Bridge. Both Hamilton and Haldane were still in their mid-20s when they made important contributions to the bridge. As if that were not enough engineers, Mott, Hay & Anderson was associated with the firm of Coode, Fitzmaurice, Wilson & Mitchell, whose Sir Maurice Fitzmaurice had conducted the preliminary report along with Basil Mott. Sir Maurice had died in November 1924, before the proper work got underway, but David Anderson still credited the firm with doing some work for the bridge.[36]

There was another important figure involved in the design of the bridge. R. Burns Dick, the Scottish-born, Tyneside-raised architect (who considered himself a Geordie), designed the external features of the bridge's towers. Those huge towers would house passenger and goods elevators and cavernous warehouse space. Burns Dick had also designed buildings as diverse as the Laing Art Gallery in Newcastle, Whitley Bay's Spanish City and Armstrong Whitworth's Walker Naval Yard. As the consulting architect on the Tyne Bridge, Burns Dick gave the towers an art deco design described by David Anderson as "simple and extremely effective".[37]

Burns Dick's initial vision was much grander. His original designs show the top of the bridge towers would have been more ornate. Beyond that, he envisaged a magnificent triumphal domed entrance gateway at the north end of the Tyne Bridge leading to a redeveloped Newcastle that he hoped "might become a modern Athens or Rome". Unfortunately, Burns Dick's remarkable plans were scuppered by a lack of funds and by a reluctance to tamper too much with the classical Newcastle of the Georgian and Victorian eras. "Is not Newcastle still trading on the brains of Grainger and Dobson and Clayton?" complained Burns Dick. "It has done nothing since worth mentioning in the same breath."[38]

One man who was not credited with a role in the planning of the Tyne Bridge—to his annoyance—was Thomas Webster, the engineer who had submitted plans for a new high-level bridge back in 1922. At Christmas 1925, Webster wrote to members of the Joint Bridge Committee suggesting he might receive "some tangible form of recognition" for his considerable work in connection with the new bridge. "I was the originator of the scheme," he wrote. "I suggested it, worked it up by writing to the newspapers [and] various councillors both in Newcastle and Gateshead, and brought the matter before the Chamber of Commerce and showed them my plans and designs."[39] The letter was read before a meeting of Newcastle Council but was ordered to "lie on the table", meaning it would be disregarded.[40]

Supporters wrote to the *Chronicle* stating there was "no doubt whatsoever" the building of the bridge was a direct result of Webster's efforts. "Mr Webster has done something at the right time which will improve his native city and will help relieve unemployment," wrote one correspondent, "and it seems rather odd that he should have to ask for the credit which should be accorded him without the asking."[41]

The newspaper agreed, having previously published Webster's designs, that he had a substantial claim to be the man who had instigated the building of the new bridge between Newcastle and Gateshead. "The site was precisely that which is now being used," the paper noted, "while Mr Webster's scheme for a single-span structure was in design prophetic of the viaduct which is about to add a new link between the two towns."[42]

* * *

Discussion of the design of the Tyne Bridge inevitably invites comparison with the Sydney Harbour Bridge and raises the question of which came first. Sir Hugh Bell said he considered the Tyne Bridge to be only 1/27th of the Sydney Harbour Bridge because it was "about one-third of the span, one-third of the weight, and one-third of the width".[43] David Anderson thought that was rather unfair to the Tyne Bridge, which did have the largest arch span in Europe. Anderson, who did not work on the Sydney bridge, said he noticed many similar details in the two designs and suggested Dorman Long had used the Tyne Bridge as an "understudy to the larger bridge". Ralph Freeman said Anderson was "hardly right" because "although the Tyne Bridge was completed first, its design was made after that of Sydney Harbour Bridge". Both bridges were built concurrently, but the much larger Sydney bridge took longer to finish. So, to answer the question of which came first, the Sydney Harbour Bridge was the first to be designed and the Tyne Bridge was the first to be completed.

Back in 1925, the work on the Tyne Bridge was only just getting started. The surveys and borings were underway. Buildings were being demolished and roads were being rerouted. The extraordinary crescent arch bridge had yet to rise over the river. Looking at the carefully considered engineering plans drawn up by Freeman, Anderson and the other engineers helps generate even greater appreciation for the Tyne Bridge and the work that went into creating it. But they are ultimately just drawings on paper and can't tell the whole story. Every piece of steel on those plans had to be milled at the furnace, every block of granite hewed from the quarry. Every beam, bracket and plate had to be fitted by riggers, platers and riveters. The story of the Tyne Bridge is not just that of an engineering marvel. It is about the ordinary men who turned it from an idea on paper to a reality over the Tyne. It's about how they did it and what they went through, and the strength and courage they needed to get the job done. Nowhere is that more important than on the parts of the bridge that were visible on the plans but no one would ever see, the parts on which everything else depended—the foundations.

6

LAYING THE FOUNDATIONS

There were twenty men inside the pressurised steel box more than four storeys down below ground. It was dark, damp and stiflingly hot. They worked with pickaxes and shovels at the open bottom of the box, hacking away at the ground, the clanging of their tools on rock echoing around the metal chamber. They were filthy, sweating and short of breath. Each man worked twelve-hour shifts in this box, in the dim glow of electric light, below the surface and out of sight as Tyneside bustled above them. It was perilous, unforgiving and vital work. The men faced great physical danger, and it seemed they had to slog twice as hard down there than on the surface. But everything that was built afterwards depended on the work they did in their underground chamber. This was a caisson, and they were using it to dig the foundations for the Tyne Bridge.

The problem with digging a hole on a riverbank is it will quickly flood with water, and its muddy sides collapse. A caisson—also used to dig foundations in riverbeds—was the solution to that problem. Think of it as an enormous open-topped riveted steel box that's flipped upside down and pushed into the ground. Men went into the caisson and dug out the earth at the bottom. Then heavy concrete was layered on the top of the caisson, causing it to sink. The caisson was filled with compressed air, like a diving bell, to maintain its integrity against the pressure of the water and underground surroundings. The air kept the water out and enabled the workers to breathe. Steel shafts and airlocks allowed the men to enter and leave the working chamber and hoist out excavated material. The more earth they extracted, the more concrete was added, and the further the caisson sunk, deeper and deeper until it was embedded in solid rock. Then the excavation could stop, and the steel caisson was filled with concrete to complete the foundation.

The caisson had originated in France (where "caisson" means "box" or "chest"). Initially, shallow caissons were pile-driven into the riverbed to allow open excavation. This type of caisson was used to sink the foundations of the High Level Bridge in the 1840s.[1] Pneumatic or pressurised caissons were used to pioneering effect during the building of the Brooklyn Bridge in New York in the 1860s and 1870s, and then during the building of the King Edward VII Bridge over the Tyne in the early 1900s. Through these projects, the dangers of working in a caisson became apparent.

Life in the caissons was hellish. E.F. Farrington, the master mechanic on the Brooklyn Bridge, described it as a disturbing and disorienting experience where "everything wore an unreal, weird appearance": "What with the flaming lights, the deep shadows, the confusing noise of hammers, drills and chains, the half-naked forms flitting about, with here and there a Sisyphus figure rolling his stone, one might, if of a poetic temperament, get a realizing sense of Dante's inferno."[2]

At the Brooklyn Bridge, caisson workers experienced unusual symptoms—ringing in the ears, difficulty breathing, muscle and joint pain and severe fatigue. As the caissons went deeper, the symptoms worsened—discombobulation, vomiting, limb paralysis and seizures. Workers collapsed in the airlocks as they returned to the surface and fell unconscious on their way home. Washington Roebling, the Brooklyn Bridge chief engineer (who had previously visited Tyneside for inspiration), was confined to his bed with debilitating symptoms after working in the caissons and was forced to supervise the remainder of the works from a window at his Brooklyn Heights home. Hundreds of Brooklyn Bridge workers were affected and at least five died as a result of a condition they called caisson disease—now known as decompression sickness, or "the bends".[3]

Some of the milder symptoms were experienced simply due to working in a pressurised environment. But the potentially fatal symptoms of caisson disease were caused by rapid decompression as the workers returned from the pressurised caisson to the surface. During decompression, as pressure reduces, bubbles of nitrogen gas

01a: Pons Aelius Roman altars

01b: Old Tyne Bridge Blue Stone

02a: The Old Tyne Bridge, 1739

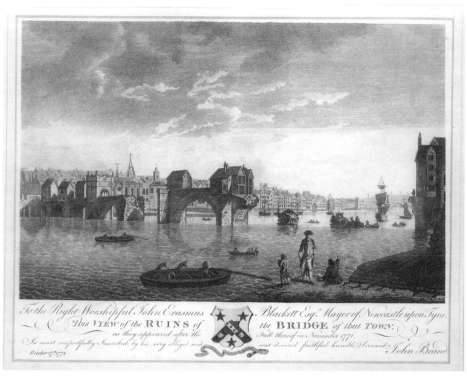

02b: The ruins of the Old Tyne Bridge, 1771

03a: The Georgian Tyne Bridge

03b: The Georgian Tyne Bridge and High Level Bridge

04a: The High Level Bridge and Georgian Tyne Bridge, circa 1865

04b: The Temporary Tyne Bridge and High Level Bridge

05a: The Swing Bridge and High Level Bridge, 1887

05b: The Swing Bridge, 1889

06a: Tommy on the Bridge

06b: Tommy attracts a crowd, circa 1905

07a: The Hell Gate Bridge, circa 1917

07b: The Sydney Harbour Bridge, 1932

08a: Tyne Bridge towers under construction, 19 Sept 1928

08b: Ralph Freeman

09a: Inside the first Tyne Bridge caisson, March 1926

09b: Inside the last Tyne Bridge caisson, June 1926

10a: Early work at Gateshead, circa Jan 1927

10b: Work progresses at Gateshead, 10 Aug 1927

11a: The Newcastle side of the arch, 2 Feb 1928

11b: The new bridge rises over the Tyne, 2 Feb 1928

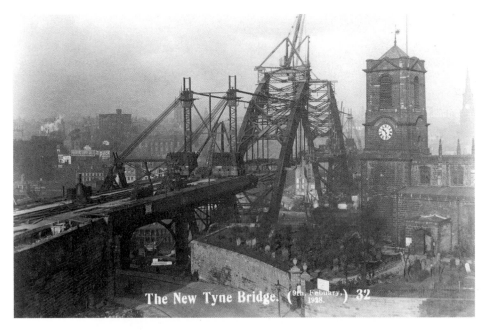

12a: View of the Tyne Bridge from Gateshead, 9 Feb 1928

12b: View from Newcastle Quayside, 9 Feb 1928

13a: The arch nears completion, 23 Feb 1928

13b: The two halves of the arch almost meet, 23 Feb 1928

14a: Tyne Bridge workers on a crane, 23 Feb 1928

14b: Tyne Bridge construction staff, 2 March 1928

15a: Tyne Bridge workers on cables

15b: Tyne Bridge workers

16a: View from the High Level Bridge, 6 March 1928

16b: Looking along the Tyne Bridge, 22 May 1928

are released into the bloodstream and body tissues. These bubbles can migrate anywhere in the body—the joints, the spinal cord, the brain—and if released too quickly can cause pain, paralysis or death. If decompression occurs slowly, and the pressure is reduced gradually, the gas bubbles are released more slowly and can be safely removed by the lungs. Much of that remained a mystery to bridge builders until the construction of the King Edward VII Bridge and the intervention of experts including Tyneside doctor Thomas Oliver.

A specialist in industrial illnesses, Oliver worked at Newcastle's Royal Victoria Infirmary (RVI). He studied the effects of compression and decompression on the caisson workers and conducted experiments in compression chambers with mice, rats and frogs. In lectures on the subject, Oliver said twenty King Edward caisson workers were hospitalised, two with life-threatening symptoms, but all recovered. Oliver identified the cause as the fast release of gases and determined that symptoms could be reduced if decompression occurred slowly. He also advised the length of time men spent in the working chamber should be reduced in proportion to the increased pressure—so they should work in shorter bursts at lower depths. Oliver published his findings from the King Edward VII Bridge in the *British Medical Journal* and was knighted by the man the bridge was named for.[4]

For the Tyne Bridge—constructed fifty years after the Brooklyn Bridge and twenty years after the King Edward VII Bridge—advanced knowledge meant the dangers of caisson disease were better understood and more effectively mitigated. Men would undergo medical checks before going into the caisson. Their 12-hour shifts were split into shorter stints, and the time taken to decompress was proportional to the depth of the caisson and the pressure in the chamber. A "hospital lock" (a hyperbaric recompression chamber) was provided for the recovery of men who showed symptoms of caisson disease.

The contractors, Dorman Long, recognised some men withstood the pressures of the caisson better than others. Some could not bear the airlock, never mind the working chamber. So the men who worked most often in the caissons were less likely to suffer symptoms. Luckily, Tyneside was full of men who seemed to have the right temperament for the caissons. There were the coalminers, used to working far below ground in dank and difficult conditions. And there were the shipbuilders, whose work in the high-pressure depths of the hulls of 100-foot-tall ocean liners might have been helpful preparation. Few unemployed miners or shipbuilders would have hesitated at working in the caissons. And those that went down proved their mettle. According to Mott, Hay & Anderson's David Anderson, "No ill effects on any of the men were recorded."[5]

* * *

Dorman Long's James Ruck was the man in charge of the whole operation. Ruck was a tall, broad-shouldered man with big hands. Now forty-four years old, he was born in Maidstone and raised in South Shields. He had worked in construction from an early age, initially as a timekeeper and then—following in his father's foot-steps—as a ganger or supervisor at sites across the country and abroad. Ruck regularly travelled to the United States to work on engineering projects in New York, including underground railway and sewer tunnels. He lived during the early 1900s at Long Island City in Queens and was there during the construction of the Queensboro Bridge and also the inspirational Hell Gate Bridge.[6]

Officially, Ruck was the contractor's agent. In practice, he was the onsite project manager, works supervisor and chief foreman. Ruck was in charge of turning the paper and ink plans into a steel and granite bridge. He was responsible for the full extent of the construction from the depths of the foundations to the crown of the arch. Ruck was trusted and respected by his superiors and those who worked alongside and under him. He wore a homburg hat rather than a flat cap and was known to wear a bow tie onsite, but he was never afraid to unbutton his collar and get his big hands dirty. Dorman Long's Sir Hugh Bell said Ruck was just the type of man they needed on such a job, but not a man you would want to "have a difference with".[7]

Ruck had an able chief assistant in the shape of James Geddie, a well-travelled Scotsman who had worked to repair blown-up bridges at the end of the Great War. Geddie was born in Edinburgh and learned engineering from night classes as a boy. He worked as a contractor on the Edinburgh Water Works, then travelled to

South Africa and Argentina, where he became a chief engineer on the countries' railways. During the war, he joined the Royal Engineers and fought in the Salonika campaign. By the time he left the army and returned to Britain, he held the rank of Major. He went to Brazil to build dams, but a bout of malaria cut short his travels and sent him home. Now forty-six, the bespectacled Geddie found a job with Dorman Long and was sent to the Tyne.[8] Hands-on and resourceful, Ruck and Geddie seemed to be cut from the same type of cloth. When their men sunk the caissons, Ruck and Geddie went down with them.

The main foundations for the abutment towers required two caissons to be sunk on each side of the river. Each caisson was 84.5 feet long and 28 feet wide, with a headroom inside the working chamber of 7 feet. The average pressure in the caissons was 27.5 pounds per square inch, about twice the normal atmospheric pressure at sea level. At that higher pressure, the lungs contract in size by a factor of two and effectively have to work twice as hard. At the deepest levels, the pressure in the caissons reached around 30 pounds per square inch, which is something like the equivalent of working inside a fully-inflated car tyre.[9]

Borings provided initial information about the ground strata for the foundations, but the men also dug trial pits to ensure the bridge was founded on solid rock. The trial pits were 10.5 feet in diameter and lined with huge cast iron rings recycled from the old City and South London Railway—the world's first underground rail system. Under the direction of Scottish steam engineers John Cochrane & Sons, workers sunk one two-foot-deep ring at a time using steam hammers.[10] The borings and trial pits revealed the ground above the sandstone at Newcastle was made up of ballast or gravel and a lot of sand. (The area is called Sandhill.) At Gateshead, it was soil, clay and shale or mudrock. To be founded in the solid sandstone, the caissons would need to be sunk to depths of about 85 feet below ground level at Newcastle and about 60 feet below ground level at Gateshead—equivalent to digging down about six storeys at Newcastle and four storeys at Gateshead.[11]

Ruck and his men successfully founded the first caisson on the Gateshead side in March 1926. It was firmly bedded in the sandstone at a depth of 66 feet. It was sunk at a rate of up to 2 feet a day, displacing about 100 tons of excavated material daily. The last 26 feet were particularly tough because they had to be excavated through black shale with veins of sandstone. On those days, the physical strength of the labourers was not sufficient, so "the ring of the pick was augmented by the deafening clatter of pneumatic hammers".[12] Altogether, the men excavated 3,500 tons of soil and clay, then 3,000 tons of shale and sandstone. As they removed that hefty mass of material, they replaced it with a similar weight of concrete. When topped with concrete, the caisson weighed more than 6,000 tons.

After the first caisson was sunk, James Ruck went down to inspect the work with James Geddie, Jack Hamilton (the assistant chief resident engineer for Mott, Hay & Anderson), and RF Hindmarsh (the chief engineer for the Tyne Improvement Commission). Two newspaper reporters went with them. Ruck explained to the reporters how air pressure of more than twice the normal level was maintained in the caisson to keep the water at bay. The men went into the airlock, and Ruck opened the air cock valve to let in the air. As the pressure increased, one of the reporters complained of a headache and difficulty breathing. Ruck lowered the pressure until the reporter regained his composure, then increased the pressure again. But the reporter soon complained of dizziness and was "on the verge of collapse". So Ruck closed the air cock, allowing the pressure to return to normal, then led the reporter out of the airlock. After a few gulps of Tyneside air, the reporter soon recovered. Ruck and the others went back into the airlock and down into the caisson, where a "flashlight photograph" was taken of the inspection party. The remarkable photo, published in the *North Mail*, showed the engineers—wearing hats and ties—inside the illuminated confines of the pressurised metal box more than four storeys underground with 6,000 tons of concrete above their heads.[13]

* * *

While digging continued underground for the Tyne Bridge's foundations, work was well underway further up the riverbanks on the high-level approaches. The bridge's road deck would sweep over the quaysides and join Pilgrim Street in Newcastle and High Street in Gateshead, more than 80 feet above the river. Preparations at Newcastle saw a large section of Pilgrim Street north of All Saints Church cleared. At Gateshead, it involved the large-scale demolition of much of Hillgate, Bridge Street, Church Street, the east side of Bottle Bank, and part of High Street.

According to a Ministry of Health inspection, Pilgrim Street was one of Newcastle's "black spots". It was one of the most ancient parts of the city, packed with cheek-by-jowl rookeries that had once been the townhouses of wealthy traders. Now they were dilapidated lodging tenements, divided into single-room dwellings that were over-occupied and unsanitary. There were no back lanes, and inspectors said the congested buildings prevented air circulation. The death rate in the area was more than three times higher than in the rest of the city. This "slum clearance" was scheduled before the war, but it didn't happen until the arrival of the new bridge. There were still questions over where the several hundred residents might be re-housed. Many of them worked on the quaysides, so the location was at least convenient, and their livelihoods might be affected if they were moved away from the river. Some property owners objected to the clearance based on their financial interests. But they also suggested the clearance scheme was "not an altogether honest one" because the compensation they were being paid didn't reflect the potential value of the land, which they suggested would almost double with the arrival of the new bridge.[14]

The clearance got underway during the early part of 1925 and continued for over a year, with more premises than planned demolished. Some of the buildings further up Pilgrim Street from the clearance zone were said to be in an "imminently dangerous state" due to the vibrations and movement caused by the nearby demolitions, with leaning chimney stacks an indication of their vulnerability. So the tenants were served with ejectment notices advising they could be removed by the police. Some of the tenants were accommodated in other houses, but those who had nowhere to go were sent to the Poorhouse.[15]

One Newcastle shopkeeper given notice to quit his premises was an ex-serviceman in failing health who identified himself in a newspaper column as "Almost Broke". His customers' homes were also being demolished, his turnover had dropped, and he felt he would have to give up his business, leaving him in a difficult financial situation. "It seems very hard after working for so many years," wrote the shopkeeper," and I feel that my nerves are getting the better of me."[16]

Over on the Gateshead side of the bridge, a particularly gruesome clearance job for the new approaches involved the removal of human remains from three sections of St Mary's graveyard. They covered a combined area of around 2,500 square feet and it was unknown how many bodies were buried within. In one of the sections, no one had been buried for almost exactly a century, and there were only three remaining gravestones—inscribed with the names Coulson, Hogget and Anderson. Descendants of those individuals, or of any other persons whose bones might be disturbed, could apply to Gateshead Council for expenses of up to £15 to move the remains and memorials to another graveyard.

In many cases, there were no surviving relatives to claim the remains. "The clanging of the pick and shovel has betrayed the grim work in progress," said one newspaper, "but so far, no relatives have attended the 'exhumation' operations."[17] However, the public showed a keen interest and were disappointed by the decision to close the church and its grounds to visitors. They inundated the verger and other church officials with questions about the work. Some "morbid sightseers" attended funerals at the church for people they didn't know in the hope of a glimpse at the disturbed remains. Eventually, carpenters erected large hoardings to screen off the graveyard from onlookers.

Around twenty workers toiled for months in the graveyard. Within the first few days, they dug up ten skulls, several bones, and a set of teeth "in a splendid state of preservation" thought to be from a grave dating from 1786. Most—but not all—of the remains belonged to adults. There were no surviving traces of any coffins. Remains were found in unexpected places. The confusion was attributed to the Great Fire of 1854 when St Mary's was severely damaged, and the graveyard was showered with huge chunks of stone, which displaced and destroyed several gravestones. In any case, the workers handled the remains with the greatest of care, placing them in a covered trench while awaiting removal to another cemetery.[18]

Near to St Mary's, workers were demolishing buildings and rerouting roads to make way for the Gateshead approach, which would run parallel to Bottle Bank, the main thoroughfare between Gateshead and the bridges for centuries. More than half of Bottle Bank's buildings—mainly on the "east raw" or east row—were demolished to make way for the new bridge. The Newcastle *Journal* suggested the clearance might help to remove a stigma that had been attached to Gateshead since 1831, when Charles Vane, the 3rd Marquess of Londonderry, objected to the town being represented in Parliament by calling it "a long, dirty lane, leading to Newcastle" and "a most filthy spot, containing the vilest class of society". It was believed that Bottle Bank had provided the grounds for the insult.[19]

Another benefit of clearing buildings from Bottle Bank and adjacent streets was that the decluttered river bank allowed St Mary's space to breathe and be admired. "The transformation is striking in many ways," said the *Journal*. "Visitors to the town, no less than the inhabitants themselves, are still commenting upon the prominence which the ancient parish church now occupies."[20]

One of the demolished Bottle Bank buildings was a famous Gateshead pub called the Goat Inn. It had existed as a watering hole since at least the early 1600s and was known as the Goat Inn from 1672. (A theory that Gateshead's name was derived from goats that grazed on its riverbank is unlikely to be true.) The pub was a community hub, accommodating everything from a magistrate's court, a masonic meeting hall, and a charity distribution centre. Its location on the main thoroughfare to the bridge meant it was regarded as a landmark for travellers, and it was said passing labourers "of the navvy type" never failed to stop for refreshments. But the old Goat Inn was showing its age. In past times, the pub "had a dignity long since gone from it", and patrons could "quaff British ale of a quality not to be obtained nowadays".[21]

The Goat Inn served users of the Old Tyne Bridge, the Georgian Tyne Bridge and the Victorian Swing Bridge—but it wouldn't survive into the era of the new Tyne Bridge. Owners Duncan & Daglish, a Newcastle brewing firm, received £4,350 compensation following its demolition.[22] The pub's gilt figure goat sign, thought to date from the Georgian bridge era, is preserved today at Gateshead's Shipley Art Gallery. At least three other pubs were demolished in Newcastle and Gateshead to make way for the new bridge—the Earl of Durham and the Ridley Arms on Newcastle's "black spot" of Pilgrim Street, and the Steamboat Inn right next to Bottle Bank on Gateshead's Church Street.

Other buildings demolished on the east side of Bottle Bank included lodging houses, a bicycle shop and a furniture store. A little further up the bank, Snowball's department store, Gateshead's "Harrods of the North", was also demolished. This was a large shop stacked with drapery and furnishings. Snowball, Son & Company received £56,500 compensation for the demolition (equivalent to around £3.3m in 2022).[23] Snowball's would open a new shop further up High Street, which one trader hoped might become "the best shopping street in the North". Gateshead's main thoroughfare was then of "unsavoury character" with many "small and unattractive shops" surrounded by "slum property". One shopkeeper said around half of the existing properties should be demolished, "but it is held that the new Tyne Bridge will improve High Street out of all knowledge".[24] As for the bridge itself, wags joked it would not stand for very long as its foundations were built on sand and snow—Newcastle's Sandhill and Gateshead's Snowball's.[25]

* * *

Back at the foundation works, while the men down in the caissons might not have suffered any lasting ill-effects, there was a tragic incident above ground—and it caused the first death of a worker on the new Tyne Bridge. Frank McCoy was a 44-year-old general labourer employed by Dorman Long to clear the earth emptied from the caissons on the Gateshead side of the river.

In the early hours of 3 February 1926, McCoy was watching a steam-powered crane lift skips of excavated material from a caisson shaft and empty them into large "muck bins" for removal. As the crane swung one emptied skip away from the bin, an attachment pin somehow slipped loose. The skip fell 10 feet onto McCoy, causing severe head injuries. Both the crane driver and the site foreman, Charles Heard and William Ette, later told an inquiry they did not think the pin was properly inserted. The pin was put in by workers down in the caisson. After the accident, Ette went into the caisson but said he could not find out which of the twelve men working down there had put the pin in. McCoy was taken to the RVI but died from his injuries. The inquiry found the pin was put in carelessly, but there was no evidence to prove who was at fault. McCoy's death—not the last to occur during the building of the bridge—was recorded as an accident.[26]

Work on the caissons was affected by the General Strike, which began at one minute to midnight on Monday 3 May 1926. Prompted by coal miners protesting against wage reductions and worsening conditions, the strike saw millions of industrial workers down tools, significantly affecting heavily-industrial Tyneside. In Newcastle, thousands of pickets filled the streets, bringing the city to a standstill. "The spectacle was only to be compared to that which was presented when Newcastle United arrived in the city with the cup," noted the *Chronicle*.[27] Buses and trams were prevented from running, and the Central railway station was overrun. A cart laden with coal was overturned, and there were running battles with mounted police. Breweries went on strike, and there were beer shortages. Pubs in Newcastle and Gateshead were ordered to close early. North of Newcastle, at Cramlington, striking miners derailed the Flying Scotsman. (Although the London to Edinburgh express train was loaded with 300 passengers, there was only one injury.)

Some work did continue. Armstrong Whitworth's Elswick Works continued to operate with reduced numbers. But the severity of the situation was visible on the Tyne, where there was virtually no river traffic and little activity in the yards. According to the *Chronicle*, "The general appearance of the Tyne is one of extreme quietness from the Newcastle bridges to the sea."[28] The situation was similar across the North East. On the Tees, the steelworks shuttered—affecting the manufacture of sections for the Tyne and Sydney Harbour bridges.

The General Strike ended after ten days in defeat for the workers. Most returned to work, but some could not. In the two-week period encompassing the strike, with industry still in turmoil, unemployment figures increased by almost 3,000 in Newcastle and by almost 2,000 in Gateshead.[29] Workers on the Tyne Bridge now seemed doubly fortunate to have their jobs.

As the caisson work continued, James Ruck and his men were also sinking foundations for the columns that would support the approach spans. There were four columns on the Newcastle side and two columns on the Gateshead side. Their foundations were sunk as huge cylinders, lined—like the trial pits—with iron rings from the underground railways. They were sunk by open excavation, with picks and shovels and a crane with a pneumatic grab. This early version of an excavator digger was described as a "rather weird instrument... with an enormous pair of steel jaws with two terrible rows of teeth" and drew crowds to watch it work. Like the caissons, the column cylinders were sunk deep into the ground, founded on stable sandstone, and then filled with concrete.

An alarming incident occurred during the sinking of one of the column foundations. One of the iron rings hit an obstruction and refused to budge, allowing freezing cold water to flood the cylinder. Remarkably, the hands-on James Ruck leapt into action. According to one report, Ruck "dived into the icy water in an endeavour to remove the obstruction". Whether Ruck succeeded with his bare hands or further remedial work was required, the situation was rescued, and the column foundation was successfully sunk.[30] Ruck was not hurt, but the episode must have added to the strain of what was evidently a very stressful job.

There were other alarming incidents and accidents, too. Towards the end of the foundations work, a young labourer named George Hauwell from Durham fell into a hole on the site. Fortunately, it must not have been a very deep hole. He was taken to the RVI and escaped with nothing more than a broken leg.[31]

Much more worrying was the potentially disastrous incident during the sinking of the final caisson—the west caisson on the Newcastle side. As it was being sunk, the concrete mass on the top of the caisson cracked horizontally and separated from the steel chamber. The surrounding mud and gravel flowed into an 18-inch gap between the concrete and the caisson. Thankfully, the pressurised caisson withstood the accident, although some subsidence was noted in nearby buildings. Excavation "cautiously continued" in the working chamber, and once the caisson was fully sunk and filled with concrete, new shafts were made to clear and fill the gap. The incident "occasioned considerable expense" to Dorman Long. Engineers thought it must have been caused by frost forming on the concrete in freezing conditions.[32]

That final caisson was sunk into the sandstone in June 1926. The *Chronicle* proclaimed "one of the most difficult and important parts of bridge construction" was complete.[33] A photograph published in the *North Mail* showed three flat-capped "compressed air workers" beginning to fill the last caisson with concrete from a skip. One of the workers appeared to be a young lad of no more than fifteen years of age.[34] Once the last caisson was filled, this boy and his colleagues could return to the surface and get to work on the above-ground building of the Tyne Bridge.

"For months, the work on the structure has seemed to the layman a matter of destruction rather than construction," noted the *Chronicle*. But all of this was necessary. "The subterranean engineering has been the most important of the whole contract," said the newspaper, because if the foundations of a bridge "go wrong", it was a very serious matter. Now this hidden work was complete. "Further progress will soon be visible to the casual passer-by," the paper said. "In a few weeks' time, Tynesiders will see the new bridge begin to grow under their very eyes."[35]

Although there was much work still to be done, thoughts turned to the opening of the new bridge. Rumours that a member of the royal family might lay a foundation stone had proved groundless. But it might be possible, suggested Councillor Charles Irwin at a meeting in September 1926, to persuade the King to open the new bridge. If so, perhaps it should be called the King George V Bridge in his honour, just as the King Edward VII Bridge was named in honour of his father.[36] Other possibilities were considered, too. If the Prince of Wales, Prince Edward, opened the bridge, that might leave Tyneside with two bridges named "Edward". But if the Duke of York opened the bridge, it could be called the Prince Albert Bridge. The *Chronicle* commented that Albert "clashes with nothing whatever in this district and is quite a dignified name for the bridge".[37]

After the bridge foundations were completed, James Ruck took a leave of absence as he was "feeling the strain of conducting his vast job at [literal] high pressure". Setting off for a far-away vacation, Ruck swapped one great river for another, travelling almost 5,000 miles from the Tyne to the Amazon in search of "queer things to hook and shoot". Hunting black caimans (the Amazon's biggest predators) from rickety canoes and shooting jaguars (the biggest cats in the Americas) at the edge of the rainforest were apparently "two of his most restful occupations". Once, while fishing from a boat, Ruck caught something of great size that dragged him across the deck. Three men attempted to hold the line, but it was pulled from their grasp. When the hook came up, it brought a lump of flesh that had been torn from the great mouth of some giant and unseen river beast.[38]

Ruck often fished at one of the deepest parts of the Amazon, with a line that went 100 feet down (and wearing his Homburg hat). He regularly caught a large species of fish with very thick, armoured skin—likely the *Arapaima gigas* or pirarucu, which has armour-like scales to protect it from piranha bites and can grow up to 10 feet long. Ruck thought the fish might have thick skin to withstand the pressure at depths of 100 feet, which was something he knew much about. When he returned to Tyneside in November 1926, Ruck amused reporters with stories of encounters with large reptiles and big cats and tales of natives shooting giant turtles with bows and arrows. As the *Chronicle* noted, "Some people have quaint ideas of recuperating."[39]

7

BUILDING THE BRIDGE

The weather on Tyneside was relatively mild and dry in January 1927. This was a boon for the workers in flat caps, dust jackets and bib-and-brace overalls who were constructing the 287-foot-long elevated embankment for the Gateshead approach of the new Tyne Bridge. The men built the embankment's retaining walls inside timber scaffolding from cement-and-ballast concrete. Working in small teams, they packed the 56-foot-wide void between the walls with hundreds of tons of dry-fill that they hauled and tipped using horses and carts. Then they faced the walls with soot-blackened sandstone blocks recycled from the now-demolished Newcastle Gaol.

The Gateshead embankment was the first clearly-visible section of the new bridge. The large site was open to the scrutiny of passing spectators. Motor vehicles chugged past along the partially-cleared Bottle Bank. Horse-drawn brakes clopped along the diverted and re-laid Church Street under the gaze of St Mary's, which was now restored to its due prominence. Members of the public stood on the pavement by huge mounds of dry-fill to watch the walls rise above them. The contractors held their building materials—stacks of timber beams, pallets of stone blocks, reels of steel cables—in storage yards protected by six-foot fences marked with "Dorman, Long & Co Ltd" signage. After the thump and holler of work stopped, nightwatchmen patrolled the hushed site.

At 6.45 one morning that January, before the winter sun had risen and with a web of overnight frost on the ground, a youth named Robert Aitken climbed a fence and stole four shillings worth of wood from one of the storage yards. Aitken carried it to his house on Church Street, next to St Mary's. He was spotted by twelve-year-old Robert Lewis Baul, the stepson of a Dorman Long nightwatchman.[1]

"You will not tell your father?" Aitken asked Baul. The two boys likely knew each other, and Aitken's minor theft (of potential firewood during winter) might have been committed out of desperation. Baul said he would not tell his father—but he did.

Aitken, who was about seventeen, was apprehended and brought before the magistrate's bench at Gateshead Town Hall. Baul, the young informant, was praised for his crime-fighting efforts.

"Is this the first time you have been a detective?" Gateshead's Chief Constable Richard Ogle asked Robert Baul.

"Yes, sir," replied Baul.

"You have done it very well," said Ogle.

It was the first time Robert Aitken had been an accused criminal, but it was not his first appearance before the bench at Gateshead Town Hall. A year earlier, in November 1925, he appeared at a hearing during which the coroner commended him for his efforts to save a drowning man from the Tyne. Aitken and his friend Albert Bone were on the Hillgate Quay when they saw a man throw off his cap, coat and shoes and jump into the river. Aitken and Bone attempted to rescue him with a hook and a rope. However, the man put his head under the water and sank beneath the surface. A third boy, Joseph Muckian, dived into the river and tried to retrieve the drowning man, without success. The coroner's inquiry found that the man, 62-year-old coal-hewer Joseph Edwards, had committed suicide. The coroner recommended that Aitken, Bone and Muckian should be recognised for their gallantry. He said it was "exceedingly creditable that Gateshead should have turned out three lads who can do such worthy service".[2]

The Newcastle *Journal* reported Aitken's crime under the headline, "Hero Turned Thief Brought to Book by Amateur Detective". The fact that Aitken had previously been praised for bravery led the magistrates to be lenient. The case was adjourned for three months as an incentive for Aitken to "lead a straight life"—and he does not appear to have reoffended. But the chair of the bench, Councillor William Hall, warned there would be no such leniency in subsequent cases "in view of the extensive amount of wood missed by the firm".[3]

* * *

Once the retaining walls for the embankment were filled, work began on the steel approach span on the Gateshead side of the bridge, that would carry the high-level road deck over the quay to the main arch of the bridge. The approach span structure was assembled in sections, formed with massive twin girders that were 40 feet long and 11 feet deep. Due to their size, special arrangements were made for weekend use of the railways to transport the massive steels from Teesside to the Tyne. Once assembled, the sections were pushed out from the embankment on huge rollers, 10 feet at a time, over Church Street and into position on awaiting columns. Each 150-ton section was pushed forward using a pair of massive winches operated by two teams of six men. Once each section was pushed out, another was bolted and riveted to the back, and the elongated structure was pushed further out. It would take seven sections to be fitted together to bring the approach span to the river's edge.

As the work progressed, great crowds watched the growing structure seemingly defy gravity as it inched its way out across Church Street. When the nose of the span reached its main support column, several thousand spectators watched with keen interest. More pushes would be needed, with the structure moving out over rollers on top of the main column until it reached its final extension. Those rollers were left in place to allow the completed structure to move very slightly as it expanded or contracted under varying temperatures. By March 1927, the 270-foot, 1,000-ton Gateshead approach was in position, and work began on the Newcastle approach.

With the Gateshead approach now conspicuous on the river bank, the people of Tyneside could see tangible proof of the progress of their new bridge. The work was impressive but not yet spectacular. It was watched with interest but not yet awe. The spectacle and awe were still to come. There was also some confusion. "Many people who watch the growth of the steel superstructure are under the impression that this is the main span of the new Tyne Bridge and will be gradually thrust across the river," said one local newspaper. "This is not the case. The steelwork is merely the approach, and the river will be crossed by an entirely different type of structure." The newspaper explained that this structure would be "a great steel arch", the erection of which was "the greatest feat of its kind attempted in this country". "As the arch grows from each side of the river until the two portions meet in the middle, Tynesiders will see the development of a most spectacular piece of engineering."[4]

Over on the Newcastle side of the river, workmen were digging trenches and constructing buttresses before rolling out the massive steel sections for that approach. The approach embankment on the Newcastle side was shorter than its Gateshead equivalent at 188 feet. But the Newcastle approach as a whole was much longer than the Gateshead one, and its steel structure was more than two and a half times heavier at about 2,600 tons. This considerable mass was counter-balanced during its construction with stacks of steel girders. Because the approach's retaining walls were not substantially visible to the public, they were not faced with sandstone blocks. The Newcastle approach followed a more complicated route than its Gateshead counterpart, passing over several important buildings that could not be demolished. Roofs were taken off and properties lowered, "fancy parapets" were removed, and there was a "great slaughter among the chimney-pots".[5] When it was complete, the approach would pass within a few feet over the grand mercantile offices on Akenside Hill and Queen Street.

Work continued in deteriorating weather conditions, regardless of rain and gale-force winds. The Newcastle approach structure was moved gingerly forward, at a pace of around 4 inches per minute, again with a pair of winches controlled by at least six men on each side. As on the other side of the river, the public was captivated by the work, and crowds gathered to marvel at the combination of engineering ingenuity and synchronised teamwork. "To the casual observer, this method of moving a mass weighing thousands of tons is ever a wonder," noted one newspaper.[6] Relying on manual rather than machine power was an essential strategy for such a delicate task. "The theory is that they can 'sense' any hitch or obstruction immediately, whereas a machine obviously could not do," reported another paper. The effort was "proving once again the indispensability of the human element in engineering operations".[7]

The men at work on the bridge became symbols of the hard graft that Tynesiders felt epitomised their region. It was the type of skilled physical work that was often hidden underground in the pits that pock-marked the region's landscape. Here, it was elevated and visible in the heart of Newcastle and Gateshead on the banks of the

Tyne. Local newspaper advertisements used the image of hardy bridge workers to promote Robert's Golden Twist Tobacco: "Men! The daily clangour of the work on the new Tyne Bridge is a community song of praise from sturdy men who chew and smoke ROBERT'S. In the yards on the Tyne and Wear, throughout all the North Country pits, the same song re-echoes. Nothing like ROBERT'S for Northern Men!"[8]

The labourers on the Tyne Bridge could expect to be paid slightly more than in the shipyards or, in many cases, the pits. When the building of the bridge began in 1925, the average weekly wage for a labourer on a building or engineering project was £2 6s (with a relative value of £139.50 in 2022). For a labourer in a shipyard, it was £1 18s 5d (£112). The average weekly wage for a coal miner around the same period was £1 19s 11d (£121).[9] These were hardly kings' ransoms, and workers' wages had been in decline since the start of the decade. Wage reductions and worsening conditions for coal miners had precipitated the General Strike of 1926. The Tyne Bridge workers were not well paid by modern standards, but they were at least employed, and any dissatisfaction did not seem to affect their work ethic.

After a long day by the Tyne, the grimy-handed and wind-blown workers would have enjoyed going to one of Newcastle or Gateshead's many pubs for a well-deserved drink. They might have enjoyed a new beverage that Newcastle Breweries launched in April 1927. Jim Porter, known as Colonel Porter, was a master brewer and decorated war veteran. Colonel Porter spent three years working alongside brewery chemist Archie Jones to perfect the formula for a distinctive new beer. Sitting alongside the brewery's Newcastle Pale Ale and Newcastle Mild Ale, it was called Newcastle Brown Ale. "Entirely new," proclaimed the first newspaper announcements. "You have tasted nothing quite the same as this before. A good brown ale with a rich mellow flavour. It's just the right strength—not too heavy for summer drinking, yet with sufficient 'body' to be able to satisfy the man who likes a good ale and knows when he gets it. Let your own good judgement tell you how excellent Newcastle BROWN Ale really is. Test it for yourself. Try a bottle to-night."[10] Newcastle Brown Ale quickly found popular favour, winning brewing medals and being distributed around the country and abroad. Like the Tyne Bridge, Newcastle Brown Ale would become a Tyneside icon.

The Tyne Bridge workers and their Newcastle brethren had another reason to raise a glass of Brown Ale in the spring of 1927: Newcastle United won the Football League. It was the fourth time the Magpies had won it (and, as of 2022, the last time). Club captain and centre-forward Hughie Gallacher—a brilliant but ultimately tragic wee Scot—scored 39 goals in 41 games.[11] Huge crowds attended St James' Park to cheer Newcastle on against their rivals. More than 67,000 fans saw a Gallacher goal beat Sunderland 1–0 in March. Newcastle secured the League title with a draw at West Ham on 23 April. It was the same week the Breweries launched Newcastle Brown Ale. With the Tyne Bridge taking shape, it was a special time for Tyneside. And the bridge, the beer and the football club would soon become indelibly linked.

* * *

The building of the Tyne Bridge was captured for posterity in a remarkable series of images taken by Newcastle-based photographers James Bacon & Sons. Dorman Long commissioned Bacon & Sons to record every aspect of the construction process for their archives. The result was a set of hundreds of numbered photos taken from various vantage points around the river, including the High Level and Swing bridges and the towers of St Mary's Church in Gateshead and All Saints Church in Newcastle. As the project progressed, the photographer climbed up with the workers into the rising structure to capture its growth. The photos are stunning— beautifully composed monochrome works of art, framing the emerging bridge pin-sharp against the inky Tyne under blankets of mist and drizzle.

Richard James Bacon was an artist and photographer from Buckinghamshire who moved to the North-East in the 1870s. By the 1880s, he had established "the largest and most replete photographic establishment in the North of England".[12] Bacon and his staff initially made their money from portraits, then from commercial work and industrial photography. His long-standing studio on Newcastle's Northumberland Street was adorned with evergreens and flowers.

It was one of the first premises in the city to be illuminated by electric light, leading Bacon to claim he was "practically independent of the sun".[13]

By the 1920s, the business had expanded, with studios in Leeds, Liverpool, Edinburgh and London. James Bacon was still registered as the proprietor in Newcastle, but he had moved back to the South-East. The Northumberland Street studio was now run by his son, William Herbert Bacon, born in County Durham, and the firm's principal photographer David Blount, from Elswick in Newcastle. The Dorman Long photos were stamped with "JAS. BACON & SONS, NEWCASTLE UPON TYNE", but the individual photographer was not credited. It was almost certainly not James Bacon but could have been William Bacon, David Blount or one of their staff. The photographs were never intended to be used outside of Dorman Long, although some were published in newspapers following the bridge's opening in 1928. After that, they might have been lost in the company's archives before re-emerging through the collection of chief assistant James Geddie and appearing in several major exhibitions. The Bacon & Sons photographs are a valuable pictorial account of the efforts to build the Tyne Bridge.

Back in 1927, representatives of Dorman Long were pleased with the progress their men were making. In March, Charles Mitchell arrived to inspect the project. Mitchell, a 53-year-old moustachioed Scot, was the manager of the firm's civil engineering and bridge construction department. He had travelled from Sudan, where he had overseen the construction of the Omdurman Bridge over the Nile. That seven-span bridge, including one swing span, was designed by Ralph Freeman. Mitchell had also supervised the building of the Abu-Deleig Bridge over the Atbara in Sudan and the Desouk Bridge over the Lower Nile in Egypt. Admired by colleagues for his single-minded "downright Scottish opinion", Mitchell would now concentrate on the Tyne Bridge—give or take a few supervisory trips to the other side of the world.[14] He recognised the Sydney Harbour Bridge was Dorman Long's most significant project, but told the press the Tyne Bridge was the biggest job of its kind in Europe and "involved certain unique methods in erections, as would be seen by the man in the street". Several of these methods were pioneered on the Tyne before being transferred to Sydney. Progress on the Tyne Bridge was said to be "eminently satisfactory".[15]

The Joint Bridge Committee also inspected the work—in pouring rain—and were delighted with it.[16] Newcastle's latest Lord Mayor, Arthur William Lambert, said he had "never known a project so large as that carried through with so great an absence of difficulty and suspicion, and with so much goodwill on both sides, the whole thing having been a complete success."[17]

However, there were rumours the project was heading dangerously over budget. It was true the builders had incurred extra costs, chiefly associated with additional strengthening for the Newcastle approach. Excavations had revealed a series of old basements that descended to various levels and were unknown before work began. Most likely, they were used by Quayside merchants during earlier eras of the Tyne's shipping trade, perhaps in the 16th and 17th centuries, and had become disused, blocked up, and forgotten.[18]

When newspaper reporters questioned the budget overspending, Newcastle's former mayor Stephen Easten said he had not heard the rumours and knew nothing about the matter.[19] The Mayor of Gateshead, W. Edwin Wardill, said there would always be unforeseen expenses in big schemes. However, there was no need for the public to worry.[20] Another member of the bridge committee emphasised that any extra costs had occurred due to bad luck and not bad planning. It was to be expected the project would come up against unexpected hurdles. What was important was that the bridge builders swiftly and efficiently overcame these hurdles, and construction of the Tyne Bridge proceeded at pace.

Another complication concerned the low stone railway arch that ran over Pilgrim Street at the Newcastle approach to the new bridge. Its proximity to the bridge meant there was less room for construction on the Newcastle side than there was on the Gateshead side. Consequently the Newcastle approach structure was assembled in shorter sections than the Gateshead one. Also, because the new approach road to the Tyne Bridge was set to be one of the busiest roads in the North of England, the low arch needed to be either raised—which was considered too difficult and expensive—or replaced. It seemed that, in attempting to solve one traffic problem, the Bridge Committee had created another. A proposed solution, a new road to carry traffic from the bridge up to the north of the city, was rejected on cost grounds. Traffic needed to run via the existing Pilgrim Street and Northumberland Street. That meant the Pilgrim Street railway arch would need to be dismantled and replaced. However, it was decided that traffic could be routed around the arch while the work was undertaken, without delaying the opening. A temporary steel girder railway bridge was erected while the stone arch was replaced.

A few weeks later, the *Journal* reported the suggestions of a "controversy" over the opening date. By then, Stephen Easten had been re-elected as Lord Mayor of Newcastle in a unanimous decision. He would now preside in ceremonial office over the completion of the "new bridging of Father Tyne".[21] Mayor Easten responded to the suggestions, during a meeting of the Joint Bridge Committee, that the only controversy he had seen was the one asserted by the newspaper, "without a particle of fact". The committee had been entrusted to produce a bridge at the cost of around a million pounds, said the mayor. They should not hesitate to open it at the earliest possible opportunity. If they kept it standing unused, he added, a commission should be appointed to "see about Coxlodge for them". Coxlodge was the location of the Newcastle upon Tyne City Lunatic Asylum.[22]

* * *

By the summer of 1927, the bottom sections of the bridge's white abutment towers were taking shape around the foundations that had been sunk with the caissons. The towers were built from steel and concrete, then faced with distinctive Cornish granite blocks from Penryn, near Falmouth. These carefully-selected blocks ranged in weight from 5 tons to almost 8 tons. Skewbacks—the resting places for the extremities of the arch—were built into the bases of the abutments. Hinged steel bearing supports were fixed to the skewbacks. Each bearing housed a huge pin, 12 inches in diameter and 8.5 feet long, which connected the arch to its supports. The hinges allowed the two halves of the arch to be lowered together into their meeting positions. They also allowed a small degree of natural movement due to expansion and contraction.

Once the hinges were in position, work began on the great arch, which was gradually built out from each bank to meet in the middle of the river. The arch consisted of two outer ribs, 45 feet apart, each with an upper and lower chord that sprung from the hinge pins to form the distinctive crescent shape. The ribs and their chords were connected by a criss-cross of lateral struts and diagonal braces. The road deck was slung from the arch ribs via vertical steel suspenders known as hangers.

The initial sections of the arch structure were supported by a temporary cradle. This was positioned first on the Gateshead side before being moved to the Newcastle side. Once the structure reached sufficient height—approximately road level—it was anchored to support masts on the riverbank with thick steel cables, and the cradle was removed. The temporary support masts were 70-feet high. The steel anchor cables consisted of 217 intertwined wires, each about the thickness of a pencil, and were overall around 8 inches in diameter. Each cable had a working load of 90 tons and a breaking load of 350 tons—approximately the weight of three fully-grown blue whales. During the early stages, as the initial reaches of the arch took shape, each half was anchored by eight steel cables. For the later stages, as the growing arch-halves extended further over the river, the number of cables was doubled to sixteen. The Tyne Bridge's erecting cables were subsequently re-used on the Sydney Harbour Bridge.[23]

The building of the hinged bearings, the cradle work, and the erection of the support masts took several weeks. It was September 1927 before the curvature of the arch first became visible on the Gateshead quays. Now local people could visualise what the completed bridge might look like and consider how difficult it might be to build. From an engineering perspective, much of the hard work had already been accomplished. But from a construction point of view, the building of the arch presented a significant challenge. The foundations were in place, and the steel sections were being delivered—all stamped with "MADE BY DORMAN, LONG & CO LTD, MIDDLESBROUGH". Now those steel sections needed to be assembled into the arch that would curve up and over the river.

The erection scheme—designed by Ralph Freeman with G.C. Imbault—was ingenious and fascinating. Given that no material could be lifted from the river, which had to be kept clear at all times, Dorman Long claimed it was a method that had never been used before in Britain. Engineers from all over the country were watching with great interest.[24] The scheme relied on clever crane work to raise and position each section of steelwork. A 20-ton electric derrick crane was mounted at the end of the ribs of each arch-half. This crane lifted the arch chord panels and struts and braces into position. When the derrick reached the limit of its reach, it was moved up and out along the growing arch to continue its work. Each time the derrick was moved, it had to be dismantled and reassembled. This was done with a smaller 5-ton crane using what Freeman referred to as his "leap-frog" technique. First, the 20-ton crane assembled the 5-ton crane on the arch ribs. Then the 5-ton crane dismantled the 20-ton crane, lifted it up and out along the ribs, and reassembled it. The next stage of steelwork was erected, and then the process started again—assemble the 5-ton, dismantle the 20-ton, move the 20-ton, and reassemble the 20-ton.

This work was duplicated on both sides of the river, so there were four cranes leap-frogging each other along the two halves of the growing arch. The working pattern was to advance the steelwork on weekdays and then advance the cranes on weekends. Each steel section was brought to the site in railway wagons and positioned for lifting by the cranes on bogie trucks that moved along temporary narrow-gauge tracks.

Spectators followed the workers' progress every day during the arch's construction. Their numbers were boosted on weekends when the building of the bridge became Tyneside's prime attraction—a spectacular free show. Traders moved around the crowd, selling roast chestnuts, baked potatoes and sarsaparillas. The most popular affliction on Tyneside was said to be a "crick in the neck" sustained from gazing upwards at the new bridge.[25] Even to those who saw it daily, the growing bridge was "an object of inexhaustible interest".[26]

One keen observer was Emily Watson, a young schoolgirl who watched the progress alongside her nine brothers and two sisters. "I remember the building of the bridge as a very exciting time," she later recalled. "My family never had any money to go to the pictures or anything, so we used to get a lot of entertainment from going down to the Quayside to see how the bridge was doing."[27]

Another interested spectator, a small boy, was overheard asking who was in charge of building the bridge. His father replied that it was the mayor of Newcastle. The boy considered this for a moment, then replied, "What a wonderful Meccano set he must have!" The popular model construction system, the Edwardian invention of Liverpool's Frank Hornby (also known for his miniature train sets), was often mentioned in references to the Tyne Bridge. In another overheard exchange, a "dear old lady", on viewing the emerging arch of the bridge—still without its road deck—was heard to say, "Dear me, I can understand the tramcars going over there, but it will be fearful for the poor horses."[28]

As technically innovative as the construction technique was, it was reliant on the manual workers—the scaffolders, platers and riveters—who pieced together Mayor Easten's giant Meccano set. They straddled the deck beams, 85 feet above the Tyne, to receive the steel sections. And they scaled the arch ribs to guide the sections into position and rivet them into place. They shuffled out along the steel anchor cables, their feet turned sideways to aid their balance, in a literal high-wire act that would have wowed crowds at the Bertram Mills Circus. They crawled on hands and knees along cross-beams, at heights of up to 110 feet above the deck—and more than 190 feet above the river. And they swung with their feet wrapped in loops of rope from crane jibs, riding with the massive steel sections as they were hoisted into the sky. It could take six or seven men to position each raised section. The men crowded on the extremities of the structure, each of them with one hand holding a beam or a colleague and the other grasping for the incoming section or signalling to the crane operator.

They lashed ladders to the arch ribs to aid climbing and fitted wooden handrails in some places, but there were few other safety measures. The only precaution the men might take was to tie a length of string around the waist of their jackets to stop them billowing open and casting them to the wind. It was dangerous and frightening work but also no doubt thrilling and satisfying. The region's two primary industries, coal mining and shipbuilding, were also hazardous. Mining was particularly dangerous. In 1925, while the foundations for the Tyne Bridge were being laid, 38 men were killed following an inrush of water at Montagu Pit in Scotswood, and five more were killed in an explosion at Edward Pit in Wallsend, both in Newcastle. Shipbuilding could involve working at heights of over 100 feet or deep in pressurised hulls that were insulated with asbestos. Many Tyne Bridge workers were veterans of the Great War and had substantially altered perceptions of danger and of risk. Far better, perhaps, to be balanced on a narrow beam over the Tyne than in a muddy trench on the Western Front.

And how satisfying it was for them to watch their bridge grow over the river. Few construction workers got to create such a tangible and enduring monument to their efforts. The men of the Swan Hunter shipyards were filled with pride as they watched the *Mauretania* and the *Carpathia* slide from their launch docks, but then they saw those great ocean liners steam away from the Tyne. The men who built the Tyne Bridge would be able to look upon their incredible creation for the rest of their lives. Perhaps the pitmen and shipbuilders who watched the construction of the Tyne Bridge viewed its high-wire workers with awe and a little envy.[29]

Among the most eye-catching work on the bridge was that of the riveters. This was a trade that came directly from the shipyards. Rivets are bolt-like metal fasteners used to join pieces of metal together. Each rivet was heated in a brazier until it was glowing white-hot—at around 1,000 degrees centigrade. Then the superheated rivets were flung with tongs up into the structure, where they were caught in a leather bucket or mitt and bashed into place with a pneumatic riveting hammer. As the rivet cooled and contracted, it formed a secure bond.

Riveters generally worked in teams of four, consisting of a *warmer*, a *catcher*, a *holder-up* and a *basher*. Their brazier was situated on girders directly beneath the section being riveted. The warmer heated and threw the rivet—with the necessary accuracy. The catcher reached out from his hazardous perch to catch it. If the warmer's aim was slightly off-target, the catcher would need to adjust his position quickly—and his safety hand-hold. If the rivet was dropped, it would plummet back down, still red hot, with any luck missing the workers below, and land with a splash and a hiss in the Tyne. Due to the great skill of the riveters, the rivet was usually caught, and inserted into a pre-punched hole. The holder-up held the rivet in place with a rivet set. Finally, the basher fixed it into place with the riveting hammer. The basher needed two arms and his body weight to operate the pneumatic hammer. There was no safety hand-hold for him. If there was room, a fifth man might be employed to grip on to his colleagues as they caught, held and bashed the rivets with a dead drop beneath their feet.

In answer to a Tyneside pub quiz tie-breaker question, there are 777,124 steel rivets on the Tyne Bridge.[30] It was one of the last major construction projects to rely on rivets. (Subsequent projects generally used bolts and welds.) Each riveter fitted around 250 rivets per shift—a phenomenal physical feat. One young riveter was a catcher named Jimmy Ransom. He recalled a site visit from a Dorman Long official who offered the teams an extra ha'penny for every extra rivet they fitted over their daily target. According to Ransom, the offer was rescinded after a week because, by starting early and finishing late, his team earned an extra £10 each—more than three times their weekly wage.[31]

It was particularly thrilling for the spectators on the quaysides to watch the riveters play their skilful, dangerous game of throw and catch, visible from across Newcastle and Gateshead. Their fiery braziers raged red hot against the grey Tyneside sky. As dusk fell each afternoon, the glowing rivets pinged about the skeletal structure like fireflies. The rhythmic sound of the pneumatic hammers became a familiar percussion to life on the banks of the Tyne.

The workers who crawled and climbed over the growing bridge became known to spectators as "spiders" and "monkeys". They were suspended from ropes in the wind like "a balloon[ing] spider" and scaled the arch like "an army of monkeys".[32] Some workers adopted these appellations as nicknames. One of the bridge's steel erectors was known as Spider Wilson. He worked on the Tyne Bridge alongside his father, a foreman. Spider Wilson's daughter, Julie Fox, said he was never afraid to climb the arch and walk along the steel cables without safety equipment. He was, she said, "a bit of a daredevil".[33]

Certainly, the men who scaled the Tyne Bridge's steelwork shared a particular mindset. Their toolbox of essential attributes included steady balance, unfailing hand-eye coordination and a robust nervous disposition. The requirements for a high-level bridge-builder were memorably set out back in 1877 by E.F. Farrington, the master mechanic on the Brooklyn Bridge. "No man can be a bridge-builder who must educate his nerves," wrote Farrington. "It must be a constitutional gift. He cannot, when 200 feet in the air, use his brain to keep his hand steady. He needs it all to make his difficult and delicate work secure. They must plant their feet by instinct... and be able to look down hundreds of feet without a muscle trembling. It is a rare thing for a man to lose his life in our business for loss of nerve."[34]

If the Tyne Bridge workers ever lost their nerves, they could surely restore them with a few bottles of Newcastle Brown Ale. One of their most popular drinking dens for the Tyne Bridge's spiders and the monkeys was the long-established Market Lane pub at the Newcastle end of the new bridge. The Market Lane, which narrowly escaped the demolition that cleared much of the surrounding Pilgrim Street area, still exists today. Housed in a Grade II-listed building dating from the early eighteenth century, the pub has a colourful history, which a modern restoration has embraced. There are photographs of the Tyne Bridge build on its walls. A monkey on the façade and hanging monkey lamps inside are nods to the bar's well-known nickname—"The Monkey Bar".[35]

Does the nickname refer to the bridge's high-climbing monkeys? A mural on the pub wall, which promises "the truth about The Monkey Bar", says the pub was frequented by bricklayers carrying hods during the construction of the Tyne Bridge. A bricklayer's hod was known as a "monkey".[36] According to the mural legend, the bricklayers would leave these monkeys in the entrance as security against their bar tabs, which is how the pub got its nickname. This theory may be true, although no definitive proof has been found. It seems just as likely the pub would be named for its scaffolding and riveting patrons than for their bricklaying colleagues' tools. Whatever the truth, the pub remains proudly linked to the building of the Tyne Bridge.

* * *

By December 1927, the workers had erected 1,200 tons of steel arch work—750 tons on the Gateshead side of the river and 450 tons on the Newcastle side. The two skeletal halves of the arch now suggested the eventual shape that would emerge. Snow began to fall, leaving a white dusting on the ribs and struts of the arch. It was the first flurry of what was a bitterly cold winter.

There was one fatality at the Tyne Bridge toward the end of 1927, but it did not involve a bridge worker. It happened in October after a Curry and Co furniture delivery van ran out of control on Gateshead High Street and careered down the redeveloped Bottle Bank, gathering speed as it went. Harry Morral, a 41-year-old packer from Cullercoats, leapt from the vehicle and was caught under its wheels. The van smashed into masonry at the works for the bridge. Two other men who were in the van escaped with cuts. Morral was taken to Newcastle's RVI in a police ambulance but died later that night.[37] Tragically, newspapers would soon have to report a death involving one of the Tyne Bridge's high-rise workers.

The great bridge did not yet have an official name. Was it the New Tyne Bridge, the New High Level Bridge, the Newcastle and Gateshead Bridge, or perhaps, some suggested, the George V Bridge? What about the Prince of Wales Bridge or the Prince Albert Bridge? The Deputy Mayor of Newcastle, Dr R.W. Shipman, paid tribute to the efforts of his mayoral superior, Stephen Easten, and suggested it should be called the Easten Bridge, "if justice were done".[38]

The public also made suggestions. "The new bridge across the Tyne will be a towering symbol of the age of mechanical transport," wrote Peter Shibden of Blaydon in a letter to the *Journal* in early December. His suggestion for a name seemed contrary to the fact that the new bridge was more than ten miles from the sea: "Let us name it the Marine Bridge."[39]

In the following week, on Thursday, 15 December 1927, the Newcastle and Gateshead Joint Bridge Committee met to officially christen the bridge. The chosen name was proposed by Newcastle's Mayor Easten and seconded by Gateshead's Mayor Wardill. The committee unanimously decided it should be called the "Tyne Bridge".[40]

112

8

CLOSING THE ARCH

James Ruck was standing at the apex of the steel arch, almost 200 feet above the River Tyne. In his hand was a telephone handset, its long cable running down the arch rib, over riveted panels and rigging ladders, to a control panel on the Quayside. It was typical of Ruck to be leading from the dangerous extremes of the bridge. He had scaled the skeletal trusses during the building of the arch just as he had descended into airless caissons during the laying of the foundations. It was a Saturday morning, 25 February 1928. Ruck was supervising the arch's long-awaited closure—a crucial and critical moment in the construction project. After six months of work on the epic steel arch, its two 2,250-ton halves were now just one and a half inches apart. Each arch was supported from a mast on the riverbank by 16 eight-inch-thick steel cables. At Ruck's command, his colleagues at the control jacks would subtly loosen the tension in these cables. This would allow the two halves of the arch to fall forwards gently, a quarter of an inch at a time, until they eventually met and—if the calculations were correct—took the full bearing of each other's weight. From that point, the workers could remove the cables, and the bridge would be a self-supporting structure. There would still be much work for Ruck and his men to do, but the central arch would be complete.

Such was the interest in this crucial procedure that thousands of spectators crawled out of their beds to stand watch on the Newcastle and Gateshead quaysides. They lined the High Level and Swing bridges and crowded St Mary's churchyard—now considered the prime grandstand for bridge-viewers. "They watched with something of the breathless interest of children building a house with an

old pack of cards," reported the Newcastle *Journal*.[1] The Joint
Bridge Committee, led by Lord Mayor Easten of Newcastle and
Mayor Wardill of Gateshead, stood on the pier of the Swing Bridge
and gazed up from river level at the looming structure above them.
Sir Basil Mott, David Anderson, Ralph Freeman, Charles Mitchell
and Sir Hugh Bell joined them on the pier. Unfortunately, Sir
Arthur Dorman could not be present as he was suffering from a
chill. Photographers and movie cameramen focussed their lenses on
the arch. But to all except James Ruck at the top of the arch, the
procedure was almost imperceptible. It was intended that the gap
that morning would be somewhat more significant. But, as one
workman explained, things were going so well on the previous evening they had decided they would "just finish the job".[2] The remaining gap—just a couple of finger-widths—could not be seen from
the ground. Spectators on the bridges and the quaysides could be
forgiven for thinking absolutely nothing was happening. But those
who were following the progress in newspapers knew this almost
invisibly small step was a hugely significant giant leap in the construction of the Tyne Bridge.

The great arch—with its 531-foot span and 193-foot rise—was
the culmination of twenty-three weeks of ingenious and daring
steelwork that had captivated Tyneside and the wider world. Ruck
and his hardy workforce had built it out from each riverbank in a
manner that appeared to defy gravity, using a method that kept the
river entirely free and unobstructed, in adherence to the stipulations
of the Tyne Commission. The men had worked seven days a week
with only two Sundays off—Christmas Day and New Year's Day.
"In other words," noted the *Journal*, "not a day has been wasted from
the moment the steel-erection began."[3] Ruck knew the workers he
was responsible for had endured a punishing schedule. And just
seven days earlier, they had suffered a terrible tragedy.

Far below Ruck, in a boat on the river, was another Dorman
Long employee with a very important job. John Carr lived on the
Close, right on the Newcastle riverbank. He was 52 years old and
married with four sons. He had a grey moustache and wore a large
flat cap pulled low over his eyebrows. Carr was employed to sit on
the river in a sculler-boat and fish out anything that might fall into
the water. Primarily, he was there to rescue fallen men. Dorman

Long chose him from around 250 applicants on the strength of his life-saving experience. Carr had worked on the river's steam wherries—the particular type of barges used to carry coal and other materials along the Tyne. Colleagues regarded him as a brave man and a strong swimmer who would not hesitate to dive overboard into the treacherous river to rescue anyone in difficulty. His job under the bridge was largely a waiting game. But he was ready to respond and had been called into action in the previous week in the most terrible circumstances. As anticipation grew ahead of the arch closure, both James Ruck and John Carr must have thought back to the dreadful events of the previous Saturday.

* * *

Work had progressed remarkably quickly through January and February, even as winter bit hard on Tyneside. Snow and frost made the steel structure even more hazardous than usual. A seemingly-permanent dank mist settled above the industrial river. Often, on a winter morning, only the Castle Keep, the three spires (of the Cathedral, All Saints and St Mary's) and the uppermost sections of the part-built bridge could be seen above the soggy grey blanket that lay across the river. Strong, chilly winds that whistled through the bridge's steelwork only made things more challenging. The weather was "very trying", said one worker after descending from the arch. "We have had a perishing time."[4]

According to the *Journal*, the bridge workers had the coldest and windiest jobs on Tyneside: "These master craftsmen who climb about the new bridge structure at dizzy heights, and seem only to have an eyebrow on this side of eternity, have faced the worst of weather, and push on with their jobs with grim determination whatever tricks the elements may play. They do not appear to be numerous, but their work is growing like spring rhubarb under an old bucket."[5]

That growth was strikingly evident. Every day, almost every hour, spectators could see the two arch halves stretching further over the river and closer to each other. At the beginning of January, the gap between the two halves was around 250 feet. By the beginning of February, it was 150 feet. By the middle of February, it was 90 feet. Then the race to complete the arch entered the home straight as Ruck and his army of monkeys and spider-men advanced the bridge nearer and nearer towards closure at a pace of almost 10 feet a day.

One of the workers toiling on the steel arch was Nathaniel Collins, a scaffold erector from South Shields. He was 33 years old and lived in a terraced house on H.S. Edwards Street, named for prominent local shipbuilder Harry Smith Edwards. Collins was married to Alice, and the couple had two children. He was born in Dunbartonshire, on the banks of another great shipbuilding river, the Clyde. His family moved to the Tyne when he was an infant. His father was a ship's plater, and Collins followed him into the shipyards as an apprentice plater at an early age.

Like many Tyne Bridge workers, Collins was a veteran of the war. He joined the Territorial Force as a part-time volunteer at the age of 17 in 1912 and was sent into battle in April 1915. He served with the 1st/7th Battalion (the first of four companies of the 7th Battalion) of the Durham Light Infantry under the command of Lieutenant Colonel Ernest Vaux of the Sunderland brewing family. The 1st/7th suffered heavy casualties in the trenches at Ypres, then served on the Somme and at Arras and Passchendaele. Private Collins received the 1914–15 Star, the British War Medal and the Victory Medal.

After the war, Collins worked as a steeplejack and high-rise scaffolder. He came to specialise in demolishing or felling chimney stacks, which involved shoring up a chimney with scaffolding before removing bricks from the base to cause its collapse. He was well used to working at heights. Friends and relatives described him as "a good climber", "a very steady man", and "one who has never suffered from giddiness". According to one family member, Collins "knew no fear".[6] Thanks to his experience in erecting scaffolding at heights, he was employed to work on the Tyne Bridge in December 1927. Two months later, he was working at the highest extremity of the Gateshead half of the arch, about 175 feet above the water, when tragedy struck.

It was three in the afternoon on a cold and bright Saturday, 18 February 1928. Strong westerly winds were gusting up the river, whistling between the incomplete ribs of the bridge. From his privileged vantage point, Collins would have been able to see St James'

Park football ground and likely hear the roar of 29,000 fans as reigning league champions Newcastle United kicked off their match against Bolton Wanderers. Along with two other scaffolders, Collins was attempting to raise a loose staging plank from below the fixed scaffold. He took hold of the plank in one hand and reached to support himself with the other. But he reached short of his support hold and grabbed only fresh air. The plank started to slip and spun him around. "Oh dear! Oh dear!" he uttered.[7] Collins lost his footing and fell headfirst from the arch—to the horror of hundreds of spectators. He appeared to hit a horizontal girder on the way down. According to a witness, he "spun like a wheel through the air" then struck the water "with terrific force".[8] He disappeared below the murky surface for a few seconds before his motionless body resurfaced.

A cry of "Man overboard!" and the terrified shrieks of onlookers alerted John Carr, who turned in time to see Collins plunge headfirst into the water.[9] Carr swiftly sculled out into the river. Battling a strong ebb tide, the boatman grabbed hold of Collins but could not pull him out of the water and into the moving boat. Carr then fought desperately against the current to maintain his grip on the stricken man. All Carr could do was keep Collins' head above the water as the current swept the sculler-boat downriver for a considerable distance. Soon a second boat, launched from the Newcastle Quayside, reached the sculler and steadied its position, allowing Carr to heave Collins from the water. The two boats hurried the injured man to the Gateshead bank of the river, where an ambulance was waiting to transfer Collins to hospital. Collins was still alive and conscious, but his severe injuries included a fractured skull. "His rescue from the water was effected in thrilling fashion," reported the *Journal*, "but despite his expeditious removal to the Newcastle Infirmary, he died shortly after admission."[10]

A policeman and a representative of Dorman Long went to South Shields that afternoon to inform Collins' widow. "It seems my husband had to die in the public service," Alice Collins later said. "He went through the Great War from 1914 to 1918 without injury, only to fall from the new bridge. Well, he died in the service of Tyneside. To myself and my two children, the new Tyne Bridge will be a monument to his memory."[11] Privately, Alice was less magnanimous. She never got over her husband's death, and she raised their children alone, never remarrying. According to her grandson, Robert Collins, Alice forever hated the bridge for what it had done to her family.[12]

At an inquest before the Newcastle coroner, Collins' co-worker and fellow scaffold erector Thomas Pearson said the job of raising a staging plank was one they had done many times. Although the weather was cold and damp, Pearson said the planks were dry and not slippery. John Carr was called to give an account of the river rescue and was praised for his bravery. A medical testimony said Collins had died from a fractured skull. The jury returned a verdict of accidental death, and the coroner added there was no blame attached to anyone. John Sinton, a solicitor acting for Dorman Long, said he wished to express the deep sympathy of the company to Collins' relatives. Overlooking the death of Frank McCoy two years earlier, Sinton said this was the first serious accident since the commencement of work on the bridge, "thanks to every precaution being taken." (Sinton likely meant it was the first accident to a worker since the commencement of the arch work.) Sinton said Dorman Long were "very sorry that such an event should have taken place before its completion".[13]

John Carr became something of a hero for his "magnificent record of life-saving". Newspaper reporters interviewed his wife, and Carr was photographed—wearing his large cap—for the national *Daily Mirror*.[14] Several newspapers said Carr had rescued fifty-seven people from the river, of whom Nathaniel Collins was the only one to have died.[15] Reports implied all of Carr's rescues had taken place during the building of the Tyne Bridge. It seems more likely they occurred during his entire career on the river. Whatever the circumstances, Carr was undoubtedly an incredibly courageous life-saver. He was subsequently awarded a Royal Humane Society medal for his bravery.[16] Tales of Carr's rescues resurfaced in newspapers when he died in 1939, aged 63.

The tragic death of Nathaniel Collins reminded Tyneside that its colossal building project, with its tons of steel and towering cranes, relied on the labour of individual men—ordinary men who lived in the same streets as those who came to gaze up at the growing structure. "It would have been a splendid achievement had the bridge been completed without loss of life," commented the *Journal*. "Such big enterprises seldom are, alas, and occasionally the human sacrifice is very heavy."[17]

According to an old superstition, a bridge was safe only if it had claimed a life. In a rather gruesome builders' rite, some cultures would make human sacrifices and bury the victims in the foundations of bridges and other buildings to secure their stability. In Greek mythology, after labourers struggled to construct the Bridge of Arta, over the Arachthos River in western Greece, the head builder's wife was sacrificed to establish good foundations for the bridge. In subsequent centuries, a fatal accident to a bridge builder might even be considered a blessing. This belief lingered in the thoughts of observers during the building of some of the modern world's greatest bridges. When the Brooklyn Bridge designer John A. Roebling died following an accident in the early stages of construction, the *Brooklyn Daily Eagle* newspaper called him a martyr whose blood had "baptized and hallowed" that bridge.[18] The newspaper told its readers the success of the bridge was now assured. There were no such claims in the Tyneside papers regarding Nathaniel Collins and the Tyne Bridge. However, the memory of Collins would forever be linked to its construction.

Collins is recorded in the annals of Tyneside as the only man who died while building the Tyne Bridge. However, this is not true. Collins was the only man who died while constructing the arch. But Frank McCoy was killed during the sinking of the foundations. And a third man was killed while building the abutment towers.

Norman Muller, a 26-year-old joiner's labourer from Sunderland, was killed on 19 June 1928. He was removing scaffolding used for the concreting of one of the abutment towers at about 60 feet above ground. Asked by a colleague to fetch something, Muller went to cross a 9-inch-wide wooden plank. Workers had crossed the plank many times that day, using the abutment wall as a hand-hold, and considered it safe. But Muller slipped and screamed as he fell to the ground. He was hurried to the RVI with a fractured skull. He never regained consciousness and died about two hours later. Like Nathaniel Collins and Frank McCoy, Muller was found at a coroner's inquest to have suffered an accidental death.[19]

Mercifully, no other workers were killed during the building of the Tyne Bridge. But bridge-building remained a dangerous pursuit,

119

and Dorman Long would have to bear more losses away from Tyneside. Sixteen men would die during the construction of the Sydney Harbour Bridge before it was completed in 1932.

Back in February 1928, James Ruck and his workers had little time to mourn Nathaniel Collins. They continued their work on the bridge without pause or, it seemed, fear. By now, the gap between the two sections of the arch was "no wider than a man could jump"—although no worker saw fit to test that measurement.[20] Down on the quaysides, spectators looked on, some of them, no doubt, with ghoulish fascination. They saw a remarkable display of fortitude by men who must have had the tragic fate of their colleague at the forefront of their minds. But the top of the Tyne Bridge was no place to dither. There could be no hesitation or doubt. Their work could only be completed with assurance and self-belief. A *Journal* reporter paid tribute to the "supreme spirit" of the men. Their attitude as they worked "with nothing apparently between an improvised foothold and death" was "sufficient to cause a shiver down the spine".[21]

Within a few days, the gap between the two arch halves was down to 9 inches. Now workers could step across the gap and, for the first time, cross the bridge. Dorman Long's photographer took a picture of the company's workers inspecting the gap. Standing in the mist at the apex of an arch rib, they seemed utterly relaxed about the fact they were a very considerable distance above the cold, dirty surface of the Tyne. As the *Journal* noted, "They stepped across those 9 inches, with a sheer drop of 200 feet to eternity, as calmly and leisurely as though striding across their own door-steps."[22]

* * *

On 25 February 1928, seven days after Nathaniel Collins' death, James Ruck was at the top of the arch, John Carr was on the river, the dignitaries were on the pier, and thousands of spectators were getting cricks in their necks. Ruck uttered instructions into his telephone, the jack operators made their adjustments, and the arch quarter-inched its way towards closure. When the two halves finally met, there was no thunderous boom or quaking reverberation. To most of the gathered there, nothing perceptible had happened. But then came confirmation. High above the murky water and the expectant crowds, Ruck gave a signal: "All right!" Down on the pier, Sir Basil Mott "ejaculated a fervent 'Thank God!'"[23]

Celebrations duly followed. Maroon rocket fireworks shot into the air and exploded with a bang and a shower of stars above the steelwork. Flags were raised triumphantly to flutter in the winter breeze. Hats were waved, and three cheers were offered to the new Tyne Bridge. The spectators had perhaps expected a little more spectacle. Nevertheless, they had witnessed "a historic event in the life of Tyneside".[24]

"Congratulations are due to all concerned," said the *Journal*. "This new demonstration of the triumph of mind over matter and the powers of nature is an impressive achievement, and Tynesiders who have watched the growth of the massive structure should be inspired in the prosecution of infinitely more humble tasks to which they turn their hands. The bridge will stand as a symbol of daring enterprise and successful endeavour against problems the nature of which the lay mind can have little real conception. Men vision, measure and calculate these great works, but always there is the element of risk in their undertaking, which has to be faced boldly if there is to be progress."[25]

The Bridge Committee, led by Mayors Easten and Wardill, watched the fireworks from the Swing Bridge and then inspected the completed arch, along with Ralph Freeman, David Anderson and Charles Mitchell. Mayor Wardill, wearing his chain of office, joined a party of "venturesome" designers, engineers and workmen who climbed to the very top of the arch.[26] Dorman Long's intrepid photographer was there, perched on the opposite arch rib, to capture the moment Mayor Wardill reached the top and shook hands with Newcastle's Councillor Arthur Lambert. Gathered around the Mayor on his narrow steel perch was a crowd of more than twenty men—engineers in bowler hats and overcoats and workers in flat caps and overalls. Some leant casually on the handrails, and others sat with their legs dangling over the edge. There were smiles and evident pride. This was a remarkable achievement.

Afterwards, Mayor Easten hosted a dinner for the Bridge Committee and representatives of the design and construction firms. Toasts were raised to the Tyne Bridge and its workers—"men of skill and craft, of seeing eye and unending pluck" who had "braved the elements".[27] Mayor Easten also raised a toast to the engineers and contractors who he said were men at the top of their professions. Basil Mott, David Anderson, Charles Mitchell and James Ruck were all praised in dispatches. Amid laughter, someone suggested the modest Ruck looked like he wished to cower beneath his dinner table. Most likely, Ruck wanted to get back to work. He knew there was still much to do.

During the celebrations, Mayor Easten stated the bridge had first been proposed at a city council meeting four years ago, in 1924. This comment reignited a dispute in newspaper correspondence columns regarding the bridge's origin. Newcastle postmaster James Webster pointed out that his younger brother Thomas Webster had already proposed a bridge on the same site two years earlier in a plan published in local newspapers and in personal visits to councillors from both Newcastle and Gateshead. "Let credit be accorded where it is due," said James Webster. Another correspondent, "On-looker", also suggested Mayor Easten should take the trouble to look back at the correspondence from Thomas Webster, from when he had proposed the idea in 1922 and asked for recognition in 1925.[28] A few days later, Thomas Webster himself wrote to the *Journal*. Webster admitted the Tyne Bridge would not have come into being had it not been for Mayor Easten. But, he said, "the same can be said with equal truth of a lot of people, including myself, who set the scheme going".[29] Webster furthered his claim to be remembered by publishing a book, *The New High-Level Bridge and its Origin*, and by highlighting his proposal during a discussion about the bridge at a meeting of the Institution of Civil Engineers.[30]

However, other claims regarding the origin of the bridge went back much further. A correspondent named Oscar Dahl pointed to a 1903 book by Archibald Reed that considered "a second high-level bridge from the south end of Pilgrim Street to Gateshead." Dahl thought the book was "somewhat prophetic".[31] Then C.T. Marshall wrote in to say it might interest readers to know he had proposed a similar new high-level bridge back in 1898.[32] Another name mentioned was that of Benjamin Plummer, the former secretary of the Chamber of Commerce, whose much earlier plans for a high-level Tyne Bridge dating back to the 1860s had found favour in subsequent decades with Gateshead Council. "How the memory of his labour seems to have vanished!" wrote a correspondent. "Have we another example in this of the pioneers who blaze the trail? They pass and are forgotten; later comers claim the glory, and sometimes get it."[33]

* * *

On the following Sunday, 4 March 1928, Ruck and his men fitted the final pieces of their steel jigsaw—the last six cross girders for the road deck. This was regarded as "one of the most astonishing feats recorded in connexion with the new Tyne Bridge", and extra-large crowds gathered early in the morning to watch.[34] Each girder measured 60 feet long and weighed almost 60 tons. To place them safely and securely at such a critical point, with the integrity of the whole structure at stake, Dorman Long had to obtain an important concession. Although the terms of their contract prohibited them from using the river, they sought special permission from the Tyne Improvement Commission for an exception. The Commission agreed to offer Dorman Long a window of four hours, very early on a Sunday morning, during which they were allowed to raise the girders from the river. To minimise the disruption, the Commission provided launches to regulate the river traffic.

Sunday market stallholders joined the crowds of early risers to watch as the huge girders were loaded into a steam barge and then ferried out one at a time into mid-river. James Ruck coordinated the procedure like the conductor of an industrial orchestra. John Carr watched from his sculler on the water, no doubt hoping he would not be called into action. The girders were attached to rope slings hanging from the derrick cranes on the arch. They were hauled up into the structure, manoeuvred into position, and fitted and riveted into place. Workers rode with the girders, clinging to the rope slings and ascending and descending the structure like the spiders to which they were often compared. By the time one girder was fitted, another had been fetched and ferried by the barge, and the process began again. All six girders were placed into position within the allocated four hours. The successful operation was regarded as "an object lesson in organisation and co-operation".[35]

A few days later, despite heavy snow, James Ruck, Ralph Freeman and David Anderson were present to supervise a crucial technical procedure—the jacking of the bottom boom. This represented the completion of the horizontal platform that spanned the river at deck level. The girders that made up the boom were shifted into place using four powerful hydraulic jacks. This was considered to be the final significant engineering hurdle for the construction of the Tyne Bridge, and it was overcome "without a hitch".[36]

* * *

Within days of the steelwork being completed, a *Journal* reporter named Eileen McIntyre scaled the arch, accompanied by one of the resident engineers. He advised her not to look down. McIntyre began her ascent by following the engineer up the ladders tied to the Gateshead side of the western arch rib, negotiating posts and platforms as she went. When she asked if the ladders were securely fastened, she was "laughingly reassured". On reaching the road deck level, 84 feet above the river, McIntyre paused for breath. Then she negotiated a "rather awkward corner" and began to climb the upper part of the arch. "We ascended by means of stout slats of wood nailed across the arch, and at intervals there was a handrail," she wrote. "At length, after I had grasped at a wholly visionary rail, almost decapitated myself on some cable tubes, and endeavoured to scramble under, instead of over, a projecting bar, we stood in ecstasy on the very summit of that arch, 200 feet above the river."[37]

The view was worth the effort: "Even about smoky, loveable Tyneside was an air of romance, remote but very real, for all the buildings, dominated on the north by the castle, were veiled in a soft, grey, wraith-like, moveless mist that obliterated the grime and squalor and gave even to the hard lines of the other bridges—all far beneath our level—a softly sculptured beauty."

McIntyre descended by the same route, pausing to watch the riveters and their pneumatic hammers. "The astonishment of the men at the presence of a girl on the bridge was in no degree greater than my own at the way in which they lightly and quickly, yet not less surely, moved at all angles about the massive cross-beams," she wrote. The most awkward part of the descent was a backwards climb down a long and almost-vertical ladder—while resisting the temptation to look down. Eventually, though, a relieved McIntyre was safely back on the ground. It was a thrilling, white-knuckle experience: "The exhilaration I had felt remained with me long after I had touched solid earth."

The *Journal*'s headline claimed McIntyre was the "First Woman to Scale Arch of New Bridge". However, on the following day, a letter appeared to dispute that claim. "I am sorry to have to disappoint the lady in question," wrote E.R. Williams of Newcastle, "but the distinction she claims belongs to Miss Ruth Kew of Gateshead, who made the ascent under the same conditions last Sunday morning, accompanied by her brother, also a resident engineer and the undersigned." The *Journal*'s editor responded: "We offer her our congratulations on a covetable distinction."[38]

In a further response, the same newspaper published an overheard exchange between a two men on a tramcar, presented in local dialect. "Aa've h'ard iv a young lass gannin' ower the arch iv th' new Tyne Bridge," said the younger man.

"Aye, lassies noo are deein' ivorything. Sixty yeor ago they dorn't hev tried it," said the older man.

"Hoo's that?"

"Th' wind wad hev meyd parachutes iv thor claes, and they'd iv landed at Jarra'." ("The wind would have made parachutes of their clothes, and they'd have landed at Jarrow.")[39]

* * *

At the end of March 1928, the Tyne Bridge became the symbol for a fundraising effort—a use that would become familiar in subsequent decades. Newcastle's Royal Victoria Infirmary, which had opened in 1906, was struggling with debt, overcrowded wards and lengthening waiting lists (all of this two decades before the creation of the National Health Service). An appeal for a fund of £150,000, launched in the previous September, had raised only £13,505. Now that the Tyne Bridge had "fired the imagination" of Tynesiders, the fundraising effort was rebranded as "A Bridge to Health".[40]

"Untold thousands of patients have by its means crossed from the darkened lanes of pain and suffering into the bright avenues of health and happiness," noted the *Journal*. The Tyne Bridge represented unity, hope and accomplishment. It represented the best of Tyneside and was a great source of pride. If the people of Tyneside could come together to build their bridge, they could come together to fund their hospital—a neglected but essential institution.

There was more fundraising involving the bridge in the following month, this time as part of a Newcastle students' rag parade to raise £6,000 for another hospital—the Fleming Memorial Hospital for Sick Children, in Jesmond. The "New Tyne Bridge" was a 15-foot-tall model constructed by a group of third-year engineering students who styled themselves "Long Dormant and Co Unlimited". "Collecting Quids For Kids" and "Coughing Up For the Fleming" were the twin mottos of the students' rag efforts, which involved "pestering" passing pedestrians and motorists for small change.[41] The model Tyne Bridge was wheeled through the streets of Newcastle as part of a parade that featured students dressed as sailors, doctors, pirates, legionnaires, and robots.[42] Crowds gathered around with great interest, and "everybody seemed to enter into the fun of the thing".[43]

For their part, the real Dorman Long wrote to "Long Dormant" stating they were sorry they had built their bridge before studying the "more up to date" methods used by the students, which would have allowed the bridge to be moved up and down the river at will. They also enclosed a donation to the fund.[44]

The highlight of the parade was a ceremony outside Central Station in which the model Tyne Bridge was opened by a fake Winston Churchill. And on the same day, the real bridge was visited—and admired—by the real Churchill, then Chancellor of the Exchequer.[45] Churchill was accosted by rag students, and genially agreed to help with a donation. The Swing Bridge was opened for his benefit, and motorists who were held up by its opening joked with each other that both their delay and their increasing petrol costs were attributable to the Chancellor.[46]

* * *

Although the steelwork was complete, there was still a great deal to do. And the work was given added urgency after Mayor Easten announced the bridge would be officially opened in October by King George V. The King had last visited Tyneside in 1915 when he

came to inspect the war effort in the shipyards and munitions factories. This occasion would be more celebratory, and he would be
accompanied by Queen Mary. The people of Tyneside awaited the
visit with "pleasurable anticipation". The presence of the King and
Queen, the *Journal* noted, would "lend greatly enhanced interest to
an event which in any case must rank big in Tyneside history."[47] In
a rare and pioneering undertaking, coverage of the visit would be
broadcast live on the BBC's 5NO Newcastle radio service.

Over the next few months, work proceeded at what James Ruck
called "high pressure".[48] Steel floor plates were bolted and riveted
onto the deck and covered with Trinidad Lake asphalt to prevent
corrosion.[49] (That job was slightly delayed when twenty Tyne
Bridge asphalters went on strike during a dispute over hours and
wages. The men claimed the contractors were undercutting their
wages by appointing miners to do the work at 5d less per hour.)[50]
The roadway was paved with creosoted wood boards, framed by
Scottish granite setts and kerbs. Pipework to carry gas, water and
electrical services over the river was laid. Cast-iron balustrades and
lampposts, from the Walter Macfarlane and Co Saracen Foundry in
Glasgow, were fitted along the span of the bridge.[51]

The grand abutment towers were taking shape, although a delay
in delivering some of the Cornish granite meant the Gateshead tower
would not be completed in time for the bridge's opening. The interiors of the huge abutment towers were considered valuable spaces
that should not be wasted. It was intended to fit them out as warehouses with industrial lifts to convey merchandise between the quaysides and storage levels. However, in April, the Bridge Committee
decided that work to fit out the warehouses would be postponed due
to the "unsatisfactory state of trade and the reduced demand for such
accommodation".[52] The committee emphasised that the work had
not been abandoned and would resume when demand improved.
However, that never happened, and the towers would always remain
empty. It was also announced that work to build a passenger lift in
the Gateshead tower would be postponed.[53]

Meanwhile, the Tyne Bridge's vast web of steelwork was being
painted. Thirty paint manufacturers applied for the contract, each
of which was invited to coat to their specifications a steel plate,
which was hung in the river at a point considered particularly cor-

rosive due to the mix of salt and fresh water, industrial waste and sewage. The plates were fully immersed at high tide and exposed to the air—and acidic fumes—at low tide. After four months of exposure, only one plate remained unaffected by the conditions. That plate was treated with a three-coat scheme from J. Dampney and Co. Ltd of Gateshead. Dampney's had recently painted the Redheugh Bridge, so they were well aware of the trying conditions presented by the industrial River Tyne.[54]

The Tyne Bridge paint scheme began with a first coat of Dampney's Genuine Non-Setting Liquid Red Lead. The second coat was of Dampney's Natural Colour Miraculum Graphite Paint. And the third and final coat was of Dampney's Superlative Middle Green Paint. (Unseen portions of the bridge were painted with three coats of Dampney's Asphaltene Super Bituminous Paint.) According to Dampney's, their Superlative Paint was "the most waterproof and weatherproof paint in existence". It had enough elasticity to withstand expansion and contraction, and enough durability to provide "years of faithful service". So, during the three stages of its initial painting, the Tyne Bridge went from red to graphite to green.[55]

The bridge's middle green colour has become enduringly familiar on Tyneside, and it's easy to underestimate how arresting such a broad swathe of colour must have been over the grey industrial river between two soot-black towns. When electric lampposts and tram standards across Newcastle were painted green to match the new bridge, the *Journal* hailed the "welcome touch of colour" as a "commendable transformation".[56] "The bridge presents a strikingly impressive embodiment of grace and strength," the newspaper added. "The permanent colour of the steelwork is a pleasing shade of green. That anything and everything giving an appearance of brightness will be approved and appreciated surely goes without saying."[57]

In September, Mayor Easten received a telegram from Balmoral fixing the date of the King's visit for Wednesday, 10 October 1928.[58] The Joint Bridge Committee stepped up their preparations. James Ruck helped Mayors Easten and Wardill and other committee members inspect the Newcastle end of the bridge, where a stand was built to accommodate the royal party. Tramlines were finished, and cranes were dismantled. The last few hundred tons of gleaming white granite were stacked on the Newcastle abutment tower. The

Gateshead tower remained frustratingly half-finished, but otherwise the grand bridge was nearing completion. Mayor Easten declared that 10 October should be a public holiday. The whole of Tyneside would be able to see George V open the new Tyne Bridge.

9

THE GRAND OPENING

It was one of the greatest celebrations Tyneside had ever seen—and perhaps would ever see. Hundreds of thousands of men, women and children crowded the pavements, scaled lampposts, dangled from windows and clambered onto roofs. They waved flags and handkerchiefs and cheered and sang. All along the royal procession route, down through Newcastle's Northumberland Street and Pilgrim Street to the great steel arch, then up and along Gateshead High Street, buildings were draped with colourful banners and buntings. Adventurous folk claimed dizzying vantage points, from the top of Grey's Monument and the rooftops of the Town Hall and Moot Hall to the towers and tiles of All Saints and St Mary's churches and all manner of chimney stacks and roof ridges in-between. The quaysides were thick with flat caps and bonnets, and the Swing Bridge and High Level were packed with onlookers. It was a Wednesday morning, 10 October 1928, and the crowds were here to see King George V open the new Tyne Bridge.

They came from across the North East. LNER offered cheap rail tickets for journeys to Newcastle from all stations within an 80-mile radius. It seemed unlikely any previous event—bridge opening, royal visit or football homecoming—had ever drawn such a vast crowd. "It is questionable if a free passage of the main streets has ever been more difficult," wrote one reporter. "All Tyneside seemed to be filling the pathways, standing on each other's toes, and showing even greater enterprise in the scaling of every height in the city... Tyneside meant to see King George and Queen Mary—and most of the many thousands did."[1]

Tyneside (and particularly Newcastle) had been traditionally royalist since the era of the Old Tyne Bridge, and George V was particularly popular for his wartime leadership and his apparent consideration and support for working people. More plainly, King George and Queen Mary were Britain's (and perhaps the world's) biggest celebrities, and this was an extremely rare opportunity for Northerners to see them in the flesh. The royal procession route was marked with white lines, which the public was requested to keep behind. Tons of grit were thrown on the roads to prevent the King's horses from slipping. According to a Newcastle *Journal* reporter, the constant tramp of thousands of feet crunching across grit made an extraordinary sound—"like the spirits of the Tyne whispering together and marvelling at the changes wrought since the day when Hadrian's men of Rome thundered over the timbered Tyne".[2]

The streets along the route were decorated with flags, flowers and banners. Shop windows were filled with displays of red, white and blue. Soot-blackened facades were covered with coloured paper streamers, giving the industrial avenues a cheerful makeover. "Newcastle and Gateshead have clothed themselves like the biblical Joseph," remarked the *Journal*, "only the hues must be much more varied and vivid than his coat." The people of Tyneside were seen to walk around their newly-decorated streets with looks of "pleased wonderment". Union Jacks and flags of many other nations were flown on both sides of the river. Street vendors sold small flags and rosettes and made a very good trade. The biggest Union flag on view was suspended across the frontage of Fenwick's department store in Newcastle. One young boy was seen to hurl down his small flag, point up at Fenwick's and yell, "Boo hoo, I want that flag, ma!"[3]

Fenwick's and other local shops sold all manner of souvenirs, including China mugs and ashtrays and embroidered tea cosies and tea cloths bearing colourful images of "our Wonder Bridge".[4] Newsboys sold "official" programmes printed by a Newcastle publisher for sixpence, plus commemorative postcards. Due to heavy demand, the *Journal* republished a souvenir supplement given away free with the paper earlier in the week containing Bacon & Sons photos of the bridge alongside a timetable for the opening ceremonies.[5]

Also in the *Journal*, on the day of the opening, Newcastle tobacco company Gallaher Ltd placed an advert for its War Horse tobacco. This was among the first of a century-worth of ads for numerous businesses and products to feature the silhouette of the Tyne Bridge.

"The opening of the New Bridge will be a big occasion on Tyneside," read the ad. *"We will all be smoking an extra pipe or two today. And for most of us, it will be an extra pipe of War Horse—the tobacco that's as natural to us on Tyneside as our pride in the new bridge."*[6]

Among the proud spectators gathered to watch the royal opening was Robert Grant, a cabinet maker, wood carver and painter from Newcastle. Grant, then seventy-seven years old, had just celebrated a half-century of business in the city and was also known for his efforts to support charities for the blind by selling his watercolour paintings in bespoke wooden frames. He was particularly interested in the opening of the Tyne Bridge because he could recall witnessing the openings of the Swing Bridge, the King Edward VII Bridge, the two Redheugh Bridges, and the temporary wooden Tyne Bridge (plus, further upstream, the Scotswood Railway Bridge and the Wylam Railway Bridge). Grant also recalled seeing the River Tyne frozen over during the later years of the Georgian Tyne Bridge and watching locals skating on the ice. Grant said he had often gone swimming in the Tyne and—in the days before it was properly dredged—had waded across it near the Elswick works. All told, the Tyne Bridge was the eighth bridge Grant saw opened over the great river.[7]

Towards the other end of the age spectrum among the spectators was Kitty Brightwell, who was six years old and attended the parade with her parents and younger brother. Recording her memories in 2011, she recalled standing among the thousands of people lining the route and being so excited she didn't feel the cold. Kitty had only seen the King and Queen in newspapers and on silent cinema reels. "To be honest, I didn't have much interest in the bridge," she recalled. "I was going to see the King and Queen, and that was enough for me."[8]

Also waiting to see the opening was Emily Watson, the nine-year-old schoolgirl from Byker who had enjoyed watching the building of the bridge instead of going to the pictures. Emily stood on the Newcastle Quayside to watch the ceremony with other pupils from Ouseburn School. Unbeknown to her, standing across the river on the Gateshead quay was a young lad called Chris Hopper. Emily and Chris did not know each other and would not meet for more than a decade, at Newcastle Races. They would be married in 1940 and spend the rest of their lives together.[9]

Meanwhile, engineers from the BBC's 5NO Newcastle regional radio station busied themselves setting up microphones and running cables for a rare and pioneering outside broadcast. On the previous evening, 5NO had broadcast a specially-written play, *The Bridge of Tyne*, by Lieutenant Colonel George Spain. A fantasy in five episodes, the play began as the Romans built the first bridge over the Tyne and followed the evolution of its crossings through to the construction of the new bridge, "when man may be said to have conquered the river". Now, 5NO would broadcast an hour of live commentary, culminating in the King's speech from the bridge.[10]

The only thing that seemed likely to spoil the occasion was the weather. It had been "dull, damp and depressing" on the previous day, and there was "no wish more generally expressed" on Tyneside than for sunshine. "May it be vouchsafed!" remarked the *Journal*.[11] And it was. An early morning mist lifted to reveal a cold but beautiful day, casting the newly-painted green arch in perfect light. All along the bridge, patient throngs of expectant spectators lined the pavements. Tyneside's well-to-do sat in the royal stand at the Newcastle end of the bridge, and local bigwigs waited on the ceremonial stage. Far above, at the apex of the recently-closed arch, a pair of flags—a Union Jack and a Royal Standard—stood proud in the Tyneside sun.

* * *

King George and Queen Mary arrived on the royal train at Jesmond station at 10.15 am—five minutes ahead of schedule. The King wore a morning suit with a top hat and carried a walking cane. Queen Mary wore a periwinkle blue coat and toque hat. ("Oh, she's in blue," women in the crowd were heard to say. "I'm glad she's in blue. Doesn't blue suit her?")[12] After being welcomed by Newcastle's Lord Mayor Easten and other local dignitaries, the royal couple transferred to their open landau, which was pulled by four dapple-grey horses and accompanied by two scarlet-clad outriders and a formation of mounted police.

The first stop was the recently-built boys' and girls' Heaton Secondary Schools, where a huge, cheering, flag-waving crowd of as many as 24,000 Newcastle schoolkids was waiting.[13] Inside the school hall, King George said the affectionate reception deeply touched him and the Queen, and the new schools—like the Tyne Bridge—represented a great step forward for Newcastle. Speaking to those gathered in the hall, the King said it was a source of much grief to him to know that the people of Tyneside were suffering under a cloud of depression due to the post-war struggles of the heavy industries that had made the River Tyne famous. The construction of the new bridge, he said, was "a characteristic act of courage", demonstrating the belief that the industries would recover and Tyneside would return to its former glory. "I trust that this day may be the beginning of a new era of prosperity," he said.[14]

Then, amid ear-troubling cheering, the King and Queen left in their carriage and headed towards the "primary object" of the visit— "the magnificent new bridge whose rainbow arch links the twin boroughs of Newcastle and Gateshead in one span". As the royal party approached the section of the route where Kitty Brightwell stood, voices shouted, "Here they come!" Then, as the landau came into view, the crowd emitted a colossal roar. "It was only equalled," said Kitty, "by the roar from St James' Park when Newcastle United scored a goal."[15]

On the bridge itself, excitement was building. In front of the royal stand, Sir Hugh Bell shared a joke with the Bishops of Newcastle and Durham that left them red-faced with restrained laughter. Sir Arthur Dorman stood smiling in the stand, packed with other "men of name and fame in the North-County—steel men, coal men, builders of tall ships and mighty engines".[16] Also in the royal stand was Alice Collins, the widow of Nathaniel Collins, who had been killed while working on the bridge six months earlier.

Above the bubbling hubbub of expectation, kilted bagpipers and a military band filled the air with music as armed forces veterans marched across the bridge. Then, at 11.40, a battalion of Northumberland Fusiliers sprang to attention to form a guard of honour. Cheers tumbled through the streets of Newcastle, becoming louder and louder as they approached the bridge. According to one story, the royal procession was momentarily delayed by a milkman who insisted on getting through with his cart because he had deliveries to make. But then came the mounted police and the outriders and the royal landau. The cheers became roars. Necks were

135

craned, and flags, handkerchiefs and hats were waved. An express train leaving Central Station stopped on the High Level Bridge to allow its passengers to watch the spectacle.

King George and Queen Mary stepped from their carriage to the sound of countless "hoorays". They were led to the royal stand, where they were presented to scores of clergymen, councillors, businessmen, and some of the bridge builders and designers, including Arthur Dorman and Hugh Bell, Basil Mott, David Hay and David Anderson, Ralph Freeman, R. Burns Dick, Charles Mitchell and James Ruck. Dorman Long had commissioned Northern Goldsmiths to produce a set of 2¼-inch silvered medals to commemorate the opening, and the King presented this keepsake to several of the builders. The medal featured a handsome image of the new bridge on the face, and dates and dimensions on the reverse. Then the opening ceremony got underway with dedications from the Bishops of Newcastle and Durham, broadcast through loudspeakers to those present and via wireless to those at home.

Lord Mayor Easten—so keenly involved in the Tyne Bridge project—addressed the King and Queen and explained that the new bridge could not have been built without the support of His Majesty's government. "The Tyne Bridge is one of the latest triumphs of bridge-building," said Mayor Easten, "being the largest single-span bridge in Europe, and appreciation of the engineers' skilful design and the contractors' ability is expressed on all sides". Easten acknowledged Tyneside was passing through a period of great industrial depression but said the building of the bridge was evidence of "our faith that the present gloom will soon be dispelled". He said the satisfaction Tyneside felt at the completion of the bridge was only enhanced by the presence of the King and Queen, and he formally invited the King to open the bridge.[17]

Donning spectacles and reading from a small piece of paper, King George approached the microphone and began to speak, slowly and deliberately:

"Twenty-two years ago, my dear father opened the King Edward VII Bridge. Now it is with great pleasure that I dedicate an even more imposing structure to public use."

"Few cities combine more favourably than Newcastle the advantages of highway, railway, river and sea transport, advantages which have ever placed you foremost in commercial developments and progress. But while a river is in some respects an aid, in others, it is a barrier to land communications, and generation after generation, the men of the Tyneside [sic] have grappled energetically with the problem of bridging the Tyne without hampering the movements of shipping."

"I congratulate you most warmly upon this bridge, constructed by the joint labours of Newcastle and Gateshead. With its wide single span and spacious approaches, the Tyne Bridge not only adds dignity and convenience to your city but also bears lasting testimony to the unrivalled capacity of the British engineering trade and its workers of all grades."

"It is my earnest hope that this notable improvement in the facilities of transport may help to bring back to your city the full tide of prosperity which your courage and patience under recent difficulties so justly deserve. I have much pleasure in declaring the Tyne Bridge open for the use of the public."[18]

Then, Mayor Easten handed King George a gold dagger-shaped key, which the King pushed into a switch box, activating a set of flag-draped electric gates that lifted swiftly up and opened in the middle of the bridge. At that moment, canons fired a thunderous salute, church bells rang, and boats on the river cranked their whirring sirens. It was "the greatest din ever heard on Tyneside".[19] "The whole city seemed to quiver and rock," noted a reporter from the *Guardian*. "The birds sped shocked through the air, and an aeroplane swooped down upon the bridge." Despite feeling members of the press ("the eyes and ears of most of the King's subjects, and in a sense his messengers") were not given reasonable access and were placed at an inconvenient vantage point on the bridge, the reporter described the event as having "the air of some medieval occasion of joy".[20]

Back in their landau, the King and Queen crossed the new bridge to the sounds of cheers and church bells and headed up the High Street into Gateshead to a reception at the Shipley Art Gallery. Behind them on the Tyne Bridge, the crowd began to disperse—with some difficulty as many of those who had stood in the surrounds now wanted to cross the new bridge. In Gateshead, the royal party was greeted by more well-wishers, including 10,000 Gateshead schoolchildren. At the Shipley, the King made his third speech of the day. He once again recalled the visit of his father to open the King Edward VII bridge and warmly congratulated Gateshead on joining with Newcastle to build the new bridge, which he said "so nobly" spanned the Tyne.[21]

After the Gateshead reception, the royal party travelled to Durham via Chester-le-Street, then re-joined the royal train for the journey back to London, arriving at King's Cross at 6.30 pm. It was subsequently revealed that the train that carried the King and Queen to Newcastle was operated by two drivers and two firemen who had not slept for thirty hours due to a quick turnaround and lack of lodgings. The men worked with "sore bones and weary eyes" but still apparently took every precaution for safety.[22]

The BBC's radio broadcast of the opening and the King's speech from the bridge was hailed as a great success that was heard with great clarity. Credit was due to the outside broadcast engineers, noted the *Journal*'s wireless correspondent, "Crystal", and also to the King for his distinct enunciation. King George, said Crystal, "may be classed as an excellent broadcaster".[23]

A recording of the King's Shipley Art Gallery speech ("The Speech of HIS MAJESTY KING GEORGE V at the Opening Ceremony of THE TYNE BRIDGE") was released by the Columbia Gramophone Company, at a "popular price" of 4s 6d, with proceeds split between Newcastle's RVI and the Gateshead Children's Hospital. The 78rpm shellac disc was etched with an image of the Tyne Bridge, alongside the Newcastle and Gateshead coats of arms, making it an attractive collector's item. The recording began with a welcome address, followed by a "very clear and faithful reproduction" of the King's brief speech in which he said he had noted with "deep solicitude" the depression affecting the town's industries and was gratified to see that, much as the people of Gateshead had suffered, "you have shown your enlightened public spirit in proceeding with this great civic enterprise". The recording cut off abruptly before the crowd's applause.[24]

The national press regarded the disc as a "sensation".[25] The only previous recording of the King's voice had been made from Buckingham Palace by HMV for Empire Day in April 1923. That was made using old mechanical devices, while the 1928 speech was recorded using a new electrical system. The rare opportunity to hear the King speak proved very appealing, no matter how provincial the message. This recording of a speech made at a small Gateshead venue on the day of the opening of the Tyne Bridge was regarded as a historic document and sold well across the Empire. "The record is a living thing," said one reviewer. "The vibrant tones of the King's voice are recorded with a realism that will reveal a new understanding of his personality."[26] The disc was added to the collection of the British Museum.

Back on Tyneside, as the crowds emptied from the route, motor sweepers and "an army of broom and shovel men" moved in to clear the grit from the streets. Almost 200 St John Ambulance Bridge volunteers had patrolled the route, and they attended to 72 casualties.[27] One of those was James Shopland, a retired gardener from Jesmond, who collapsed in the crowd and was taken to the RVI. And 17-year-old Thomas Elliott from Elswick was taken to the same hospital with leg injuries after being knocked from his bicycle by one of the first motor cars to cross the Tyne Bridge—the earliest of many traffic accidents on the new crossing.[28] Elliott spent two weeks in hospital recovering. (The first fatality on the new bridge occurred two days later, on Friday 12 October 1928, when 66-year-old John Donnolly from Gateshead was struck by a Northern motorbus while attempting to cross the road.)[29]

Once all the dust and grit and ticker-tape had settled, newspaper correspondents would suggest the opening ceremony had sidelined some very important individuals. Few of the bridge workers were introduced to the King, despite their huge efforts. "Could not something be done for them?" asked a correspondent named Rosalind Gare, who suggested a party or some entertainment could be laid on for the men and their wives. "We must consider the risks many of them took and the anxiety their families must have felt. Could no fund be raised to show these brave men how much their fellow citizens honour them?" Also absent from the ceremony was Thomas Webster, whose "strenuous and successful efforts" had kick-started the scheme. "Surely it was to be expected that he would figure largely in the opening proceedings," wrote a correspondent using the pen name "Gratitude". "And yet amid all the speech-making and rejoicing he was not allowed to play any part whatsoever."[30]

* * *

On the day after the grand opening, the new Tyne Bridge was "green as a grasshopper and as active", as road traffic, trams and pedestrians crossed incessantly between Newcastle and Gateshead.[31] Visitors came from all over the North-East to see the new crossing, and its remarkable scale and views were "a revelation". "From these lofty heights one may look serenely upon the flowing river below and across the intervening roofs at the not unpicturesque vista of the city," noted a *Journal* reporter. The new bridge provided new views of prominent landmarks such as the Castle, the Cathedral, and the churches of All Saints and St Mary. Not all of the views were as pleasant. There were derelict buildings under the Newcastle side of the bridge and "unprepossessing hovels" under the Gateshead end. On both sides of the river were warehouses and wharves and billboard signs for all manner of businesses. When large steamers passed beneath the new bridge, spectators crowded at the balustrades to watch. Street vendors did a brisk business selling postcards commemorating the King and Queen opening the bridge. There was a constant flow of motor cars, trams and buses. "The scene indeed," said the reporter, "was an animated one until a late hour at night."[32]

The High Level Bridge, meanwhile, was "the most friendless looking thing on Tyneside".[33] Observers said the High Level had never been so quiet, with only the occasional clomp of a pedestrian's boots or clip-clop of a horse-drawn cart echoing across the road deck. Tram services across the High Level had been cut by half, with the remainder being shifted across onto the Tyne Bridge. Things were similarly quiet down on the Swing Bridge. Only vehicles with business on the quaysides bothered with the low-level crossing, and when it swung open to let boats pass, the road traffic waiting at each side could be counted on the fingers of one hand. One of the aims of the Tyne Bridge project was to reduce the congestion on the river crossings, and it appeared this was successful—although some congestion was now seen on the new bridge.

Local and national newspapers published detailed reports and photographs of the event. "King Opens £1,250,000 Bridge", said the *Daily Mirror*.[34] "Cheering Thousands Line Royal Route," said the *Dundee Courier*.[35] The *Yorkshire Post* referenced the King's comments with "Courage of Tyneside".[36] The headline in the Newcastle *Journal* was "Tyneside's Welcome to the King and Queen".[37] "A great city and wider district given up wholly to rejoicing is an inspiring spectacle under any circumstances," said the *Journal*'s editorial, "but in the circumstances of this area is perhaps more inspiring than any." The new bridge, the paper said, signified a "stimulus of hope".[38]

Once sightseers had finished gazing at the actual bridge, they could look at a remarkably accurate Meccano model displayed at Newcastle's Clayton Street branch of the Halford's cycling company. The model, praised for its excellence by Dorman Long, was built at the shop under the direction of district manager G.W. Horn. It was pictured in the international *Meccano Magazine*, which called it "a masterpiece of constructional work".[39] Another remarkable model of the bridge was built by a railway engine driver from Blaydon named Ernest Hanson. With the assistance of his 13-year-old son, Hanson constructed his model from hundreds of pieces of carved wood using plans loaned to him by Dorman Long. The incredibly detailed model was displayed in a window of the Lowe and Moorhouse department store on Newcastle's Northumberland Street and then sold to raise funds for the Newcastle Eye Hospital.[40]

Within twenty-four hours of the grand ceremony, patrons of Newcastle's New Westgate cinema (now the O2 Academy concert venue) could watch "special pictures" of the royal visit and the opening of the Tyne Bridge (alongside "tip-top western picture" *Hound of Silver Creek* starring Dynamite the Dog). The Tyne Bridge film was likely a silent Pathé News reel, or perhaps an amateur film recorded by the Newcastle and District Amateur Cinematographers' Association.[41] A more prominent film of the occasion would soon emerge. Fox Movietone had secured footage of the opening and intended to release it with sound as "His Majesty's First Talking Picture".[42]

A few days later, visitors to the nearby Newcastle's Stoll Theatre (now the Tyne Theatre and Opera House) enjoyed a talk on "The Tyne Bridge and Other Wonderful Bridges" by famous author and radio broadcaster Edward Cressy. Well known for his popular takes on science and engineering, Cressy presented a history of bridge-building from the "far-off days when the people of Babylon put up structures of mud" through to the wonder of the new Tyne Bridge. "When you think of all that the building of the bridge has involved,"

Cressy told the audience, "you are bound to recognize that it is not merely a matter of immensity, grace, or utility, but a symbol of enterprise, of imagination, knowledge, skill, endurance and indomitable will."[43]

The Fox Movietone talking newsreel of the opening of the Tyne Bridge was released toward the end of 1928, but few Tynesiders would see it. The special film was made by matching silent movie footage with an audio recording to create a rare "talkie".[44] The film was sent to New York to be developed, and there were 600 prints made, but the difficulty of preparation caused a delay and led Fox to double its usual licence fee for Movietone topical newsreels to £100.[45] Some British cinemas refused to show it, and others had no facility to show talkies. So the six and a half minute film, "one of the finest talking picture subjects yet made", was initially shown exclusively at the Empire Theatre in London's Leicester Square and then exclusively "in the provinces" at the New Oxford Theatre in Manchester.[46] It was not shown on Tyneside, but *King of England Makes a Speech* drew crowds for several months afterwards in other parts of the world, including New York and other US cities. Such was the interest that some American newspapers transcribed the full text of the speech from the film. In Australia, at Melbourne's Auditorium Theatre, movie-goers yelled "offensive remarks" during a newsreel featuring Benito Mussolini but "loudly cheered" the film of George V at the Tyne Bridge.[47] Although the film was barely seen in Britain in the months following its recording, it helped make the Tyne Bridge famous around the world.

Both the Movietone film and the Columbia record were released during a period of great anxiety regarding George V's health. In November 1928, the monarch fell seriously ill with a complicated case of pleurisy. There was no official suggestion that the visit to Tyneside worsened his condition, but there were implied suggestions that the film and record might represent the last chance to see or hear him speak. This, of course, increased demand—and boosted the number of people who got a look at the Tyne Bridge. Such was the level of public concern for the King that, during a showing in London of the Movietone film, the audience rose and stood silently to attention during his speech. King George came close to death and never fully recovered. He stepped back from public duties and spent much of the next few years attempting to recuperate. George V died on 20 January 1936.

* * *

Although the bridge was open and carrying traffic from October 1928, it was not yet complete. Work continued on the Gateshead abutment tower for several months. Also at the Gateshead end of the bridge, workers constructed the unusual octagonal-shaped building known as Number One Church Street. This elegant little structure, with arched openings, oak doors, and a glass dome roof, was designed by Gateshead Council architect Arthur Bashford. Overlooked by many of the thousands that pass it as they cross the Tyne Bridge, it fulfilled a very useful purpose, because Number One Church Street—which still stands today—was a rather grand public convenience (or, in Tyneside dialect, a *netty* on the bridge).

The Newcastle tower's two passenger lifts were officially opened by a party led by the ex-Lord Mayor and once-again Councillor Stephen Easten in the middle of December. However, the opening did not go to plan. "While we may risk our own unworthy lives in making a test of the lifts," joked Easten, "it is not desirable we should risk the lives of the general community that keeps us in existence until we have had them adequately tested." Then his party, including Mayor Wardill of Gateshead and James Ruck, paid their halfpenny toll and stepped into one of the lifts while representatives of the press stepped into the other. The lift containing the pressmen ascended swiftly from the Quayside up onto the bridge deck. However, Easten's lift would not "rise to the occasion", and the embarrassed party was forced to use the other lift to reach the bridge.[48] The Tyne Bridge was finally completed—with working lifts but absent ceremony—on 27 March 1929.

A pair of embossed plaques were fitted to the balustrades at opposite sides of the midpoint of the bridge. Both can still be seen today, painted—like the rest of the structure—with a heavy coat of middle green. The plaque on the west side explains that the bridge was erected by the corporations of Newcastle and Gateshead (and the Ministry of Transport). It names Dorman Long as the contractors, Mott, Hay & Anderson as the engineers and R. Burns

Dick as the architect. The plaque on the east side bears the names of Lord Mayor Easten and Mayor Wardill and says: "TYNE BRIDGE, OPENED BY HIS MAJESTY KING GEORGE V, 10TH OCTOBER 1928."

The total cost of the Tyne Bridge was £1,035,000 (equivalent to around £64m in 2022).[49] This included the cost of construction at £693,000 plus expenditure on land at £342,000. The construction cost was about 20 per cent higher than Dorman Long's tendered bid due to architectural and other work sanctioned after the contract was awarded. The total cost, including land, was around 10 per cent higher than Mayor Easten's estimate of £970,000. The main arch cost £158,772. The most expensive sections of the bridge were the abutment towers, which cost £252,241—partly due to the enormous efforts required to sink the foundations. There would be more costs related to the bridge. The diverted Newcastle approach, which temporarily avoided the under-renovation railway bridge, still needed to be re-routed. At the time of the opening, newspapers estimated the overall cost of the bridge and its approach works at as much as £1,250,000 (around £77m in 2022).[50]

But what happened to the men who built the Tyne Bridge? The former Lord Mayor of Newcastle Stephen Easten, who was so influential in getting the bridge built, was awarded a knighthood for his efforts in 1929. Sir Stephen died at his Jesmond home, "Esperance", after contracting pneumonia in 1936, aged 69. Mayor of Gateshead W. Edwin Wardill, another leading advocate of the bridge (and who had climbed to the very top following the closing of the arch), was also knighted, in 1929. Wardill died in 1938.

Sir Arthur Dorman and Sir Hugh Bell, the twin leaders of Dorman Long, had hoped to live long enough to see the completion of both the Tyne Bridge and the Sydney Harbour Bridge. They did attend the opening of the Tyne Bridge, but both of them died in 1931, with the Sydney Harbour Bridge still unfinished. Sir Arthur was 82, and Sir Hugh was 87. The *Northern Daily Mail* used the same stark headline to announce both deaths four months apart: "North's Loss".[51]

Following the deaths of Dorman and Bell, Charles Mitchell, the manager of the company's bridge-building department, became managing director and then chairman of Dorman Long. Mitchell held the role of chairman during the firm's completion of the Sydney

Harbour Bridge.[52] Dorman Long continued to trade successfully and built many other bridges around the world through to the 1960s, when the company—and much of the British steel industry—was nationalised. Following subsequent denationalisation and numerous mergers and acquisitions, a last trace of the Dorman Long name was removed when the famous Teesside Dorman Long steelworks tower was demolished in 2021.

Basil Mott of Mott Hay & Anderson received a knighthood in 1930. Sir Basil and David Hay both died in 1938. ("Responsible for Tyne Bridge" was the headline of one obituary for Sir Basil.)[53] David Anderson, the "Great Scots Bridge Designer", continued as lead partner, often working alongside Ralph Freeman. Mott, Hay & Anderson worked on the Wearmouth Bridge, the Mersey Tunnels and the Tyne Tunnels. Sunderland's Wearmouth Bridge—superficially similar to the Tyne Bridge but with a different design—was opened in 1929.[54] The Tyne's pedestrian and cyclist tunnel (1951) and original traffic tunnel (1967) were both designed by Mott, Hay & Anderson. Sir David Anderson was knighted in 1951. He died in 1953, aged 72, with obituaries highlighting his role in designing the Tyne Bridge. In 1989, Mott, Hay & Anderson merged with Sir M. MacDonald & Partners to become Mott MacDonald.

R. Burns Dick designed the Tyne Bridge's art deco towers but never got to see his vision of the grand entrance gateway to Newcastle realised. He had to be satisfied with designing the city's former police and fire station on the corner of Pilgrim Street and Market Street, a Grade II listed classically-featured chunk of Portland stone that gives an indication of what his redeveloped Newcastle might have looked like. After retirement, Burns Dick left Tyneside for Surrey. He died in 1954.

Ralph Freeman's work on the Tyne Bridge was overshadowed somewhat by the much larger Sydney Harbour Bridge, which opened in March 1932. He travelled to Sydney to inspect progress in 1926 and then again in February 1929, as the final blocks were being placed into the towers of the Tyne Bridge. He explained to the Sydney press how this type of bridge and its method of construction was tested on Tyneside and added that Australians would be familiar with the Tyne Bridge as it was the subject of the popular Movietone "talkie".[55] But his arrival for the second visit triggered a dispute between Freeman and the chief engineer for New South Wales, Dr J.J.C. Bradfield, over who had designed the bridge. After Dr Bradfield claimed he was the designer, Freeman responded with a lengthy and detailed rebuttal stating the design was entirely his. Freeman had put in two solid years designing it, his staff created thousands of drawings under his direction, and not a single feature was inspired by Dr Bradfield. In the end (after Dorman Long threatened legal action), a commemorative plaque on the completed bridge credited both Bradfield for supervising the "general design and specification" as chief engineer and Freeman as "consulting and designing engineer for the contractors".[56] Freeman was knighted in 1947. (It's notable that so many of the men behind the Tyne Bridge were honoured in this way.) Sir Ralph died in 1950, aged sixtynine. His son and grandson, Ralph and Anthony, were also civil engineers and bridge builders.

Sir Ralph Freeman was not the only bridge builder who travelled from Tyneside to Sydney. Some of the riveters and riggers who worked on the Tyne Bridge were brought out to Australia by Dorman Long. But they also became engaged in a dispute. The men found they were earning only half as much in Sydney for more arduous and dangerous work. The rivets used in Sydney were the "heaviest in the world" and were fitted in extremely risky conditions due to the bridge's great span and height. The workers said they had not realised the difficulty of the work when they travelled from the other side of the world.[57] One worker, James Dickson, said he was constantly working at heights and was liable to fall into the water from 200 feet, or 300 feet when working on the jib of a crane. He was also liable to injury from men dropping metal from above.[58] While the dispute was ongoing, an Australian worker named Thomas McKeorn died after falling from the bridge.[59] The workers threatened to strike, and an arbitration court ordered their wages should be raised by up to 75 per cent to account for their unusually hazardous and demanding work.[60]

One Sydney newspaper printed an anonymous poem titled *The Bridge Builders* that referenced the dispute between Freeman and Bradfield and also credited the manual workers from Tyneside:

"*Who built the bridge?*
I, said the rivetman, I came from the Tyne

To tighten the rivets and keep it in line—
I built the bridge.[61]

Other Tyne Bridge workers travelled to different parts of the world. Duncan MacDonald, a senior foreman from Gateshead who worked on the Tyneside crossing, went to India to work as a "specially engaged expert" on the Bally Bridge (now the Vivekananda Setu) over the Hooghly River at Calcutta (now Kolkata). Unfortunately, shortly after his arrival, in December 1928, he was killed in an accident involving the dreaded caissons. In the dark of night, one of the underwater caissons suddenly collapsed, tipping 20 men into the river. Searchlights were turned on, lifebuoys were thrown, and all the men were saved—except for MacDonald, whose body was later recovered by a diver. He was thirty-eight years old.[62]

The indomitable James Ruck went to Thailand to supervise Dorman Long's building of the Bangkok Memorial Bridge over the Chao Phraya River. This was the biggest double-leaf bascule bridge (or drawbridge) in the world. Ruck travelled to Bangkok with his family in December 1929 and, while travelling through Thailand, experienced a terrifying incident involving his young daughter Jessie. The 12-year-old girl was wrapped in a blanket in a bunk on a sleeper train when she somehow fell out of an open window while the train was hurtling along the track. As soon as she was found to be missing, the alarm was raised, and a search party went out on a railway trolley. The party covered almost a hundred miles of track before they eventually found Jessie safe and well, sheltering in the hut of a local family. She had fallen from the train onto soft ground and rolled down an embankment, then pulled her blanket around her and gone back to sleep before being picked up and taken to the hut.[63]

After completing the Bangkok crossing, Ruck built several other bridges for Dorman Long, including the Storstrøm Bridge in Denmark and the Birchenough Bridge in Zimbabwe, which Ralph Freeman designed as a two-hinged through-arch bridge—like the Tyne and Sydney Harbour bridges. Ruck returned to Tyneside, but was living in York when he died in 1968 at the age of 83.

One other man involved in the Tyne Bridge project should not be forgotten—and in the end, he was not. Thomas Webster had proposed the bridge over the Tyne in 1922 but never received the credit he felt he deserved. Almost four decades later, in 1961, he proposed another new bridge of a similar design between Newcastle and Gateshead at Pelaw at the cost of £5m. "Tyne Bridge No 2 From Mr Webster", announced the Newcastle *Chronicle*, which called him "the man whose insight and perseverance was largely responsible for the building of the Tyne Bridge".[64] His "Tyne Bridge No 2" was never built. Webster died at his home in Corbridge in the following year. The headline in the *Journal* belatedly gave him his due: "'Father' of the Tyne Bridge is Dead".[65]

10

CROSSING THE BRIDGE

George Wilson was one of the men who built the Tyne Bridge, but unemployment drove him from Tyneside. He was a hardworking man who couldn't stand idle, but after suffering two years of unemployment, he went just about as far as it was possible to go without crossing the sea, to Penzance in Cornwall. But prospects in the South West of England were little better than in the North East. He couldn't find work and, after several more years on the breadline, was driven to desperation. In 1935, after reading surprising reports of improving prospects on Tyneside, he decided to head home. But Wilson had almost no money and no means to pay for a train or coach. The only option, he decided, was for him and his wife—with their infant daughter—to trek the best part of 600 miles from Penzance back to Tyneside, via London, on foot.

Wilson was born on Pilgrim Street at what would become the Newcastle approach to the Tyne Bridge. He was a former soldier, a Queen's Own Cameron Highlander, who served his country for over a decade and fought on the Western Front and at Salonika. He was wounded three times during the Great War—twice at the Somme. Wilson left the army in 1923 and returned to Tyneside, where he laboured on the bridge. However, he suffered another traumatic injury when he was jammed between a lorry and a wall, and was unable to work for five months.

Wilson, his wife and their daughter set off on their return journey on 1 July 1935. The couple had just a few shillings between them. All of the family's possessions were tightly packed into a kit bag that Wilson carried. His wife carried the child. They planned to ration their food, leave shelter to chance, and cover twenty miles each day. But it was an even more difficult undertaking than they had anticipated. Both Wilson and his wife suffered terribly with their feet, and progress was slow. They were forced to beg or raid nature's larder for food and sleep in barns or in the open. They spent one night in a workhouse—paying in casual labour for a night's accommodation. Wilson bunked next to a young man, an unemployed sailor, and they spoke enthusiastically about the trek to Tyneside. In the morning, the young man was unresponsive, having died in his sleep. Wilson recognised his "ghastly pallor" from his wartime experiences.

In London, Wilson went to the satellite office of Tyneside news-paper the *Sunday Sun*. He secured accommodation and two days' worth of provisions in return for an exclusive on his story once he got home. On the family went, via a circuitous route through Birmingham, Liverpool, Manchester and Leeds. The weather, which had been fine, turned against them. The trio were soaked with rain, and Wilson's daughter came down with a bad cold. Then, in Manchester, Wilson fell ill with what he described as a flare-up of malaria he had caught in Salonika during the war. He was forced to use the last of the family's money to pay for two nights' accom-modation while he recovered. During the rest of the journey, Wilson and his family spent several nights at police stations, where they were given a cell for the night and a meal. Then, finally, after more than a month on the road, home was in sight.

"It didn't mean a cheery welcome," recalled Wilson. "We had no place of our own to go to on Tyneside. But it was Tyneside, and that in itself was cheering enough."[1]

As Wilson and his family came through Gateshead, they saw on the north side of the river "the grey acres of Newcastle with their familiar spires and steeples and chimney stacks". And then, after 35 days of suffering, the sight he had longed for: "At last, the great span of the Tyne Bridge—the bridge I helped build—could be seen. I held my breath. We were *home*."

This was a sentiment many travellers at the end of much less gruelling journeys would share—the sight of the Tyne Bridge sym-bolised their return home. Wilson and his family were in rags. Their boots were worn out, and their feet were covered in blisters. "We were utterly exhausted," he said. "But we knew a strange feeling of triumph." He began looking for work and felt hopeful: "I do not think I can fail now that we have been through so much." Wilson gave his story to the *Sunday Sun*. By the time it was published a few days later, he had a new job at Pelaw in Gateshead and viewed life "with a new and happier interest". It was a long-overdue piece of luck because there were few jobs to be found in the shadows of the big steel arch.

* * *

In the aftermath of the grand opening, the new bridge was hailed locally and around the globe as a great masterpiece of civil engineering. But, while it was a triumph of industry, the new bridge did not bring the Tyne back to life. As the bridge was being completed in early 1929, there were more than 70,000 unemployed adults on Tyneside—20,000 more than when Mayor Easten proposed the project five years earlier.[2] There were still hopes of a revival of industry, which wishful thinkers expected might create a shortage of skilled workers. But skilled work continued to disappear, the coal trade continued to decline, shipyards continued to close, and many of the bridge workers went back on the dole. Within a year of the bridge's opening, much of the world slid into the Great Depression.

In an effort to stimulate and promote local industry, Tyneside hosted the North East Coast Exhibition from May through to October 1929. Held at what is now Newcastle's Exhibition Park, the World's Fair-type expo attracted almost 4.4 million visitors. Its huge site housed three main buildings—the Palace of Engineering, the Palace of Industry and the Palace of Arts (which still stands today)—plus a festival hall, an athletics stadium, an amusement park and sculptured gardens. A new Art Deco-styled bridge was built over the park's lake, where the reproduction of the Old Tyne Bridge had stood during the Jubilee Exhibition back in 1887. All across the site were many marvels of engineering and ingenuity. Still, there was no doubt Newcastle's most outstanding attraction was the newly-completed steel arch that stood a mile south of the exhibition over the great river.

Ahead of the exhibition in Newcastle, a big clean-up began. Soot-covered stone was scrubbed, flaking paint was scraped, and shiny new coats of colour were applied. Locals had to avoid walking underneath decorators' ladders and tempting bad luck. Onlookers were said to rub their eyes when they saw the transformation of the city's once-grimy facades into bright-as-new stone. "I wonder what our visitors will think of the city?" wrote one Tynesider to a friend. "For it seems to me to be one of contrasts; with the old Castle, grim and massively strong, the loveliness of St Nicholas's Cathedral, and the all-compelling wonder of the Tyne Bridge."[3]

And it *was* a wonder, to be enjoyed by locals and visitors alike. One newspaper, referencing the seven wonders of the world, suggested the Tyne Bridge ought to be included among the "seven wonders of the North".[4] Several national papers published striking photos of the bridge on their front pages under headlines such as "Wonderful New Tyne Bridge".[5] Abroad, *Le Pont de la Tyne* was pictured on the front page of French newspapers and, more than 5,000 miles away from Tyneside, on the front of the *Los Angeles Times*.[6]

Over in Australia, with the Sydney Harbour Bridge still more than two years from completion, the *Sydney Morning Herald* praised its "English prototype". Alongside size, weight and cost comparisons, the newspaper explained how difficult problems—from design calculations to the construction of the arch—had been solved on Tyneside. It was noted with some jealousy that the Tyne Bridge's towers incorporated passenger lifts, while Sydney's did not. The *Herald* was particularly impressed with the Tyne Bridge's paintwork: "To see the bridge with the sun shining on its beautiful glossy finish is a sight not easily forgotten."[7]

Back in Britain, Cardiff's *Western Mail* said the Tyne Bridge was a "very majestic structure", and there was consideration for the plight of its builders amid the employment crisis. "It is proof of the adaptability of the British working man," the newspaper added, "that the majority of the constructional work on the bridge was carried out by Tyne shipbuilders who otherwise would have been unemployed."[8]

The Tyne Bridge had been built with the steel and rivets of the shipyards, and it was already looking like a monument to lost industry. In 1933, the once-mighty Palmers shipbuilding company of Jarrow, which had launched over a thousand ships and employed almost ten thousand men, collapsed. This devastating closure was one of the economic disasters that led to the Jarrow March.[9]

When J. Baker White, a reporter from London newspaper *The Sphere*, visited Tyneside in 1932, he travelled in a launch from Tynemouth to Newcastle. He described how the depression in the coal, shipping and shipbuilding industries had hit the great river: "Rows of colliers and freighters, idle, rust-streaked and deserted. Giant cranes, black and motionless against the sky above the empty grass-grown slipways. Here and there a little activity in the yards, but most of them empty, the cargo-less, crew-less ships swinging in the tideway mute evidence of their state."[10]

But Baker White saw something that gave him hope. "Through the smoke and the river-haze there came in sight the great new bridge spanning the Tyne, standing out in strong contrast to its dingy surroundings," he wrote. "Very impressive this bridge, one of the finest in the world, and strangely symbolic. A triumph of British engineering, it seems to arise phoenix-like from the ashes of the Industrial Revolution, typifying new industry growing from old." No one wanted ships anymore, and the coal trade was on its knees. But Tyneside was trying to diversify—building motor vehicles, diesel engines, oil-fired locomotives. "The North is not down, nor out," wrote Baker White. "It is fighting back, trying to build new industries for old, its symbol the great bridge across the Tyne."

* * *

The outbreak of the Second World War temporarily revived Tyneside's shipyards and related industries as they busied themselves building and repairing ships and manufacturing armaments for the war effort. In November 1939, a couple of months after the start of the war, a Newcastle office clerk named George Duke was arrested for taking a photograph of the Tyne Bridge. Duke, who was fifty-seven and from Elswick, was spotted taking the photo by two passers-by, who apprehended him and took him to a policeman. "Apparently, some people do not know they cannot take photographs of bridges," Newcastle's Inspector Allison told the city's Police Court. Duke said he knew military objectives could not be photographed, but he thought this meant "soldiers' guns and camps". He didn't think he was doing anything wrong, as picture postcards of the bridge were being sold across Tyneside. But he now realised he had been indiscreet. The court fined him £5 plus costs.[11]

The prominent Tyne Bridge was a conspicuous visual reference—and a prize target—for Nazi bombers. The first deadly raid came in broad daylight, at 5.30 pm on 2 July 1940, when a small party of aircraft flew in from the North Sea and up the Tyne towards Newcastle. One of the targets was determined to be the Tyne Bridge. A Royal Observer Corps spotter followed one of the raiders through binoculars. "Plane approaching from East," reported the spotter. "Steep dive… pulled out… Dornier 17… two explosions heard… columns of debris clearly seen… sirens heard… anti-aircraft fire."[12]

The bomber's payload narrowly missed the Tyne Bridge and sailed over the Swing and High Level bridges. One of the bombs hit Spiller's Old Flour Mill on the Close, just to the west of the High Level. Off-duty Royal Artillery Bombardier L. Hamilton was walking across the High Level with his fiancée when the bomb dropped. "It certainly was a near miss, and we were lucky to escape," he recalled.[13]

Thirteen people were killed in the raid, including several children, and 123 were injured. Tyneside's newspapers, restricted from publishing information that might be useful to the enemy, reported only that "a high explosive bomb fell on the poorer quarter of a North-East town" and damage "seems to have been confined to a disused flour mill, latterly occupied by an extra warehouse by a local transport firm". Warehouse workers had just left the old mill when the bomb dropped. One told a reporter, "I was lucky to get out in time".[14]

In August 1940, as many as 300 German aircraft crossed the North Sea. The RAF shot down up to seventy-five of the raiders, but the remainder dropped hundreds of bombs on Tyneside and Wearside. According to one story, an off-course Luftwaffe bomber that was supposed to target the Tyne Bridge accidentally flew ten miles upriver and tried to blow up the Wylam Railway Bridge. Also known as the West Wylam or Hagg Bank Bridge, this 1870s-built through-arch bridge is visually similar to the Tyne Bridge, although it is much smaller and of a slightly different design. In any case, the bomber missed the bridge and dropped its payload harmlessly in the surrounding fields.

One night in September 1941, a few days after a particularly devastating raid and with blackout regulations in force, the electric lights on the Tyne Bridge suddenly began to blaze, illuminating the potential target for all to see. A steeplejack quickly scaled the bridge and extinguished one light, but was called down by police before he could move on to the others. Eventually, after half an hour of perilous illumination, council officials switched off the lights and plunged the bridge back into darkness. The cause of the inadvertent illumination was never revealed.[15]

On top of the threat of bombing raids, there were fears of an invasion along the North-East coast. This meant vital structures were primed for deliberate demolition to slow the Nazi advance, one of which was the Tyne Bridge, and the man with his finger on the detonation button was known as Andrew Clayton. Speaking long after the war, Clayton (a military and security advisor who declined to give his real name) revealed British Intelligence expected the Nazis to land on the Northumberland coast and proceed south through Newcastle. "The bridges across the Tyne would have been so vital," recalled Clayton. "Had they been able to cross the river, they would have advanced without interruption."[16]

When the invasion started, Clayton would receive a telephone call containing a code word: "Humbug." This was the signal for him to blow up the Tyne Bridge—plus the other bridges and Central Station. He could have been forgiven if he felt something of a shiver run down his spine at two o'clock one morning in 1940 when his phone rang and a voice on the other end said, *"Humbug to you. I repeat: Humbug to you."*

Clayton hurried to his assembly point, along with around a thousand other men with different roles to help repel the invaders. But, before Clayton began his deadly mission, he was advised to stand down. This Operation Humbug had been a false alarm, "a little test dreamed up by Churchill to make sure everyone was on their toes". But the plan to blow up the Tyne Bridge was genuine. "Happily, in the end, there was no destruction," said Clayton. "However, we were more than ready."

The Tyne Bridge was not destroyed by Nazi raiders nor by British defenders. There were further deadly bombing raids on Tyneside—around thirty-one in total between 1940 and 1943—that killed and injured scores of men, women and children and destroyed hundreds of homes and other buildings. "And throughout all of this, the Tyne

Bridge stood firm," the Newcastle *Chronicle* later reflected, "a symbol of the determination of the people of Tyneside to withstand all that the Nazis could throw at them."[17]

* * *

The Tyne Bridge received its first new coats of paint shortly before the war, in the summer of 1938, a decade after it was first painted. Tyneside firm Structural Painters Ltd employed twenty local men to carry out the work. It took eight weeks to apply almost 12 tons of paint—two coats of black bitumastic to the underside, and an undercoat of red lead and a topcoat of green oil paint to the upper structure.[18] Onlookers craned their necks as they crossed the bridge to watch "the men who look the size of ants" paint the enormous arch.[19] The Tyne Bridge remained green, but that would not always be the case.

After the war, a shortage of specialist labour and speciality paint delayed a full paint job, and the bridge was simply patched up. It wasn't until 1950 that the bridge was completely repainted, with Gateshead manufacturer Bowran's green "Bowranite".[20] It was said to still be in excellent condition a decade later when Newcastle Council announced that, as part of a scheme to "tidy up the Tyne", the Tyne Bridge would no longer be painted a "drab" green colour. It would instead be painted with a brighter colour scheme that would be harmonised across all council-owned structures. Gateshead Council said the plan was long overdue.[21] There was controversy over the councils' plan to appoint a professor of art and design at the Royal College of Art to advise on the colour scheme— at the cost of £420. That too-expensive plan was shelved, and Newcastle's chief planning officer and city engineer picked the colours. These were Persian blue (actually a blue-green teal), ash grey, crimson red and Wedgewood blue (a very pale greyish blue).[22]

The outsides of the main arch and deck span were painted in the Persian or teal blue—a noticeable variation from the original green—and the verticals and diagonals were ash grey. The handrails and other parapet details were painted crimson red, and the lampposts Wedgewood blue. The repaint, which began in August 1961, took a team of twenty men four months to complete. "What is this man up to, dangling precariously high in the girders of the Tyne

Bridge?" asked the Newcastle *Chronicle* next to a photo of "one of the army of 'spidermen' painters who are bringing a splash of colour to the drab Tyneside scene".[23]

The painters lashed ropes to the bridge ribs and held onto them as they negotiated the arch. The foreman was Tommy Ferguson from West Moor in North Tyneside. He had worked on most of the Tyne's bridges and on the previous job on the Tyne Bridge. The only danger, he suggested, involved passers-by getting hit with the odd splash of paint. "I spend most of my working life swinging from the bridges," he said. "To me, it's just as safe as standing on a pavement... It is a healthy open-air job, and I enjoy every minute."[24]

The bridge got another repaint in 1970 with a similar colour scheme. In an advance on safety, the painters used scaffolding and cradles rather than ropes and hand-holds, and wore hard hats instead of flat caps. This time it was painted in two shades of blue—the teal blue and the greyish blue, with crimson red parapets. So the Tyne Bridge was not green but blue from 1961 until 1985. Then it was announced that the bridge would receive a new £275,000 repaint and "the most famous landmark on Tyneside will turn green—its original colour".[25] In fact, the bridge was painted a very specific British Standard paint colour, BS 4800 14 C 39, mid-green, also known as Holly Green or Hollybush.[26]

The 1985 repaint made national news—not for the colour change, but for the antics of one of the painters. Terry Donnelly was pictured in the *Daily Mirror* performing a handstand on the top of the arch, 193 feet above the river. Donnelly, who was 38 and from Killingworth, had been unemployed for ten years before starting the Tyne Bridge job but had been a structural painter since leaving school. "I have done this sort of thing before, such as standing on the top of pylons, electricity towers, just for my own satisfaction to see if I can do it," he said. "But the gaffer wasn't amused by it."[27]

When his bosses at painting contractor Taziker and Co. saw the photo, Terry got the sack—officially for not wearing a safety harness while working on the top of the bridge. "There's no way I can have that sort of thing going on," said managing director Tom Taziker. "He would be better off working in a circus."

* * *

Thomas Scott was a 48-year-old handyman from Jarrow who was married with six children. In August 1939, he fell 84 feet from the road deck of the Tyne Bridge onto the roof of a parked car on Newcastle's Queen Street, landing with a "terrible thud".[28] Passers-by were astounded to find he was still alive. "What did I fall over?" he asked, before groaning and pulling his cap over his eyes. Scott had been unemployed for almost ten years, since the time of the completion of the Tyne Bridge. That morning, he had left home on his daily search for work with his dole cards in his pocket. He was taken to the RVI with serious injuries. National newspapers printed photos of the damaged car under the bridge, with the 84-foot drop clearly labelled. But this was not a tale of miraculous survival. Although he was conscious when his wife visited him in hospital, where he told her he could not remember what had happened, Scott died fourteen hours after the accident. The coroner recorded a verdict of suicide. Tragically, Scott was one of four men to take their lives at the Tyne Bridge in the space of ten days in August 1939. One newspaper labelled it "the Bridge of Death".[29]

The first suicide at the Tyne Bridge occurred in January 1929, before the abutment towers were completed. Richard Wilkinson, an unemployed crate maker from Gateshead, threw himself from the road deck at the Newcastle end of the bridge and landed on the pavement in front of a group of schoolchildren. He broke almost every bone in his body and died from a fractured skull.[30] The fact that both Scott and Wilkinson were driven to desperation by Tyneside's unemployment crisis was not coincidental.

There were several other attempts during the bridge's first year of opening. At least one of them was thwarted. In June 1929, Edith Simpson was walking across the bridge towards her home in Byker with a friend when she saw a man climbing over the parapet. Telling her friend to fetch the police, Simpson rushed towards the man and grabbed the back of his neck, just as he was about to jump into the Tyne. Although the man struggled, Simpson managed to pull him back over the parapet to safety. James Denny, who was deaf and used sign language, later told magistrates the attempt had been a mistake. The 39-year-old was remanded for fourteen days for medical observation. The magistrate's clerk described Edith Simpson's heroism as "a very courageous act".[31]

Attempts continued in subsequent years and decades with alarming regularity. One summer's day in 1957, Elsie Emmerson, a 22-year-old accountant from Kibblesworth in Gateshead, was working in her office in the Exchange Buildings on Newcastle Quayside when she looked out of her third-storey window and locked eyes with a man on the Tyne Bridge. He was just a few yards away, and was perched precariously on the outside of the parapet. "What a funny place for a workman to be," thought Emmerson. Then she realised—the man was about to jump. Staring into the man's eyes, she shook her head firmly and tried to plead: "Don't! Don't!" But, still staring back at her, the man—a 55-year-old docker named George Brown—slowly spread his arms and jumped.

"I realized what he was going to do and screamed and turned my head away," Emmerson told an inquest. She had not slept since it happened and could not say much more. Her manager, Madge Counsell, explained that Emmerson had been at the same window only a fortnight before when another man jumped from the bridge and crashed to his death just a few feet from her car. "Elsie was very brave, but she does not like being left alone in that room anymore," said Counsell. "I think we'll have to put a curtain over the window."[32]

In 1963, a different clerk in a different Quayside office watched five people fall to their deaths from the bridge in as many months. River police pulled sixteen jumpers from the river that year—and only four survived. Local businesses and residents protested to the local authorities and demanded safety barriers be erected on the Tyne's "death bridges". The Newcastle and Gateshead Joint Bridge Committee discussed the idea but rejected it after learning it would cost £7,500 to fit the requisite barriers. Newcastle's Lord Mayor Peter Renwick said the proposal was too costly and impracticable and wouldn't solve the problem. "If people can't jump off the bridges, then they'll just go and jump off a tall building," he said.[33]

That wasn't necessarily true. All across the world, people in desperate situations are drawn to bridges. Iconic structures from the Golden Gate Bridge to the Sydney Harbour Bridge have inadvertently become suicide spots. Back in the 1960s, Newcastle *Journal* reporter John Ritson attempted to find out what drew people to attempt to end their lives at the Tyne Bridge and to understand the "fatal fascination of the Coaly Tyne". He spoke to a psychologist and a police spokesman about the dramatic symbolism of the bridge and the deadly allure of the river. "The height, the water, the loneliness of the Tyne Bridge all combine to make it attractive for the person who wants to commit suicide," concluded Ritson.[34]

A decade later, in 1972, after pressure from the fire brigade, parts of the Tyne Bridge were painted with special anti-climb paint. The design of the bridge, with the arch rising gradually out of the road deck, had previously allowed those with the inclination to clamber up the ribs of the arch. To prevent this, a six-foot-square area at the bottom of each rib was treated with the new paint, manufactured by Sunderland's Camrex Ltd, that was "slippery as sheet ice". "It is now impossible to climb up," said Camrex's Guy Readman, who added that the paint would also deter mischievous children from playing on the arches.[35]

Today, Samaritans, the suicide prevention charity, has signs on the Tyne Bridge urging anyone in distress to talk to them in confidence.[36] The signs were installed in December 2007 and are credited with reducing the number of tragic deaths on the bridge. But suicide attempts continue. Many are prevented by the good work of the police, Samaritans and passers-by.[37] Attempts are not always reported, partly due to the risk of influencing other vulnerable people. But the people of Tyneside are aware that whenever the Tyne Bridge is closed due to a "police incident", a tragedy may be unfolding.

* * *

Not all dramas on the Tyne Bridge have ended in tragedy. Shortly before Christmas in 1964, a 12-year-old boy named Brian Hepple fell from the bridge twice within the space of a few minutes. Hepple, from Winlaton in Gateshead, climbed over the parapet of the Tyne Bridge to try to spot his friend down on the Quayside. But he slipped and fell from the bridge. Luckily, he landed on the sloping rooftop of a Quayside building about 15 feet below the bridge and about 70 feet above the ground. Hepple edged his way around a chimney stack and found a long wooden ladder, which he propped up against the edge of the bridge and began to climb. Unfortunately, the ladder snapped, and Hepple fell for the second time, again landing on the roof.

"After that, I thought I had better sit still until the police came," Hepple later recalled. "I didn't want to chance my luck a third time." The police and fire bridge lowered a more reliable ladder down from the bridge. A fireman carried Hepple to safety, and the police put him on a bus home. Hepple said he had not been afraid, and he knew he would be safe because he was wearing a St Christopher's medal he had just purchased at the Quayside Market. Evidently a keen climber, Hepple hoped to become a steel erector when he grew up. After putting him to bed that night, his mother, Megan Hepple, said, "There's never a dull moment with Brian."[38]

There was more excitement in February 1968 when a huge bull escaped from Maughan's Auction Mart in Gateshead, chased shoppers down the High Street, and then barrelled its way across the Tyne Bridge, causing motorists to swerve out of its path. Harry Jobling, a traffic warden on duty at the Gateshead end of the bridge, couldn't believe his eyes when he saw the animal approach. "I ran into a sweet shop and dialled 999," he said. "It was a big beast." A police patrol car swiftly arrived, and spectators watched the unusual sight of a panda chasing a bull over the Tyne Bridge. The bull made its way down to the Newcastle Quayside and was eventually captured near the Swing Bridge after a two-mile dash.[39]

And there was more incredible drama one afternoon in February 1972, when an RAF rescue helicopter was called in to rescue a man and his dog from the apex of the Tyne Bridge arch. Described as a "lovelorn, half-naked nightclub busker", Don Crown clutched his black and white terrier Susie to his bare chest as he "cavorted about" at the top of the bridge.[40] Crown had recently returned to his native Newcastle after becoming a minor celebrity during a decade in London. (Susie was part of Crown's busking act, performing tricks—alongside a dozen trained budgerigars.) Traffic was stopped, and spectators looked on as the hovering helicopter lowered a winchman, in strong winds, onto the arch. Crown refused to move, but the winchman managed to grab Susie and bring her to safety.

Later, with the helicopter (and the terrier) on the ground, a scaffolder who was also a church minister scaled the arch and tried to convince Crown to come down, without success. Finally, after three hours of chaos, police brought Crown's girlfriend Sonya Maughan to the bridge, and the couple attempted to communicate at a great distance. "I love you," Crown shouted. "Will you marry me?" Sonya's response was not recorded, but Crown quickly disappeared from view, reappeared on the outer chord, and hurried down the arch to road level. There, he rushed up to Sonya and embraced her—before being apprehended by police. Crown later apologised for the trouble he had caused and offered to put on a show in the city centre with Susie and the budgerigars. "With the nice weather coming," he said, "it would be marvellous for everyone to see these lovely budgies performing in the sunshine and then they'll know I'm not really a bad guy."[41]

In more recent times, climbing the Tyne Bridge has occasionally been used as an ill-advised method of protest. In 2008, protestor Simon Anderton scaled the arch to unveil a banner for the Real Fathers for Justice group. He spent three days on the bridge before being talked down. Then in 2015, Anderton went back up and spent eleven days on the bridge, waving to passers-by and posting on social media. (He also posted a five-star review of the Tyne Bridge on TripAdvisor, praising the "spectacular views" but complaining it was "a bit draughty".)[42] Supporters winched food parcels up to him using ropes. Anderton—then 56—had planned to stay aloft longer, but his stay was cut short by a dangerous thunder and lightning storm.

* * *

Through to the 1960s, traffic ran from Gateshead High Street across the Tyne Bridge and up Newcastle's Pilgrim Street and Northumberland Street along what was then the A1 Great North Road. But the rapidly increasing number of vehicles on the road meant the volume of traffic passing through the centres of Gateshead and Newcastle was becoming intolerable. So, through the 60s and early 70s, Tyneside underwent another transformation, driven largely by controversial Newcastle City Council leader T. Dan Smith. A former painter and decorator, Smith planned a brutalist regeneration to turn Newcastle into "the Brasilia of the North".[43]

Smith's vision was of a multi-level concrete city incorporating a series of central motorways that would pass through underground tunnels and flyovers. Part of the plan involved a proposed new Bypass Bridge to the east of the Tyne Bridge, but this was never built. The overall plan was curtailed due to a lack of funds, and Smith was later jailed for corruption. But some of the work was completed, and the approaches to both sides of the Tyne Bridge were entirely renovated.[44]

In Gateshead, the A167 Gateshead Highway diverted traffic away from the town centre. In Newcastle, only one of Smith's planned motorways was built, the Central Motorway East or A167(M), which similarly diverted traffic away from the centre and up past the east of the city.[45] The Central Motorway, which was built from 1972, bears east at the Newcastle end of the Tyne Bridge and passes underneath Swan House (now 55 Degrees North), a concrete ten-storey 1960s telecoms centre (now an apartment building) standing on a busy roundabout that represents a rather disappointing gateway to the city, particularly in comparison to the proposed triumphal arch envisaged by R. Burns Dick back in the 1920s.

Not to be outdone, Gateshead built a high-rise on its side of the bridge, the 13-storey Tyne Bridge Tower. The 1960s office block was demolished in 2011, but for five decades the Tyne Bridge was bookended by a pair of buildings that many viewed as eyesores. The surviving former Swan House and its concrete surrounds are still seen as a carbuncle at the north end of the bridge, and representative of the worst of Tyneside planning, in contrast to the beloved bridge. T. Dan Smith and his town planners and architects are firmly blamed for this and for the destruction of treasured properties such as John Dobson's Royal Arcade. But some form of bypass was essential if Newcastle and Gateshead were not to be overrun by traffic, and the development's walkways, tunnels and flyovers do have fans among enthusiasts of brutalist architecture.

* * *

On 10 October 1978, Tyneside celebrated the 50th anniversary of the opening of the Tyne Bridge, the golden jubilee of the landmark that had come to symbolise the North-East. Church bells rang, bands played, balloons were released, and a procession of fifty vintage 1920s vehicles plus schoolchildren in period costumes crossed the bridge from Gateshead to Newcastle in intermittent rain. The bridge was specially floodlit to mark the occasion, and there was an exhibition of photographs showing the bridge's construction in the passenger lift in the Newcastle tower. The lift attendant at the time was Eddie Stobbart, an RAF veteran who manned the wood-panelled lift for ten hours a day. "Oh, it has its ups and downs, you know," he said.[46]

Alongside the mayors of Newcastle and Gateshead, guests at the celebration included a handful of men who had worked on the project in the 1920s—men who could say, "We built the Tyne Bridge." Among them was Jack Hamilton, the assistant chief resident engineer, who had been in his twenties when the bridge was built. He regarded the Tyne Bridge with particular fondness. His main memory was from the day he stood on the top of the bridge as the arch was successfully closed. "There was a great sigh of relief," he recalled. "I was due to get married at that time. I turned to my superior and asked him, 'How long can I have for my honeymoon?'"[47]

Jack Dunford, who was 85 in 1978, had worked at Dorman Long steel works in Middlesbrough. He was involved in the fabrication work and never saw the bridge actually being built. "I saw it for the first time shortly after the official opening," he said. "I came to Newcastle for the derby match with Middlesbrough. I remember looking at the bridge and thinking, 'Well, the lads have done a good job there…'"

The Newcastle *Chronicle* invited readers to send in their memories of the opening of the bridge, and many did. *Chronicle* reporter Eric Forster wrote that the bridge was, after fifty years, "already part and parcel of Tyneside legend." "It has come to typify a region, represent its aspirations, symbolise its industrial tradition," he wrote. "There was never a native-born Geordie who did not feel that little thrill which spoke of home when the Tyne Bridge hove into view."[48]

Correspondents recalled attending the ceremony as children and worrying about how the royal horses would get over the steep incline of the bridge's arch. Margaret Baty said she presented a needlework set to Queen Mary as a schoolgirl on the opening day. And John Henry Swan also remembered the opening. "I was staying at the Salvation Army Men's Palace," he wrote. "I had no work. Dole was 12s 6d a week, and I paid 6d for my bed. Looking out the window, I saw the royalty coming over the bridge. Their stomachs would be well filled. Mine was not. I thank God times are much better now for everyone."[49]

One correspondent was Thomas Elliott, the lad who ended up in hospital after being knocked from his bike by a motor car on the bridge following the opening ceremony. "The accident made front-page news," he recalled. "All the paper lads were shouting, 'First accident on the new Tyne Bridge!' I often think about this. I am now 67 years old."[50]

Another correspondent, May Wright, wrote that the Tyne Bridge was a monument to the efforts the members of Newcastle and Gateshead councils had made to improve the region. May Wright's maiden name was Easten. She was the last surviving child of former Lord Mayor Stephen Easten and had served alongside him as Lady Mayoress during the building of the bridge. On behalf of the Easten family, she thanked the newspaper for the "spectacular" anniversary memories, saying, "How nice it is that there are those who wish to remember."[51]

11

A CULTURAL ICON

Geordie Peacock walks across the Tyne Bridge, between the mid-dle-green balustrades and steel arch hangers, a granite abutment tower behind him, the coaly Tyne below. He wears a buttoned-up white shirt, an oversized suit and a large pair of plastic-rimmed spectacles. His long, straggly blonde hair blows across his haggard face. It is 1995, and Geordie has recently escaped from prison. He has returned to Tyneside to see his lifelong friends Nicky, Mary and Tosker. Geordie pauses at the railing. *Don't Look Back in Anger* by Oasis begins to play. The camera pans back. Then Geordie resumes his walk across the bridge, towards Gateshead and whatever awaits. He walks past the camera and out of shot. A slow procession of traffic moves across the bridge. Fade to black. Roll credits. The end.

This is the final scene of *Our Friends in the North*, the classic BBC drama written by Peter Flannery and starring Daniel Craig, Christopher Ecclestone, Gina McKee, Mark Strong and the Tyne Bridge. Based on Jarrow-born Flannery's stage play, the series, which aired in early 1996, follows the four Tyneside friends over more than thirty years against a backdrop of social and political tur-moil. The series is often named on lists of best-ever TV shows (including lists produced by the British Film Institute, *Radio Times* and *The Guardian*). And the poignant final scene is among the most memorable of all TV moments, combining an almost-unrecognisa-ble pre-James Bond Daniel Craig, the Oasis song that was number one in the UK charts when the episode aired, and the unmistakable backdrop of the iconic Tyne Bridge.[1]

The bridge was a film star from the day it was opened, initially in the Movietone "talkie" of the opening ceremony, which was shown around the world. There was also another spectacular film from those earliest days. *The Building of the New Tyne Bridge Between Newcastle and Gateshead* was produced by Dorman Long and might have been filmed by the project's official photographers James Bacon & Sons. Essentially a promotional film, it wasn't widely released but was shown on Tyneside in April 1929 and then at educational lectures at various technical colleges.[2]

This remarkable 45-minute silent film combines footage of the construction work with animated diagrams to explain key stages. The standout images are those of the death-defying workers walking along support cables, climbing vertical beams and balancing on the top of the arch so high above the river. But there are also shots of the caisson excavators entering the shafts one at a time via the air lock, then digging with shovels and pickaxes inside the pressurised chamber. We see the approach spans being launched across their support columns, the road deck being constructed, and the final member being inserted into the top of the arch. The moment the arch is closed, with celebratory flags unfurling and fluttering in the breeze, is also captured. The film ends with footage from the opening ceremony, followed by a charming scene of the bridge in use, featuring trundling motor cars, clip-clopping horses and carts, inquisitive pedestrians, and a passing cyclist who seems dangerously distracted by the camera.

In subsequent decades, the Tyne Bridge became a popular backdrop for movies and television, often as shorthand to place the location on Tyneside. The 1939 film noir *On the Night of the Fire* and 1950's *The Clouded Yellow* both feature the Tyne Bridge. Most notably, the gritty 1961 heist movie *Payroll* gives the bridge a starring role in several key scenes. A decade later, 1971 saw the release of *Get Carter*, which has become Tyneside's most famous film despite barely featuring the Tyne Bridge. (*Get Carter*'s most famous filming location was Gateshead's now-demolished Trinity Square car park.)

If *Get Carter* is Tyneside's most famous film, *The Likely Lads* is its most famous TV show. *The Likely Lads* (and superior follow-up *Whatever Happened to the Likely Lads?*) used Tyneside locations, from demolished terraces to new-build estates, to show a region in transition and to reflect the contrasts between its characters, working-class Bob and upwardly-mobile Terry, played by James Bolam and

Rodney Bewes. The Tyne Bridge—a symbol of home for both characters—appears prominently a couple of times in the 1976 *Likely Lads* movie, which was shot while the bridge was wearing its alternative colour scheme of blue, grey and red.

The Tyne Bridge also features in another classic TV show, *Auf Wiedersehen, Pet*, the comedy-drama about British construction workers who find work in Dusseldorf, notably in the second series in which the gang, including Jimmy Nail's Oz, return to Tyneside.

Both *(Whatever Happened to) The Likely Lads* and *Auf Wiedersehen, Pet* are social documents capturing the changes that occurred on Tyneside in the 1970s and 1980s. The *Likely Lads* characters both trained as electricians, but Terry is mostly unemployed after leaving the army, while Bob has a comfortable job as a civil engineer (perhaps allowing him to appreciate the bridge from a professional as well as a personal viewpoint). In *Auf Wiedersehen*, the characters are manual workers who might once have worked on projects like the Tyne Bridge but are now forced to work abroad due to the unemployment crisis on Tyneside. In the wider Tyne and Wear region, there were 67,000 job losses in the four years between mid-1979 and mid-1983. By February 1984 there were more than 95,000 people out of work in the region.[3]

The bridge made another prominent screen appearance in Mike Figgis's 1988 debut movie *Stormy Monday*, which sees Wallsend-born Sting (as nightclub owner Finney) face-off with Tommy Lee Jones (as New York gangster Cosmo) on the High Level Bridge, with the green-again Tyne Bridge conspicuous in the background. Figgis grew up in Newcastle and was determined his movie would show the real Tyneside.[4] The movie's cinematographer was multi-Oscar-winning Roger Deakins, who magnificently captured the rugged splendour of the river and its bridges.

Then came *Our Friends in the North* and appearances for the bridge in numerous other TV shows, including the Ant and Dec-starring *Byker Grove*, crime drama *55 Degrees North*, soap opera *Quayside* and reality show *Geordie Shore*. Martin Shaw's *Inspector George Gently* was called on to investigate a dead body found below the Tyne Bridge, and Brenda Blethyn's *Vera* has solved several crimes against the backdrop of its famous arch.

The bridge is certainly more of a visual icon than an aural one and features much more often in TV and film than in music. It does feature in the lyrics of poignant Tyneside favourite *Home Newcastle* by Busker from 1981, in which the late Gateshead singer-songwriter Ronnie Lambert wishes he was on the Quayside looking at the old Tyne Bridge (as opposed to the *Old* Tyne Bridge). The cover of the single features a sketch of the bridge—and a Newcastle Brown Ale label. In the song *The Immigrant Lad* from 1968 by Eric Burdon and the Animals, Burdon imagines building a bridge of steel to cross the expanse of Tyne between two separated souls.

One of the most prominent musical representations of the Tyne Bridge appeared in 1969 with The Nice's *The Five Bridges Suite*, although it's not entirely clear which of the suite's five movements represents the Tyne. A recording was released as an album in 1970 with a "fisheye" photo of the Tyne Bridge on the cover. At the time, there were five bridges between Newcastle and Gateshead. As Emerson later noted, "While more planets have been discovered and some dismissed since Gustav Holst wrote his *Planet Suite*, there are now a few more bridges in Newcastle."[5]

* * *

Back in the late 1970s, as the Tyne Bridge celebrated its fiftieth anniversary, a new bridge was being constructed over the river between Newcastle and Gateshead. Fittingly, the Queen Elizabeth II Metro Bridge was opened by Queen Elizabeth II, alongside the Duke of Edinburgh. And the Queen recognised that the bridge's most striking feature was the view it provided of its neighbours. "When I was last here in Jubilee year, Britannia was moored at the quayside, from where we had a splendid view of the Tyne bridges," said the Queen in her speech. "Today, we have an equally striking view from the vantage point of a train crossing the latest bridge, which I have just opened and to which I have gladly give my name."[6]

The new bridge provided the fastest way to cross the river and provided those terrific elevated views of the High Level, Swing and Tyne bridges. Commuters would come to appreciate the Metro bridge for those reasons, but otherwise, it is something of an over-looked sibling among its more elegant neighbours. The Pevsner architectural guide describes the Metro Bridge as "rather inelegant". (The High Level is "superb", the Swing is "attractive", and the Tyne

Bridge is "Newcastle's modern-day symbol".)[7] Originally white, the Metro Bridge was painted blue in 2006 and fitted with 140 colour-changing LED lights as part of a permanent art installation.[8]

As the Metro Bridge was coming into service, another bridge was being built between Newcastle and Gateshead, a quarter-mile upstream. This was the third Redheugh Bridge, following the previous crossings of 1871 and 1901. Designed—like the Tyne Bridge—by Mott, Hay & Anderson, the new Redheugh Bridge was built right next to its predecessor by contractors Nuttall between 1980 and 1983. A post-tensioned concrete construction, it's supported by two river piers and has a main span length of 526 feet—just 5 feet shorter than the Tyne Bridge. Pevsner calls it "a good example of modern medium-span bridge design", although it is unlikely to be named at the top of anyone's list of favourite bridges over the Tyne. The new Redheugh Bridge was opened by Diana Princess of Wales in May 1983.

As the most westerly bridge between Newcastle and Gateshead, the Redheugh is subject to the full force of the wind blowing down the Tyne Valley, and its open deck design can cause problems for high-sided vehicles. In December 1986, a United double-decker bus was travelling over the Redheugh from north to south when it was side-swiped by a great gust of gale-force wind. The bus smashed into the bridge's safety barriers and teetered on the edge of an 85-foot drop into the Tyne. Driver Gary Mains and his passengers managed to escape, and the bridge was closed while the bus was tethered to the bridge to prevent it from falling. "I thought at one stage that it would definitely go over," said Mains. "The winds were incredibly strong. The bus suddenly lunged through the safety barrier, ripping off the front section and ploughing through the barriers for some distance. The windscreen smashed as we crashed into things, and I feared that we might go right over the side."[9]

* * *

On 28 June 1981, 12,264 people ran across the Tyne Bridge in T-shirts and vests with numbers pinned to the front. Among them were elite athletes, wheelchair users and fun runners. They were participating in a half-marathon from Newcastle to South Shields. It was the UK's first mass-participation half-marathon road race, held just a few months after the inaugural London Marathon (and with almost double the number of runners). The winner was Elswick Harrier and future Olympic medallist Mike McLeod. In 20th place was (supposedly retired) Gateshead Harrier and Olympic medallist Brendan Foster. Now Sir Brendan Foster, he was the Tyneside athletics great who co-founded this ground-breaking and much-imitated road race—the Great North Run.

It was always intended that the Great North Run should start at the Tyne Bridge, which has become an indelible part of the race—a thrill for the runners to pound their way across and a famous backdrop for photos and TV footage of the event. But taking over the Tyne Bridge for a fun run was no mean feat. "Initially, the police said no, then they allowed us to do what we wanted," recalled Foster. "Closing the Tyne Bridge was a big thing. The only time it had been closed before we got the Great North Run started was the opening with King George V, so we are in good company."[10]

The run became a huge success, tapping in to the growing popularity of running for leisure and celebrating the best of the North East—the warmth of the people, the sporting achievements and the splendid locations. Today, more than 55,000 runners participate in each year's Great North Run, many of them in fancy dress and raising funds for charities. The run is regularly oversubscribed, with places allocated by ballot.

Since 2002, that defining moment of the Great North Run has become more spectacular as the runners on the bridge have been joined from above in a flypast by the RAF's Red Arrows display team. "It's an iconic image, the Tyne Bridge," said Brendan Foster. "The key shot is the runners going over it with the Red Arrows flying across—it never ceases to amaze me."[11]

It is a remarkable scene: thousands of runners in a multitude of colours and costumes—most of them still smiling at this early stage of the race—pounding across the green steel arch, and above them the formation of red jets with their multi-coloured vapour trails. Former Red Arrows Squadron Leader Simon Stevens, Red 6, said the Great North Run flypast had a special significance for him. "Even from above you can feel the electric atmosphere," said Stevens, "and seeing all the runners packing the Tyne Bridge as we flew over is something I will never forget."[12]

George Caulkin is a senior writer at football publication *The Athletic* and a patron of the Sir Bobby Robson Foundation. He is one of many who raises money for charity via the Great North Run. Caulkin says the day of the run is the best of the year and an excellent showcase for the region and its people. "Tens of thousands of runners," he says, "everyone with a story, all running for a reason, laughing at their own achievement, crying out of loss, and everybody being cheered on their way." At the heart of the event is the Tyne Bridge. "The bridge is the set-piece, the moment you want to recall. You still feel fresh at that point, although chances are you've set off too quickly and it'll come back to bite you on the other side of the river. For a lot of the run, your body and brain are urging you to stop, to pack it in, but not here, never on the bridge. You climb from the tunnel, see the steel arch, a glint of water, a blur of faces, there's a roar in your ears, and you're just telling yourself: *Go*."[13]

* * *

One of the participants in the very first Great North Run in 1981 was footballer Kevin Keegan, who ran in a half-and-half Newcastle and Sunderland kit. A year later, Keegan was wearing an all-Newcastle kit after signing for Newcastle United. The shock transfer was backed by Newcastle's club sponsor Newcastle Breweries. Keegan, born in Doncaster with North East roots, became an adopted Geordie and an iconic figure on Tyneside after effectively saving Newcastle from relegation to the third division twice, as player and manager. And after he signed for Newcastle in 1982, he wore the Tyne Bridge on his chest. That's because the famous Newcastle United black and white shirt was adorned with the Newcastle Breweries blue star, and the blue star featured the silhouette of the Tyne Bridge. The Tyne Bridge on the black and white shirt on Kevin Keegan—an icon on an icon on an icon.

Newcastle Breweries added the five-pointed blue star to its beer labels, including its Brown Ale labels, in the year the Tyne Bridge was opened following an award-winning performance at the 1928 International Brewer's Conference. (Among seven awards, Newcastle Brown Ale won the Brewing Trades' Review Challenge Cup for best bottled beer.) A promotional booklet prepared for the

1929 North East Coast Exhibition showed on its cover a gleaming blue star shining over the silhouetted Tyne Bridge, Cathedral of St Nicholas and Castle Keep.[14] The silhouette was added to the blue star to create one of beer's most recognisable logos. It can be found all over the world on beer bottles and draft pumps, window decals and neon signs, beer mats and bar towels, schooner glasses and ash trays, bottle crates and delivery vans. From Los Angeles to Auckland, from Reykjavik to Buenos Aires, there are pubs with some kind of Newcastle Breweries or Newcastle Brown Ale barware and brew-eriana—even if they don't serve Brown Ale—all featuring the famous blue star and the mighty Tyne Bridge.

Kevin Keegan, the adopted Geordie, loves the Tyne Bridge. "It epitomises the city," he said. "Everything I buy—and I've got some paintings at home—always has the Tyne Bridge on. It *is* Newcastle."[15] In July 1993, during his first spell as Newcastle manager (and with the Blue Star once more on the black and white shirt), Keegan flicked the switch to illuminate the Tyne Bridge following a cam-paign led by the Newcastle *Chronicle* and *Journal* newspapers. The campaign raised £175,000 to fund a computer-controlled system of 48 floodlights. The illumination coincided with the visit to the Tyne of 121 sailing ships for the 1993 Tall Ships Race

One of the visitors who crowded onto the bridge to watch the illumination ceremony was eight-year-old Arran Barker from Gretna. He and his family were making one of their regular pilgrim-ages to a place that had been particularly dear to their hearts since the moment Arran was born. It was just after 2 am one night in November 1984, and Arran's mother Tina Barker was in labour and on her way in an ambulance from her home in Whickham, Gateshead, to the Princess Mary Hospital in Newcastle. With baby Arran very keen to make an appearance, the ambulance pulled over in the middle of the bridge, where he was delivered by the crew. So Arran was born right in the middle of the Tyne Bridge. As lead ambulance man Bill Shields remarked, "You can't get much more Geordie than that."[16]

The family moved away from Tyneside, and Arran grew up in Scotland, but he was always told he was born exactly halfway between Newcastle and Gateshead, so he considered himself a Geordie and became a "mad keen" Newcastle United fan (and his hero was Kevin Keegan). "I always feel like it's my own bridge, nobody else's," said Arran. Every time we come back to Newcastle, I make my mum and dad drive across the bridge so I can see it."[17]

A few months after Kevin Keegan illuminated the Tyne Bridge, later in 1993, the public got a rare chance to see inside part of the structure when the bridge's north tower was opened as part of a major exhibition of contemporary art, Tyne International. The tower, a cavernous warehouse space, had been unoccupied since it was built and contained only its skeletal steel framework (and out-of-service elevator).

Another largely forgotten part of the Tyne Bridge was revived in 1994 when the former public convenience building at the Gateshead end of the bridge, Number One Church Street, was reopened as a suite of offices. The Grade II listed building—Tyneside's first (but not only) listed public toilet—had been closed to the public since 1972 and used by Gateshead Council to store cleaning supplies. In 1994, it was re-opened by architects the Jenkins Partnership. (As of 2022, the building is occupied by graphic designers Beacon Creative.)

* * *

As the 21st century approached, Tyneside got two new structures that would challenge the Tyne Bridge for the title of icon of the North-East—and only one of them was a bridge. The first was the Angel of the North, Anthony Gormley's 200-tonne steel sculpture, which was erected by the side of the A1 in Gateshead in February 1998. The Angel is 66 feet tall, and its wingspan is 177 feet wide (about a third of the width of the Tyne Bridge's arch span). Its location by a busy road and near the East Coast Main Line rail route means it is among the most-viewed pieces of public art in the world, and arguably the most recognisable piece of public art in the UK. And it is widely popular—although initial reactions to the £800,000-work were mixed. Like the Tyne Bridge, it has an instantly-recognisable silhouette, and its "rusty metal" design reflects the region's industrial heritage. With its welcoming open wings, the Angel also serves as a symbol of home.

And then came the new bridge, the seventh between Newcastle and Gateshead. The Gateshead Millennium Bridge was floated into place on the Tyne by the giant Asian Hercules II crane in front of large crowds of spectators in November 2000, although it didn't open to the public until 17 September 2001. As its name suggests, it was conceived to celebrate the new millennium by Gateshead Council. The eye-catching design by Wilkinson Eyre with Gifford & Partners is an innovative tilting bridge that, crucially, echoes the arch of the Tyne Bridge. The pedestrian and cyclist crossing tilts open in a "blinking eye" movement to allow the passage of river traffic (which included, in 2008, the departing *Tuxedo Princess*). It's comprised of two white prefabricated steel arches—one being the pedestrian and cycle deck and the other a counterbalancing support. The bridge span is about 345 feet long, and when open, it provides clearance over the river of 82 feet.[18] The bridge was officially opened by Queen Elizabeth in 2002 during her Golden Jubilee tour.

As the first bridge over the Tyne built purely for leisure and aesthetic purposes, the Gateshead Millennium Bridge symbolises the changes that have taken place on Tyneside, of reinvention and regeneration following the decline of traditional industries. The High Level and Swing bridges were built for heavy industry, and the Tyne Bridge was built from it. But the Millennium Bridge was built for recreation and tourism, to be enjoyed by locals and visitors. Positioned right by the Baltic Centre for Contemporary Art (formerly the Baltic Flour Mills and opened in 2002) and the Sage Gateshead music venue (designed by Sir Norman Foster and opened in 2004), the Millennium Bridge makes a significant contribution to the cultural landscape of Gateshead and the riverscape of the Tyne. Although very different to its adjacent crossings, the Millennium fits perfectly into Tyneside's suite of bridges. It's easy to take a photo of the Tyne Bridge framed by the Millennium Bridge, with the Swing and High Level bridges behind (and, with a good lens, the Metro, King Edward and Redheugh in the distance).

Like the Tyne Bridge and the Angel of the North, the Millennium Bridge has become a symbol of Tyneside and an icon of the North-East. It also has a recognisable silhouette that looks nice on a tea towel. (In 2007, to mark the 80th anniversary of Newcastle Brown Ale, Scottish and Newcastle Breweries changed the blue star design on its Brown Ale labels by incorporating the Millennium Bridge over a slightly-reworked silhouette of the Tyne Bridge.)[19]

When the Baltic opened in 2002, as part of its inaugural exhibition, the gallery commissioned American artist Chris Burden to make a scale model of the Tyne Bridge from Meccano—just as the enthusiasts at Halfords cycle shop had done back in 1928. Burden's impressive model was 1/20th of the size of the actual bridge, with a span of around 26 feet. And it was positioned by plate glass windows that framed a perfect view of the Tyne Bridge, allowing visitors to compare the model and the real thing. (The model was large enough that it was also visible from the real bridge.)

The exhibition did cause controversy after it was revealed the Baltic had paid Burden £100,000 to make the model but had not secured any ownership, allowing it to be sold on to the Louis Vuitton Moët Hennessy (LVMH) fashion house for £400,000 without the Baltic receiving any recompense. (The model was placed in the reception of the company's Paris headquarters.) Critics said the money could have been better spent painting the Tyne Bridge, and the North East Meccano Society said they could have built a similar model for a fraction of the cost. Baltic also had to pay £11,000 for damage caused to another of Burden's models used in the exhibition—a scale model of the Tyne-inspiring Hell Gate Bridge, which was owned by tennis legend John McEnroe.[20]

But could the Tyne Bridge—or any bridge—really be a work of art? That question was posed by the *Daily Telegraph*, to which correspondent Alan Mole responded: "The Tyne Bridge is an instantly recognisable icon to millions of expatriate Geordies. It is a triumph of form and function created by the hand and eye of man, unsurpassed, in the black-and-white-tinted view of any Geordie, including that slightly vulgar edifice crossing Sydney Harbour. The Tyne Bridge is Art."[21]

Even when setting aside the black-and-white-tinted spectacles, the Tyne Bridge is undeniably a work of art. Beyond its engineering intricacies, it has great creative, imaginative and aesthetic appeal. It generates an emotional reaction in those who view it, whether they like it or not. And it has inspired numerous artists—film directors, photographers, painters, graphic designers, musicians, composers, novelists, playwrights. It has become embedded in the culture of Tyneside, prominent in the arts, in sport, and in the customs and ideas of local people. The Tyne Bridge is on things Geordies buy and eat and drink. It's on T-shirts and shop signs and home decorations. It is more than a bridge. It has transcended its basic function as a river crossing to become an icon of Tyneside and a symbol of the Geordie way of life.

12

THE PRIDE OF TYNESIDE

There are many great views to be had of the Tyne Bridge, and among the best is from the battlements of the Castle Keep, the 850-year-old fortified stone tower that perches on the northern lip of the steep Tyne Gorge. The Keep is more than 80 feet tall, and its battlement roof is accessed via a spiralling set of 99 steps. From the top, amid the corner turrets and fluttering flags, visitors can gaze down on the river and its crossings. The High Level Bridge stretches out ahead, the occasional train pulling across its top deck. Below is the Swing Bridge, no longer swinging but still carrying road traffic, the Tyneside sunshine illuminating its red, white and blue colour scheme. This, of course, was the site of the old Tyne Bridges—Georgian, medieval and Roman. The Castle Keep stood above them all.

Next to the Swing is the Tyne Bridge, grand in stature and epic in scale, visible here from an elevated angle that shows the entire curve of the steel arch, from pin to pin, the long sweep of the busy road deck and the art deco-stylings of the bookend towers. The constant rumble of traffic crossing the bridge thrums in the air, and the repetitive call and squawk of birds reverberates across the gorge. Behind the Tyne Bridge, framed by its arch, is the Sage Gateshead music centre. Beyond that, on Gateshead's revitalised quayside, is the former flour mill that is now the Baltic arts centre. And in front is the latest bridge to link Gateshead and Newcastle, the "blinking eye" Millennium Bridge. These four bridges combine to create a stunning riverscape. Look to the west and add in the Metro, King Edward and Redheugh, and you have an extraordinary suite of seven bridges that is unmatched anywhere in the world. Tyneside really is a place of bridges, boasting a set of jewels of which the Tyne Bridge is the emerald, the jadeite, the rarest of green diamonds.

It's no wonder the formerly coaly Tyne has become a major tourist destination, with its bridges backed by numerous other historical, architectural and cultural landmarks, leisure activities, shopping outlets, dining opportunities, and loads and loads of pubs. In 2018, 65 million people visited Newcastle and Gateshead, and Newcastle was named by Rough Guides as the top destination to visit in the world. For tourism purposes, the city of Newcastle and the town of Gateshead have been combined into a single destination named "NewcastleGateshead" by the NewcastleGateshead Initiative marketing partnership. And the quaysides and riverscape are at the heart of Tyneside's offering as a tourist attraction, where it's the bridges that really connect Newcastle and Gateshead.

On the Tripadvisor travel website, the Tyne Bridge is highly rated by visitors as a landmark attraction. "I think it's so majestic", writes one visitor. "It's a must-see bridge," says another. Other reviews call the bridge "iconic", "spectacular", "wonderful", "photogenic", and "instantly recognisable". One reviewer describes it as "bridge porn". Another visitor said she had seen the bridge on TV every year during the Great North Run, and "it was very moving to be standing right next to it". The website's top review is by a visitor from Fremantle in Australia, who calls the Tyne Bridge a "really big piece of Meccano". Fremantle is around 2,500 miles from Sydney, so there's a good chance the reviewer has never visited the Sydney Harbour Bridge. But she very much likes the Tyne Bridge: "It is an amazing sight and looks magnificent in its setting across the river." It is, of course, Tripadvisor's number-one-rated bridge in Newcastle.[1]

Visitors can obtain other fine views of the Tyne Bridge from its neighbours. From the elevated pedestrian walkway of the High Level, the Tyne Bridge can be framed against the backdrop of the Millennium Bridge, with the Swing Bridge in the foreground. From the low-level Swing Bridge, viewers can gaze up as the bridge arcs above them. And fine photos can be snapped from the Millennium Bridge, although Instagrammers might want to walk a little further along the Newcastle Quayside to capture a shot of the Tyne Bridge framed within the Millennium's complementary arch.

One great benefit of the Millennium Bridge as a low-level crossing is that it forms a loop with the Swing Bridge, allowing pedestri-

17a: Tyne Bridge towers under construction, 6 Sept 1928

17b: View from Newcastle Quayside, 6 Sept 1928

18a: Tyne Bridge roadway nearing completion, 25 Sept 1928

18b: Opening of the Tyne Bridge by His Majesty the King, 10 Oct 1928

19a: Herding sheep under the Tyne Bridge

19b: Tyne Bridge from Gateshead

20a: Aerial view of the Tyne Bridge, circa 1929

20b: Aerial view of the Tyne, Swing and High Level bridges, 1995

21a: The Tyne Bridge's alternative colour scheme, 1985

21b: Quayside Sunday Market, 1986

22a: *Payroll*, 1961

22b: *The Likely Lads*, 1976

23a: *Stormy Monday*, 1988

23b: *Our Friends in the North*, 1996

24a1: Newcastle Brown Ale

24a2: Newcastle v Liverpool
programme, 1984

24b: Runners on the Tyne Bridge

25a: Angel of the North

25b: The Gateshead Millennium Bridge and Tyne Bridge

26a: The Tyne Bridge from the Side

26b: Queen Street from the Side

27a: The bridge passes over Quayside rooftops

27b: The Tyne Bridge from Lombard Street

28a: North tower quayside entrance

28b: North hinge and skewback bearing

29a: Traffic on the Tyne Bridge

29b: Tyne Bridge kittiwakes

30a: North tower deck-level entrance

30b: Tyne Bridge opening ceremony plaque

31a: The Tyne Bridge at night

31b: The Tyne Bridge in reduced circumstances, 2022

32a: View from the High Level Bridge

32b: View from the Castle Keep

ans to walk right around the Tyne Bridge along the Newcastle and Gateshead Quaysides. On the Newcastle Quayside, visitors can walk a few yards from the Swing Bridge past centuries of history— the Watergate Buildings (with the remains of the Old Tyne Bridge in its cellar), the Guildhall, Bessie Surtees' House and the 17th-century merchants' houses at Sandhill. As with any historic city, the trick is always to look up. There are terrific views of the soaring Tyne Bridge from Sandhill and the Side. By heading around Queen Street to Lombard Street, visitors can walk right under the Newcastle approach and see how closely it passes the rooftops of the mercantile buildings.

Lombard Street provides more epic views of the Tyne Bridge (reminiscent of those of the Manhattan Bridge from the "most Instagrammable" Washington Street in Brooklyn, New York).[2] And Lombard Street also provides close-up views of the base of the Tyne Bridge's north tower, with the entrance door to the out-of-service lifts. (The eagle-eyed might also spot a small piece of street art on the north tower, a ceramic tile mosaic of video game character Donkey Kong attributed to French artist Invader.)[3]

Around the corner on the Quayside, the huge hinge pin and skewback abutment that bears the load of the bridge can be seen at close quarters. It's worth recalling that the stone towers have no real structural purpose and that the foundations below this spot were sunk to great depths with the hellish caissons. On the Sandhill side of the north tower, its art deco details are more easily visible, including a small balcony up at road deck level. By the doors on the Sandhill side is a plaque marking the 75th anniversary of the opening of the bridge in 2003. There is a plaque on the south tower, too.

The 75th anniversary was celebrated with another "Parade of Transport" featuring vintage vehicles, including a royal landau. (The vintage effect was slightly spoiled by the fact that regular 2003 traffic was not stopped and continued to drive across the bridge during the parade.) The passage of time meant there were no construction workers present. Instead, Newcastle and Gateshead Councils invited the families of the workers to attend a celebration dinner. Among those who attended were Robert Collins, the grandson of tragic Nathaniel Collins. "I never met him, but I remember listening to my grandmother telling stories about him," said Robert Collins.

"I'm very proud of the Tyne Bridge as we all are in Newcastle. It epitomises the Geordie spirit."[4]

Another attendee was Violet May Rose, the daughter of Kit Lattimer, one of the spidermen who helped build the arch and one of a long line of bridge builders. "The family joke is that his false teeth are still lying at the bottom of the River Tyne," she said, "because one day, when he was working, hanging upside down, his false teeth fell out."[5] Today, Kit's great-grandson Karl Lattimer laughs when he hears that story. Karl is proud of the part Kit played in building the Tyne Bridge. "Very proud," he says. "The bridge means an awful lot. It's symbolic of the city."[6]

And Kit's great-granddaughter Helen Rose is also very proud that Kit worked on the bridge at such daring heights with few thoughts of health and safety. "It's also funny telling my kids that I had a great grandad who was a spiderman," she says. Helen now lives in Brisbane, Australia, and has visited the Tyne Bridge's cousin in Sydney several times. "The Sydney Harbour Bridge is spectacular and amazing but has never had the impact of our bridge at home," she says. "The Tyne Bridge is an important part of our family."[7]

Standing at the bottom of the Tyne Bridge's north tower, more than 80 feet below the road deck and more than 190 feet below the soaring apex of the arch, it's incredible to comprehend the bravery and skill of men like Kit Lattimer. Tourists walk along the Quayside with coffee cups and ice creams and gaze up at the bridge. A Scandinavian couple stop to look and cup their eyes against the sun. A group of lads tumble out of a nearby Premier Inn and begin to take selfies by the bridge as a reminder of where they have been. A delivery driver pushes a trolley of boxes along the pavement, and a motorised street sweeper trundles into view. The rumble of traffic and squawk of birds echo off the underside of the bridge. Locals pass by on foot and in cars and cast a quick glance—perhaps one of many hundreds or thousands they have given to the Tyne Bridge. It's still reassuringly there. It's still reassuringly theirs.

* * *

Tourists are not the only visitors drawn to the Tyne Bridge. Each spring and summer, the bridge becomes home to a colony of kittiwakes—the largest inland colony in the world. The black-legged kittiwake is a small white gull with a yellow bill, grey plumage, and black-tipped wings. The birds first arrived on the Tyne in the 1960s and at the Tyne Bridge in the 1990s. By 2001 there were 134 pairs of nesting kittiwakes on the bridge. As of 2022, there are more than a thousand pairs. They nest on both sides of the river, on the ledges of the north and south towers and the metal girders in between. The north tower is a particular favourite spot, with almost every available shelf and crevice occupied during the nesting season. The birds also nest on adjacent buildings—and on structures all the way down to the mouth of the Tyne. (The Tyne Bridge kittiwakes represent more than half of the Tyne's overall population.)[8]

Considering the kittiwake (named in imitation of its cry) is included on the UK Birds of Conservation Concern Red List as critically endangered and threatened with global extinction, the Tyne Bridge colony is an environmental triumph. Many locals and visitors love to see the birds arrive with the spring. Paul Buskin from the Kittiwakes upon the Tyne group, which aims to protect and raise awareness for the birds, explains the kittiwakes need urgent conservation action. "There is a great need to help safeguard existing birds and help secure and protect their nesting sites as global populations have fallen by over 40 per cent since the 1970s," says Buskin. "The kittiwakes are also part of Tyneside's local history and heritage. For many of us, they have been part of our spring and summer months for our whole lives."[9]

The presence of such a large colony does cause some problems involving noise, dirt and smell in areas around and under the bridge. The colony produces a huge quantity of droppings, and council cleaners can be regularly seen jetwashing guano from the pavements. (Tourists walking underneath the bridge by the towers might need to quicken their step to avoid being dropped on.) Anti-bird netting, spikes and other deterrents have been used to try to keep the kittiwakes away from some parts of the bridge, but these have at times accidentally trapped or injured the birds. A sensitive solution is required because the Tyne Bridge colony is too important to be evicted from its home.

In winter, the kittiwakes head towards the North-West Atlantic, with many reaching Canada and Greenland, and the Tyne Bridge and its towers are once again vacant. But the kittiwakes are not the only wildlife that brings the bridge to life. Otter cubs have been spotted underneath the Tyne Bridge, and the cleaned-up River Tyne—after several centuries of industry—has returned to being one of the best salmon rivers in the country. What would the men who built the Tyne Bridge almost a century ago, across the still-coaly Tyne, have thought of the men who stand with fishing rods casting lines under the bridge to catch a fish supper?

* * *

Each New Year's Eve, when funding and pandemics allow, the Tyne Bridge is at the centre of a spectacular fireworks display that welcomes the flipping of the calendar—eleven hours after the Sydney Harbour Bridge celebrates in a similar manner. On New Year's Eve 2021, the fireworks were replaced by an interactive laser light display with lasers positioned on the Tyne Bridge that could be controlled by the public using their smartphones. And on New Year's Eve 2016, more than 200 revellers attended an illegal rave inside the Tyne Bridge's north tower.

The rave was rumbled in the early hours of the New Year. Loud music could be heard and lights could be seen inside the tower and, at around 2.30 in the morning, a large number of police officers arrived. Unable to gain entry, the police smashed and power-sawed through the tower's 90-year-old doors on Lombard Street. The revellers were eventually removed, and their sound and light equipment was disconnected and seized. The rave was organised via Facebook. No arrests were made. Newcastle Council said the organisers had potentially put hundreds of people in "grave danger" because the tower wasn't safe. (The long-neglected shell has no fire exits, and the accumulated bird droppings are toxic.) But it was hoped the incident could create interest in using the space for legal purposes.[10]

In 2018, bar and nightclub developer Tokyo Industries applied for planning permission to turn the north tower into an entertainment venue with event and gallery spaces and food and drink offerings. Permission was granted in the following year, with conditions to prevent it from being used as a nightclub.[11] And in 2020, Tyneside art cooperative Unit44 staged a virtual exhibition,

"Hidden in Plain Sight", in the north tower. Due to pandemic restrictions, the exhibition was entirely digital, with visitors invited to view the artworks within the space via an online 360-degree interactive tour. Despite the fact that visitors were not physically allowed inside, this was perhaps the best use of the Tyne Bridge towers since they were built.[12]

Heading towards the Millennium Bridge along the Newcastle Quayside (on a pedestrian walkway that can perhaps be called a promenade), there are more uninterrupted views of the Tyne Bridge. There are boats moored along the 500 yards or so of Quayside between the Tyne and Millennium bridges (all significantly smaller than the dearly-departed "Boat"). This is the location of the Quayside Sunday Market, which is mentioned in records from 1736 but probably originated much further back in Tyneside's history. In any case, the Quayside Market was a fixture here during the eras of the Old Tyne Bridge and Georgian Tyne Bridge, and has continued as a popular weekly attraction under the "new" Tyne Bridge.

There was once—very temporarily—another bridge across this stretch of the river between the Tyne and Millennium bridges. In the summer of 2008, the Bambuco Bridge, constructed entirely out of bamboo, was built here for the NewcastleGateshead initiative's SummerTyne Festival. This eighth bridge between Newcastle and Gateshead was actually an art installation that couldn't be crossed (other than by its creators with climbing equipment). The Bambuco Bridge was made from 20 tonnes of sustainable bamboo strung between two 25-metre-tall towers. It was lit up for its opening with 400 blazing firepots, which were illuminated by daring riggers who were suspended more than 80 feet above the river in a throwback to the bravery of the Tyne Bridge builders—but with added safety ropes and helmets.[13]

On the north side of the Quayside promenade, running up into Newcastle, are a series of chares—Trinity Chare, Broad Chare, Cox Chare—which are a particular North-East type of narrow alleyway that once ran from wooden jetties in the river. The Grade II-listed John Wesley Memorial Fountain is further towards the Millennium Bridge, opposite the Law Courts. Right next to the Millennium Bridge is a much more modern monument, the bronze River God by André Wallace, erected in 1996. There are several other art-works in this area, including, just beyond the Millennium Bridge, the Swirle Pavillion and the Blacksmith's Needle. Looking back up the river from this point, it's possible to get a good sense of the scale of the Tyne Bridge as it rises from the depths of the river's gorge.

* * *

Across the Millennium Bridge in Gateshead, the Baltic Centre for Contemporary Art has an external terrace and an indoor viewing box with excellent views of the Tyne Bridge and its riverscape. During the summer, the external terrace also provides close-up views of nesting kittiwakes on the building's north face. The curved glass frontage of the Sage Gateshead also offers unique views. (The Sage is perhaps to the Tyne Bridge as the Opera House is to the Sydney Harbour Bridge.) To the west of the Sage, St Mary's Church is now a heritage centre. And behind St Mary's is Church Walk, another prime viewing spot for the bridge. Church Walk also has an inscription stone for some embedded boulders that were flung at the church by the explosion during the Great Fire. Down at the bottom of Church Walk, at the foot of the bridge's south tower, is the plaque marking the site of Wilson's worsted factory, where the fire started. Like the north tower, the south tower is an art deco monu-ment that, in spring and summer months, is alive with the sound and flutter of nesting kittiwakes.

At the time of writing, a new £300m entertainment arena, con-ference centre and hotel complex is under construction between the Baltic and the Sage Gateshead.[14] Over on the Newcastle Quayside, a £100m Ferris observation wheel, the "Whey Aye Wheel", is planned for the former site of the Spillers flour mill near Ouseburn. The 460-foot wheel, which would be the tallest in Europe, has faced multiple delays and opposition from protestors who think it will be a very big blot on the Tyne's riverscape.[15]

Sadly, at the time of writing in 2022, the arch, the towers and the approaches of the Tyne Bridge were in desperate need of atten-tion. The paint was faded and blistered, entire panels were rusted brown, and a lack of lighting rendered the bridge almost invisible at night. There were graffiti tags and streaks of white droppings on the

186

steelwork, and the stonework was grubby and stained. There were concerns about the bridge's structural integrity, too. Up close, the handsome old icon was in dire condition. As the Tyne Bridge approached its 100th birthday, it looked every day of its age.

Seeing the dreadful state of the Tyne Bridge during the 2021 Great North Run inspired folk singer and actor Jamie Brown to write a song about it. "There's an unapologetic sentimentality and pride that most Tynesiders associate with the Tyne Bridge, and never more so than when it is teeming with runners during the Great North Run," says Brown. "In 2021, that sense of pride in the Tyne Bridge had been replaced with a sense of sadness at its state—bare metal, scabbed paint and rust, there for all to see."[16] After the race, Brown wrote and recorded *The Bonny Tyne Bridge* (a spin on the old Tyneside music hall song *The Bonny Gateshead Lass*), and it was soon picked up by local media. It celebrates *"the bonniest looking bridge that ever stood upon the Tyne"* but laments its deterioration: *"They used to say that it's iconic, but noo that soonds ironic; Though the shadow of former glories seems befitting of the time."*[17]

Newcastle Central MP Chi Onwurah raised the plight of the bridge in Parliament and called for it to be restored. Onwurah says the Tyne Bridge is much more than just a vital part of the region's transport infrastructure. "It is a symbol of North-East confidence, pride and achievement," she says. "The Tyne Bridge reflects the great engineering achievements of the North-East over the past century, and the aspirations of the people of the North-East." Praising its builders and designers, Onwurah (formerly a chartered engineer) paid particular tribute to Dorothy Buchanan, the pioneering civil engineer who produced calculations for the bridge. "She was a real trailblazer for women in engineering," says Onwurah.[18]

A further bid for funds was submitted in March 2022, and the councils also made listed building planning applications to restore the bridge and its towers.[19] Then, in June 2022, the government announced that the funding would be provided to refurbish the Tyne Bridge and the Central Motorway. The government would provide £35.3m of the £41.4m required, with the remainder contributed by Newcastle and Gateshead councils. It was expected that the work on the bridge could be completed within two years.[20] (The work would be carefully managed to avoid disruption to the kittiwake colony.) Tyneside was eager to see the Tyne Bridge restored to its proper condition—to a *bonny fettle*.

George Caulkin sees the bridge as emblematic of Tyneside and Newcastle. "In terms of truly iconic structures, I guess the city has two; St James' Park and the bridge," he says. "Both stand for home, and so they also stand for love." Caulkin is very fond of the Tyne Bridge kittiwakes. "The bridge marks the changing of the seasons for me," he says. "The arrival of the kittiwakes and their nests, the squawk, the astringent smell, is the sight and sound of spring. It's a joyous bedlam. Their slow departure is the opposite; a sad draining and the knowledge that winter is heading towards us."[21]

Musician Steve Luck, who composed the track *Steel Bridge* as a tribute to the bridge workers, says the Tyne Bridge has been an important landmark for him throughout his life, from gazing up at it during childhood visits to the Quayside Sunday Market through to running over it during the Great North Run—just as the Red Arrows flew in formation overhead. "It's an iconic symbol of the North-East," he says. "Every time I have been away from home, the sight of the green arch makes me feel proud to be a Geordie."[22]

Ben Holland is an artist who makes drawings and prints of North-East icons. The Tyne Bridge features prominently in his work, which he regularly sells from a stall at the Quayside Market. Holland is originally from the North-West but has lived in Newcastle for more than 20 years. He says the Tyne Bridge has played an important role in his life over that time: "I've drawn it numerous times, run over it with thousands of others for the Great North Run, watched on as a Fathers for Justice campaigner climbed up it, and seen just about every weather system imaginable pass by as I've sat in its shadow on a market stall every Sunday."[23]

The Newcastle *Chronicle* often publishes articles about the Tyne Bridge (and its predecessors), many of them written by the paper's nostalgia editor, Dave Morton. Those articles always do well, Morton says, and there's a lot of interest in the current and earlier bridges. "The Tyne Bridge has been an ever-present in our lives, representing permanence and strength," he says, "and without doubt, it's the most widely recognised physical symbol of our proud region." He remembers, as a child growing up on Tyneside, marvelling at the size and shape of the giant arch. "Later in life," he says, "crossing back into Newcastle on the train—from university, working down south, football awaydays, holidays—I knew I was home the moment I set eyes on it, and I felt a certain pride."[24]

Andrew Hankinson is the Newcastle-born journalist and author of *You Could Do Something Amazing with Your Life [You Are Raoul Moat]*. "When I was young, before I'd seen much of the world, it felt like Newcastle was the centre of everything, and the Tyne Bridge seemed huge and famous," he says. "Then I started to visit more places, and it made me reassess what I had thought to be true. My home city didn't feel as significant anymore. The bridge did not seem so big. People around the world did not know it, they did not have feelings about it. I realised it mattered to relatively few of us, and though it felt smaller, my feelings for it became stronger. It started to signify home."[25]

That feeling of a sign of home is echoed by Michael Chaplin, the theatre, radio and TV writer and the author of the memoir *Newcastle United Stole My Heart*. Raised in Newcastle, Chaplin has often worked and lived away from Tyneside, and he values the welcoming sight of the bridge. "Returning to the city on the train from London," he says, "you wait in anticipation as the great gorge of the Tyne opens up—and then suddenly it's there! The great arch of the Tyne Bridge, wreathed in mist or twinkling in the sun, the powerful symbol of blood, belonging and home."[26]

* * *

Standing at the midpoint of the bridge, blocking out the constant rumble of traffic, it's possible to gaze up at crossbeams and chords and the ribs of the arch, to place hands on steel panels and run fingers over rivets. Every one of those rivets stands for the industrial history and heritage of Tyneside. You can peer across at the other bridges, look up to the Keep and the spires, and gaze down at the quaysides and the flowing Tyne. The river has been revitalised, and the Tyne Bridge stands over it as a reminder of what it once was and as a symbol of what it has become.

Here on the railing is the plaque commemorating the opening of the bridge on 10 October 1928 by King George V, dedicated by Mayors Easten and Wardill. On the opposite side of the carriageway is the plaque for the constructors—Newcastle and Gateshead Councils, Dorman Long, Mott, Hay & Anderson, R. Burns Dick. There is no mention here of Thomas Webster or Ralph Freeman or Dorothy Buchanan, James Ruck or John Carr, Nathaniel Collins or Frank McCoy or Norman Muller, George Wilson or Jimmy Ransom or Kit Lattimer or the hundreds of others who toiled on the bridge. No mention of the men (and woman) who made the drawings and calculations, who supervised the project, who went down in the caissons, who scaled the arch. It's a testimony to their work and a tribute to all of them that the bridge they built is still standing and still so important to Tyneside. We cannot know what any of them would have thought of the bridge as it approaches its 100th birthday. There is no one left alive who built the bridge. Still, many of us retain a close connection to it, perhaps because we are descendants of the builders, because the bridge has played an important role in our families' histories, or because it continues to be an ever-present in the lives we live today.

Ian Hardie's great grandfather Thomas McCullough was a plater who worked on the Tyne Bridge—and narrowly escaped disaster. "He could draw or make anything, steel or wood," says Hardie. "He talked of riveting and finishing. He was literate and could read drawings, so I assume he was a lead worker." One day, while working on the arch, McCullough fell 30 feet onto a wooden scaffolding deck. He survived but bore a permanent reminder. "He had a flat back to his skull, which my great grandmother said was a result of the accident," says Hardie. "There were no ropes or safety gear, they wore caps, and that was it!" McCullough wore his best suit to the royal opening in 1928 and was presented with a commemorative medal by King George. When he died in 1991, McCullough was buried in his best suit with the medal in the breast pocket.[27]

Christine Hutchinson's maternal grandfather James Thompson was a painter on the bridge. He and his wife Jane lived on Dog Bank, near All Saints Church. Tragically, the Thompsons' two-year-old daughter Isabella became seriously ill and died on 9 October 1928—the day before the grand opening. The family could not afford to call out a doctor, and Isabella died at a workhouse infirmary of whooping cough and pneumonia. Despite this tragedy, James and Jane Thompson attended the opening ceremony with their other daughter, Phyllis, in their arms. Phyllis, Christine Hutchinson's mother, was just three months old. "Perhaps she was the youngest person to attend the ceremony," says Hutchinson.[28]

David Simmons also has a poignant connection to the Tyne Bridge. His late mother was born on the day of the opening, 10 October 1928. "In fact, the doctor who delivered her was called away from the ceremony," he says. "He said to my grandma, you should really call this child Bridget." Instead, they called her Edna. And because of her birthdate, whenever the bridge celebrates an anniversary, Simmons knows that his mother would have been that age as well. In 1988, on the Tyne Bridge's 60th anniversary and for Edna's 60th birthday, Simmons booked a Rolls Royce to drive her over the bridge and on to a party. And when the bridge celebrates its 100th birthday, he reflects, "I will know exactly how old my mother would have been".[29]

For ex-pat Geordie Mike Watson, the bridge represents a connection to Tyneside and to grandparents he never knew. His granda George Watson was a bricklayer who worked on the bridge (and perhaps left his brickie's "monkey" hod in the doorway while drinking in the Monkey Bar). His grandma Maud ran Maud's Florists in the Grainger Market. "I never knew them," Watson says, "but I always visit the bridge and the market when I'm in Newcastle and think about them."[30] Emma Jane Stanley's great grandad was a joiner who worked on both the *Titanic* and *Olympic* in Belfast, and later worked on the Tyne Bridge after moving to Newcastle.[31] And Derek Richardson's granda John Morgan was a veteran of the Somme who went on to help build the Tyne Bridge. Morgan was one of the first workers to cross over the top of the bridge after the arch was closed.[32]

Victoria Parkinson is the great-granddaughter of John Carr, the boatman employed by Dorman Long to rescue fallen men from the river. Although he was not able to save the life of Nathaniel Collins, Carr's fifty-seven rescues make him one of the great heroes of the Tyne. "I feel so very proud of John," says Parkinson. "He was a man with very little in terms of money, but he clearly was a very good person. I feel his story has been lost somewhat, although I always think about him when I go down to the Quayside, and I have been sure to pass on what I know about him to my own children. I am so glad he is being celebrated in some small way, along with the brave men who built the bridge—and Nathaniel, of course."[33]

It's easy to see why those with a personal connection are so proud of the Tyne Bridge, but that sense of pride—that heart-swelling pleasure and satisfaction—stretches deep and wide across much of the population of Tyneside. The Tyne Bridge makes Geordies burst with pride because it's so indelibly representative of the whole region. This is a place of bridges, but also of other great structures, storied histories, industrial grit, natural beauty, famous institutions, brilliant pioneers, important inventions, sporting achievements, bestselling authors, distinguished artists, music legends, movie stars, telly classics, proper dialect, rude comics, brown ale, sausage rolls. Tyneside has much to be proud of:

The High Level Bridge, the Swing Bridge, the Millennium Bridge, the Angel of the North, the Sage, the Baltic, the Castle Keep, the Cathedral of St Nicholas, St James' Park, *Howay the Lads*, Alan Shearer, Gazza, Newcastle Brown Ale, the Blue Star, the Blue Stone, Grey's Monument, Grey Street, the Tyne & Wear Metro, the Boat, the Bigg Market, *Viz*, Lindisfarne, *Fog on the Tyne*, Geordie Ridley, *The Blaydon Races*, Brendan Foster, the Great North Run, Mark Knopfler, *Local Hero*, Sting, Jimmy Nail, *Spender*, Tim Healy, Kevin Whatley, *Auf Wiedersehen, Pet*, Ian La Frenais, Terry Collier, Bob Ferris, *Whatever Happened to the Likely Lads?*, Ant McPartlin, Declan Donnelly, Spuggy, *Byker Grove*, Sam Fender, Cheryl, Jade Thirlwall, Perrie Edwards, Vicky Pattison, *Geordie Shore*, *Geordie Racer*, stottie cakes, pease pudding, Greggs, Fenwick's, Barbour, *Whey aye man*, Catherine Cookson, George Stephenson, Robert Stephenson, William Armstrong, Charles Parsons, *Rocket*, *Turbinia*, *Mauretania*, Cuthbert Collingwood, John Collingwood Bruce, James Wilson Carmichael, Thomas Bewick, Bessie Surtees, Brian Johnson, Neil Tennant, Hank Marvin, Eric Burdon, Chas Chandler, The Animals, Busker, *Home Newcastle*, Stan Laurel, Ross Noble, Sarah Millican, Chris Ramsey, Rosie Ramsey, Ridley Scott, Robson Green, Jill Halfpenny, Charlie Hunnam, Charlie Hardwick, Andrea Riseborough, Denise Welch, Peter Flannery, *Our Friends in the North*, *Get Carter*, Lee Hall, Alan Plater, David Almond, Jack Common, Kevin Keegan (honorary Geordie), Sir Bobby Robson, Jackie Milburn, Colin Veitch, Peter Beardsley, Shola Ameobi, Jossy Blair, Michael the Geordie, Clarence the Angel, Peter Higgs, Basil Hume, Basil Bunting, Mike Neville, Kathy Secker, Jimmy Forsyth,

Tish Murtha, David Olusoga, Brian Redhead, Miriam Stoppard, Mary Midgley, Lucozade, Domestos, lightbulbs, windscreen wipers, the offside trap, the Strawberry, the Crown Posada, the Old George, Ambrose Crowley, Tommy Ferens, Ronnie Gill, Alan Robson, the Metrocentre, Eldon Square, Old Eldon Square, Grainger Market, Richard Grainger, John Dobson, John Clayton, the Theatre Royal, Tyneside Cinema, the Lit & Phil, Newcastle Central Library, Newcastle Central Station, Leazes Terrace, Leazes Park, Saltwell Park, the Town Moor, WT Stead, Joseph Cowen Senior, Joseph Cowen Junior, Harry Clasper, James Renforth, Robert Chambers, Stephen Miller, Mike McLeod, Gateshead Stadium, Gateshead FC, Newcastle Falcons, Newcastle Eagles, kittiwakes, vampire rabbits, All Saints Church, St Mary's Church, Newcastle University, Northumbria University, Northumberland Street, the Chinatown Archway, the Roman altars, Segedunum, Hadrian's Wall, the Old Town Walls, *Fortiter Defendit Triumphans*, the River Tyne... and the famous icon that stands above them all: the steel arch, the granite towers, the monument to industry, the signpost for home, the symbol of Tyneside, the icon of the North-East, "*Wor* Bridge"; the Tyne Bridge.

NOTES

EPIGRAPH

1. Busker, *Home Newcastle* (Ronnie Lambert, Wildfire Music, 1981). Lyric reproduced with kind permission of Hazel Lambert.

INTRODUCTION

1. The Tyne Bridge links the city of Newcastle upon Tyne and the town of Gateshead over the River Tyne in the conurbation known as Tyneside in the North-East of England. The Tyne Bridge is most often associated with Newcastle, which is slightly unfair considering half of it is in Gateshead. Inevitably, the larger and more high-profile Newcastle receives more mentions than Gateshead does in this book. No cross-river bias is intended.
2. There are seven bridges over the Tyne between Newcastle and Gateshead. From east to west: the Gateshead Millennium Bridge; the Tyne Bridge; the Swing Bridge; the High Level Bridge; the Queen Elizabeth II Metro Bridge; the King Edward VII Railway Bridge; and the Redheugh Bridge. (Further west: the Scotswood Bridge; the Scotswood Railway Bridge (disused); Blaydon Bridge; and Newburn Bridge. These cross between Scotswood and Newburn, which are districts of Newcastle, and Blaydon, which is in the Metropolitan Borough of Gateshead but not in the town of Gateshead.
3. David Anderson, "Anderson on the Tyne Bridge", *Minutes of the Proceedings of the Institution of Civil Engineers*, Volume 230, 1930, pp. 167–188 and plates.
4. Relative values calculator, Measuring Worth, www.measuringworth. com/calculators/ukcompare
5. *Observer Literary Supplement*, 23 November 1930.

1. PONS AELIUS

1. J. Collingwood Bruce, "The Three Bridges Over the Tyne at Newcastle", read April 1872, published in *Archaeologia Aeliana*, 2nd Series, Vol. 10, 1885, pp. 1–11. (Also see *Old Tyne Bridge*, Newcastle *Journal*, 2 May,

1872.) Bruce calls the Roman bridge and settlement at Newcastle *Pons Aelii*, which some historians still prefer, but most sources call it *Pons Aelius*.

2. The River Tyne is formed by the confluence of the North Tyne and the South Tyne. The source of the North Tyne is in a field near Deadwater and Peel Fell in Northumberland, a few hundred yards south of the Scottish border. The source of the South Tyne is a North Pennine spring at Garrigale, Alston Moor in Cumbria. The confluence is at Warden, near Hexham in Northumberland. (Steve Ellwood, *River Tyne*, Amberley Publishing, 2015; "Get to Know Your Rivers", *River Factfiles: The Tyne Catchment*, Environment Agency, undated).

3. Gainsford Bruce, *The Life and Letters of John Collingwood Bruce*, Edinburgh & London: William Blackwood and Sons, 1905, p. vii.

4. At 73 miles long, Hadrian's Wall is the same length as the full River Tyne when followed from either of its North and South Tyne source points. The North and South Tyne are each 38 miles long, and the main body of the Tyne is 35 miles long ("Get to Know Your Rivers", undated).

5. D.J. Smith, *Museum of Antiquities, Newcastle upon Tyne: An Illustrated Introduction*, Department of Archaeology, University of Newcastle upon Tyne, 1974, p. 27.

6. Bruce, *Life and Letters*, 1905, p. 157.

7. "The Life of Hadrian", *Historia Augusta* (*Historiae Augustae*), vol. 10, no. 2, Loeb Classical Library, Cambridge, MA: Harvard University Press, 1921. John Speed wrote that the wall was built to "defend the incursions of the wilder Britons and ill neighbours that daily molested the peace of the Romans". (John Speed, *The History of Great Britaine*, William Hall and John Beale, 1611.)

8. Another Pons Aelius, known as the Ponte Sant'Angelo in its modern form, was completed over the Tiber in Rome in 134.

9. Bruce, *Three Bridges*, 1885, p. 1.

10. George Chambers, *Caledonia, Or An Account, Historical and Topical, of North-Britain*, London: T Cadell and W Davies, 1807, p. 49; John Phillips, *The Rivers, Mountains and Sea-Coast of Yorkshire*, London: John Murray, 1853, p. 200.

11. Bruce, *Three Bridges*, 1885, p. 2.

12. J. Collingwood Bruce, *The Roman Wall*, 2nd ed, London: John Russell Smith, 1853, pps. 96, 98.

13. Today, a line of cobblestones set into the ground near the Keep marks the supposed outline of the settlement, and what is thought to be a small section of the stone fort can be seen under a nearby railway arch.

14. Bruce, *Roman Wall*, 1853, p. 96.

15. P.T. Bidwell & N. Holbrook, *Hadrian's Wall Bridges*, London: English Heritage, 1989, p. 100, fig 72.

16. Ibid, p. 100. "It must be concluded that no definite remains of the Roman bridge have ever been seen."

17. Bruce, *Roman Wall*, 1853, p. 102.

18. Ibid, p. 102.

19. "Roman Altar Found Near the Tyne Bridge", *Tiverton Gazette*, 3 August 1875, and R.G. Collingwood & R.P. Wright, *The Roman Inscriptions of Britain*, Oxford: Clarendon Press, 1965.

20. "Roman Britain in 1903", *Milgavie and Bearsden Herald*, 19 January, 1904.

21. Although the altars appear in their present form as naturally-coloured stone, traces of paint indicate they were originally brightly coloured. ("Roman Britain in Colour", Great North Museum: Hancock, https:// greatnorthmuseum.org.uk/whats-on/roman-britain-in-colour).

22. Bruce, *Life and Letters*, 1905, p. 383.

23. "Cathedral of St Nicholas", Historic England, https://historicengland. org.uk/listing/the-list/list-entry/1355309

24. J. Collingwood Bruce, *Hand-Book to Newcastle-on-Tine* [sic] London: Longmans, Green & Co and Newcastle upon Tyne: Andrew Reid, 1863.

25. *Vita Oswini*, Surtees Society, 1838.

26. The also-surviving Black Gate, the castle's fortified entrance, was built around 75 years later, in the reign of Henry III. Construction of the Town Walls began around 1265.

27. Rev J.A. Giles (translator), *Matthew [of] Paris's English History: From the Year 1235 to 1273*, Vol 2, London: Henry G. Bohn, 1853, p. 278.

2. THE OLD TYNE BRIDGE

1. James Clephan, "Old Tyne Bridge and its Story", *Archaeologia Aeliana*, Volume 12, 1887, pp. 135–147.

2. Ibid.

3. John Smeaton, "Report of John Smeaton, Engineer, Upon the State of that Part of the Tyne Bridge Belonging to the Town of Newcastle (1771)", *Reports of the Late John Smeaton*, Vol II, London: M Taylor, 1837, p. 315.

4. John Leland, Lucy Toulmin Smith (ed), *The Itinerary of John Leland in Or About the Years 1535–1543*, London: G Bell, 1910, p. 126.

5. John Nichols, *The Progresses, Processions, and Magnificent Festivities, of King James the First...*, London: JB Nichols, 1828, p. 70.

6. William Grey, *Chorographia, Or a Survey of Newcastle upon Tyne* [sic], Printed by S.B., Newcastle, 1649, p. 38.

7. Celia Fiennes, *Through England on a Side Saddle, 1698 Tour of England*, London: Field & Tuer, Leadenhall Press, 1888, p. 178.

8. Henry Bourne, *History of Newcastle upon Tyne*, Newcastle: John White, 1736, p. 130.

9. The statue of Charles II survived and was relocated to the stairwell of Newcastle's Guildhall.

10. The carving of the Newcastle coat of arms also survived (along with a carving of the coat of arms of the Prince Bishop of Durham, which had adorned the Drawbridge Tower). It was removed during the demolition of the ruins of the Old Tyne Bridge to a garden wall and then a delivery yard, both on Pilgrim Street. By the 1970s, following the redevelopment of Pilgrim Street, it was held in the Castle Keep. ("Old Tyne Bridge Relics", *Newcastle Chronicle*, 22 May 1888; Percy Corder, "Notes on Two Sculptured Panels...", *Proceedings of the Society of Antiquaries of Newcastle-upon-Tyne*, Third Series, Vol 1, Jan 1903 to Dec 1904, R. Simpson & Sons, 1905, pp. 147–149.)

11. Dan Jackson, *The Northumbrians: North-East England and Its People*, London: C. Hurst & Co, 2019, p. 33. Wallace was hated on Tyneside for his brutal invasion of Northumberland, during which he burned the villages of Corbridge, Wylam and Ryton along the Tyne, causing women and children to be evacuated to the relative safety of walled Newcastle.

12. Richard Welford, "Francis Anderson: The Story of the Fish and the Ring", *Monthly Chronicle of North County Lore and Legend*, vol. 1, no. 6, August 1887, pp. 243–244.

13. "The Tower on the Bridge", *Monthly Chronicle of North County Lore and Legend*, June 1887, p. 181; William Hylton Dyer Longstaffe, *Memoirs of the Life of Mr Ambrose Barnes*, Durham: Andrews & Co, 1867.

14. *Gephyrologia: Or Historical Account of Bridges, Ancient and Modern*, unknown publisher, 1751, quoted in Clephan, "Old Tyne Bridge and its Story", 1887. The Old London Bridge was visually similar to the Old Tyne Bridge but was around three times longer with many more buildings.

15. Daniel Defoe (as "A Gentleman"), *A Tour Thro' the Whole Island of Great Britain*, Vol III, London: G Strahan, 1727, p. 191.

16. Eneas Mackenzie, *A Descriptive and Historical Account of the Town and County of Newcastle upon Tyne*, Newcastle upon Tyne: Mackenzie and Dent, 1827.

17. "Bookselling on the Tyne", *The Bookseller*, 4 January 1871.

18. Mackenzie, *A Descriptive and Historical Account...*, 1827.

19. Bourne, *History of Newcastle*, 1736, p. 158.

20. Thomas Pennant, *A Tour in Scotland*, London: Benjamin White, 1776.

21. James Clephan, "A Romance of the Tyne Bridge: The Story of Dr Oliphant", *Monthly Chronicle*, July 1887, pp. 202–206.

22. James Oliphant, *The Case of Mr James Oliphant, Surgeon...*, B. Fleming, 1768.

23. *An Account of the Great Floods in 1771 and 1815...*, Emerson Charnley, 1818. Variously attributed to both William Garret and John Bell, it is thought the original account of the 1771 Great Flood was written by the Rev. Isaac Farrer, the curate of Eggleston.

24. John Smeaton & John Wooler, *A Report Relative to the Tyne Bridge*, Newcastle upon Tyne: Thomas Saint, 1772, p. 1.

25. "A Contemporary Account of the Fall of the Tyne Bridge", *Monthly Chronicle*, July 1887, pp. 206–207.

26. *Newcastle Chronicle*, 30 November 1771; James Clephan, "Chronicles of the Tyne Bridge No III", *Newcastle Chronicle*, 20 April 1867. Some sources use the spelling "Weatherley", but an advertisement placed by the shoemaker in the *Newcastle Chronicle*, 11 January 1772, uses the spelling "Weatherly".

27. Alexander Carlyle, *Autobiography of the Rev Alexander Carlyle*, Edinburgh and London: William Blackwood & Sons, 1860.

28. *An Account of the Great Floods*, 1818, p. 1.

29. John Sykes, *Local Records; or Historical Register of Remarkable Events…*, Newcastle upon Tyne: John Sykes, 1824, p. 127.

30. Smeaton & Wooler, *A Report Relative to the Tyne Bridge*, 1772, p. 5.

31. James Clephan, "Chronicles of the Tyne Bridge No V", *Newcastle Chronicle*, 4 May 1867. Clephan suggests the skeleton and coffin were found separately, but a report from the time states workmen found "the remains of a human body in a stone coffin". (*Newcastle Chronicle*, 8 July 1775). The original account of the finding of the scroll was in the *Newcastle Courant*, 25 January 1772.

32. *Newcastle Chronicle*, 11 January 1772.

33. James Clephan, "Old Tyne Bridge and Its Cellars", *Archaeologia Aeliana*, Vol IX, 1883, p. 237.

34. *Newcastle Chronicle*, 9 June, 1887.

35. *Newcastle Chronicle*, 27 June 1887.

36. *Newcastle Chronicle*, 28 May 1887.

3. A PLACE OF BRIDGES

1. "Tommy on the Bridge", *Newcastle Chronicle*, 12 June 1866 and 4 January 1907; "North Country Wit & Humour", *Monthly Chronicle*, December 1889, p. 566.

2. Mackenzie, *A Descriptive and Historical Account…*, 1827, p. 214. The balustrades had an unpleasant effect, particularly in winter when bridge passengers found them to be "a very inconvenient and injudicious kind of ornament" that caused them to be "attacked at every opening by a disagreeably violent gust of wind".

3. *Newcastle Chronicle*, 20 April 1889.

4. Translation: "Well Tommy, I'm very pleased to see you've got an inside job." After visiting the waxworks, the pitman crossed the Swing Bridge, where he was surprised to encounter the real Tommy, and shouted, *"Whaat! Oot already? Wey, ye greet slavering cull, ye must be daft te leave yon*

inside job for his caad yen!" ("What! Out already? Well you big dribbling fool, you must be foolish to leave your inside job for this cold one!") ("Local Anecdotes", *Newcastle Chronicle*, 12 October 1889; "North Country Wit & Humour", *Monthly Chronicle*, December 1889, p. 571).

5. Ralph Beilby, plan of the temporary Tyne Bridge, c.1772, found inside Smeaton & Wooler, 1772.

6. *Newcastle Courant*, 29 April 1775.

7. *Newcastle Courant*, 18 September 1779.

8. *Newcastle Chronicle*, 11 September 1779.

9. *Newcastle Courant*, 2 October 1779.

10. Mackenzie, *A Descriptive and Historical Account...*, 1827, p. 214.

11. Moses Aaron Richardson, *The Local Historian's Table Book*, Newcastle upon Tyne: M.A. Richardson, 1844, pp. 153–155.

12. *Tyne Mercury*, 22 January, 1828.

13. Other famous Tyneside rowers of the era included James Renforth and Robert Chambers, both world champions.

14. "Great Boat Race on the Tyne", *Newcastle Journal*, 29 November 1845.

15. *Tyne Mercury*, reprinted in *Carlisle Journal*, 18 January 1845.

16. In the views of William Gladstone, John Betjeman and listeners of BBC Radio 4. (David Morton, "Newcastle's Grey Street: Built in the 1830s and the Finest in the City", *Newcastle Chronicle*, 14 October 2015).

17. *Gateshead Observer*, 25 November 1854. Gateshead was made a municipal borough in 1835 (and a county borough in 1889).

18. "High Level Bridge", Historic England, https://historicengland.org.uk/listing/the-list/list-entry/1248568

19. David McCullough, *The Great Bridge*, New York: Touchstone, 1972, pp. 166–167.

20. "Marvellous Escape from Death", *London Daily News*, 6 August 1849.

21. *Newcastle Journal*, 25 August 1849.

22. "Arrival at Newcastle", *Illustrated London News*, 6 October 1849.

23. *Tyne Mercury*, 5 October 1850.

24. *Illustrated London News*, 14 October 1854; *An Account of the Great Fire and Explosion*, Newcastle upon Tyne: M. and M.W. Lambert, 1854; James Rewcastle, *A Record of the Great Fire in Newcastle and Gateshead*, George Routledge, 1855.

25. Frank Manders & Richard Potts, *Crossing the Tyne*, Newcastle upon Tyne: Tyne Bridge Publishing, 2001, p. 50.

26. "Tyne Bridge", *Newcastle Chronicle*, 13 August 1864.

27. *Gateshead Observer*, 5 June 1854.

28. "Tyne Bridge", *Newcastle Chronicle*, 20 December 1864.

29. *Newcastle Chronicle*, 18 September 1866.

30. *Shields Gazette*, 9 January 1871.

31. "The Old Tyne Bridge Blue Stone", *Newcastle Chronicle*, 2 December 1887.
32. *Newcastle Journal*, 2 May 1872.
33. "Swing Bridge over River Tyne", Historic England, https://historiceng-land.org.uk/listing/the-list/list-entry/1390930. Although originally operated by hydraulics, the Swing Bridge's steam pumps were replaced with electrics in 1959. During the 2020s, around £1m was spent on the Swing Bridge's upkeep. However, at a proposed reopening in August 2021, the bridge mechanism failed. The Swing Bridge was no longer swinging.
34. *Shields Daily News*, 16 June 1876.
35. Translation: "Ah, dears, the works of god are wonderful, but the works of man are far more so!" *Berwickshire News*, 29 August 1876.
36. "The New Hydraulic Swing Bridge over the Tyne", *Newcastle Chronicle*, 16 June 1876.
37. "Tommy o' the Bridge", *Newcastle Chronicle*, 13 January 1887.
38. "Tommy on the Bridge", *Newcastle Chronicle*, 20 April 1889.
39. Thomas Allan, *Allan's Illustrated Edition of Tyneside Songs and Readings*, Newcastle upon Tyne: Thomas & George Allan, 1891. Translation: "Two and a half pence out of all the hundreds of folks that have gone over the bridge."
40. "Tommy on the Bridge", *Newcastle Chronicle*, 19 April 1889; 22 April 1889.
41. Allan, *Allan's Illustrated Edition...*, 1891. Translations: "petition the Corporation to get the bridge altered" and "making a living".
42. "Tommy on the Bridge at Court", *Newcastle Chronicle*, 7 May 1906.
43. "King Edward Railway Bridge", Historic England, https://historiceng-land.org.uk/listing/the-list/list-entry/1242100
44. *Newcastle Chronicle*, 4 January 1907.

4. A NEW TYNE BRIDGE

1. *Newcastle Journal*, 9 September 1922 and "Trans-Tyne Traffic Problem", *Newcastle Chronicle*, 12 September 1922.
2. Armstrong's works merged with the engineering firm of Joseph Whitworth in 1897 to form Armstrong Whitworth. Sir William Armstrong died in 1900.
3. *Newcastle Journal*, 5 September 1918.
4. *Newcastle Chronicle*, 12 September 1922.
5. "Proposed New Bridge Across the Tyne", *Newcastle Chronicle*, 28 July 1883.
6. "Proposed New Tyne Bridge", *Newcastle Chronicle*, 13 July 1892.
7. "The Proposed New High Level Bridge", *Newcastle Chronicle*, 3 August 1899.

8. "Genesis of Undertaking", *Newcastle Journal*, 9 October, 1928.

9. "The Proposed New Tyne Bridge", *Newcastle Chronicle*, 14 September 1899.

10. Newcastle upon Tyne & Gateshead total populations, A Vision of Britain Through Time, www.visionofbritain.org.uk

11. "HC Deb 09 August 1920 vol 133 c12", *Hansard*, 9 August 1920, https://api.parliament.uk/historic-hansard/commons/1920/aug/09/newcastle-on-tyne

12. "HC Deb 12 December 1922 vol 159 cc2855–91", *Hansard*, 12 December 1922, https://api.parliament.uk/historic-hansard/commons/1922/dec/12/unclassified-services-2

13. "Discussion on Bridges", *Minutes of the Proceedings of the Institution of Civil Engineers*, vol. 230, no. 1930, 1930, pp. 189–194.

14. "Tyne Bridge No 2 From Mr Webster", *Newcastle Chronicle*, 27 April 1961.

15. *Newcastle Chronicle*, 12 September 1922.

16. "Trans-Tyne Traffic", *Newcastle Chronicle*, 13 September 1922.

17. "Epoch in Tyne's History", *Newcastle Chronicle*, 11 January, 1923.

18. "New Bridge Needed for Tyne", *Shields Daily News*, 29 January 1923.

19. "What the Unemployed Want", *Newcastle Chronicle*, 8 February 1924.

20. "Three New Bridges and a Tunnel", *Shields Daily News*, 6 October 1923.

21. *Sunderland Echo*, 4 October 1923.

22. "Sir Stephen Easten", *Newcastle Journal*, 30 October 1936.

23. *Berwick Advertiser*, 5 October 1923.

24. *Newcastle Journal*, 30 October 1936.

25. *Berwickshire News*, 20 November 1928.

26. "North's Engineers", *Shields Daily News*, 31 January 1925.

27. *Northern Daily Mail*, 9 January 1924.

28. "New Tyne Bridge", *Shields Daily News*, 6 March 1924.

29. "Some Particulars of the New Tyne Bridge", *Shields Daily News*, 8 February 1924.

30. "Tyne Development", *Shields Daily News*, 29 October 1924.

31. "Tyne Bridge", *Shields Daily News*, 19 March 1924.

32. "Newcastle Cheers the English Cup", *Daily Mirror*, 30 April 1924.

33. "The Cup Winners", *Northern Daily Mail*, 29 April 1924.

34. "New Tyne Bridge", *Shields Daily News*, 30 April 1924.

35. *Shields Daily News*, 30 August 1924.

36. "New Tyne Bridge", *Shields Daily News*, 3 September 1924.

37. "New Bridge Borings", *Shields Daily News*, 29 October 1924.

38. Webster's new design featured arch ribs that were inclined together, which he later said would have been advantageous for the completed bridge in resisting lateral wind stresses. ("Discussion on Bridges", 1930).

5. AN INGENIOUS PLAN

1. "World's Heaviest Bridge", *New York Sun*, 21 January 1917.
2. "Great Hell Gate Bridge", *New York Sun*, 26 September 1915.
3. "Engineers Inspect Hell Gate Bridge", *Brooklyn Standard Union*, 3 November 1913.
4. "Engineers View Hell Gate Bridge", *Brooklyn Citizen*, 3 November, 1913.
5. Ralph Freeman, "The Design of a Two-hinged Spandrel-braced Steel Arch", read 9 March 1906 and published in *Minutes of the Proceedings of the Institution of Civil Engineers*, vol. 167, 1907, pp. 343–367.
6. Sir (Charles) Douglas Fox died in November 1921. Freeman became senior partner despite the continued presence of two other Foxes, Francis and Bertram. The firm became Freeman, Fox & Partners in 1938.
7. Ralph Freeman, "The Massive Main Span", *Sydney Morning Herald*, 19 March 1932.
8. "Harbour Bridge", *Sydney Morning Herald*, 11 March 1929.
9. *Sydney Morning Herald*, 19 March 1932. According to their company publications, the name of the contractor is styled "Dorman, Long & Co Ltd" or "Dorman Long".
10. "New Tyne Bridge", *Shields Daily News*, 4 December 1924.
11. Ibid.
12. "Dorman, Long & Co Ltd", *Guardian*, 18 December 1930.
13. *Sydney Morning Herald*, 19 March 1932.
14. "Great Hell Gate Bridge", *New York Sun*, 26 September 1915.
15. Anderson, "Anderson on the Tyne Bridge", 1930.
16. "Discussion on Sydney Harbour Bridge", *Minutes of the Institution of Civil Engineers*, vol. 238, 1934, pp. 402–436.
17. Crescent arch design (1905) drawing published in O.H. Ammann, "The Hell Gate Arch Bridge and Approaches…", *Transactions of the American Society of Civil Engineers*, vol. 82, no. 1, 1918, pp. 873. Calculations from this report were used by the engineers of the Tyne Bridge, as stated in Anderson, "Anderson on the Tyne Bridge", 1930. Ammann mentions the Garabit Viaduct in Cantal, France, and Maria Pia Bridge in Porto, Portugal, as pioneering examples of bridges that use crescent arches (although the decks of both run across the top of the arches rather than through them). Both bridges were designed by Gustave Eiffel, meaning there is an engineering link between the Tyne Bridge and the Eiffel Tower (and the Statue of Liberty).
18. "Discussion on Sydney Harbour Bridge", 1934.
19. Rare examples of crescent arch bridges where the deck runs through the arch include the Jerome Street Bridge near Pittsburgh in Pennsylvania and the Adomi Bridge (originally the Volta Bridge) at Atimpoku in

Ghana. The latter was built by Dorman Long and designed by Freeman, Fox & Partners during the 1950s—after the death of Ralph Freeman but perhaps inspired by his work.

20. "Discussion on Sydney Harbour Bridge", 1934. The "leap-frog" cranes used on Tyneside were not used in Sydney. Freeman said that would have been "out of the question" due to the broader width between the Sydney bridge ribs and the large expense of the cranes.
21. *Sydney Morning Herald*, 11 March 1929.
22. A case of mumps delayed Donaldson's graduation, and in the meantime her fellow Edinburgh student Elizabeth Georgeson became the first woman to obtain a degree in engineering.
23. Mike Chrimes, "Buchanan, Dorothy Donald [Dot] (1899–1985)", Oxford Dictionary of National Biography, 12 July 2018, www. oxforddnb.com
24. Institution of Civil Engineers membership records, 17 May 1927 and 4 January 1928, via Ancestry.co.uk.
25. "Home Before Career", *Shields Daily News*, 9 July, 1931.
26. *New Civil Engineer*, 6 July 1978, pp. 15–16.
27. *Shields Daily News*, 9 July 1931.
28. "New Task", *Sydney Sun*, 12 July 1931.
29. "Engineer Girl Can Cook!", *Evening News* (Queensland), 16 July 1931.
30. *Sydney Morning Herald*, 11 March 1929.
31. "A Great Scots Bridge Designer", *Dundee Courier*, 20 October 1928.
32. "North's Engineers", *Shields Daily News*, 31 January 1925.
33. As stated in Anderson, 1930, calculations were from Ammann, 1918.
34. *Dundee Courier*, 20 October 1928.
35. "Discussion on Sydney Harbour Bridge", 1934.
36. Anderson, "Anderson on the Tyne Bridge", 1930. Following Fitzmaurice's death, the firm became Coode, Wilson, Mitchell and Vaughan-Lee, although it is still credited as Coode, Fitzmaurice, Wilson & Mitchell on the 1928 erection plaque mounted at the centre of the bridge.
37. Ibid.
38. "The Unknown Architect", *Newcastle Journal*, 1 November 1982.
39. "The Bridge's Beginnings", *Newcastle Chronicle*, 6 January 1926.
40. "Who Thought of It", *Newcastle Chronicle*, 15 April 1926.
41. "The Bridge Idea", *Newcastle Chronicle*, 16 January 1926.
42. "Who Thought of It?", *Newcastle Chronicle*, 14 March 1927.
43. "Discussion on Sydney Harbour Bridge", 1934. Comparative Dimensions: Tyne Bridge: arch span 531 ft; total length 1,276 ft; weight (of steel in arch) 7,122 tons; width 56 ft. Sydney Harbour Bridge: arch span 1,650 ft; total length 3,770 ft; weight (of steel in arch) 39,000 tons; width 160 ft.

6. LAYING THE FOUNDATIONS

1. R.M. Laffan, "Notes upon the High Level Bridge at Newcastle", *Report of the Commissioners of Railways*, London: W Clowes & Sons, 1848, pp. 83–84.
2. E.F. Farrington, *Concise Description of the East River Bridge*, New York: C.D. Wynkoop, 1888, as quoted in McCullough, *The Great Bridge*, 1972.
3. McCullough, *The Great Bridge*, 1972. During Washington Roebling's absence from the Brooklyn Bridge construction site, his wife Emily Roebling took on much of the day-to-day project management. Despite his health problems, Washington lived to the age of 89 and died during the building of the Tyne Bridge in 1926.
4. Sir Thomas Oliver, "Physiology and Pathology of Work in Compressed Air", *British Medical Journal*, 30 January 1909, p. 257.
5. Anderson, "Anderson on the Tyne Bridge", 1930.
6. Passenger records show Ruck crossed the Atlantic on both the *Mauretania* (built at Swan Hunter on the Tyne) and the *Lusitania* (sunk by a U-boat in 1915, a year after Ruck's voyage).
7. "Bond of Unity", *Newcastle Journal*, 27 February 1928.
8. Jack Geddie, *The Families Geddie & McPhail*, Fort Worth: Henry L. Geddie, 1959, pp. 60–63.
9. *Newcastle Journal*, 27 February 1928. The standard atmospheric pressure at sea level is about 14.7 pounds per square inch.
10. "New High Level Bridge Across the Tyne", *Dundee Evening Telegraph*, 20 February 1925.
11. David Anderson said the abutments were founded at 59.74 feet below OD (Ordnance Datum or mean sea level) at Newcastle and 36.50 feet below OD at Gateshead. The ground level at both Newcastle and Gateshead quaysides is about 25 feet above OD. (Anderson, "Anderson on the Tyne Bridge", 1930).
12. "Gateshead End of New Bridge", *Newcastle Chronicle (North Mail)*, 8 March 1926.
13. Ibid.
14. "City's Black Spot", *Shields Daily News*, 17 December 1924.
15. "Houses in Danger", *Shields Daily News*, 6 June 1925.
16. "Improvements That May Mean Ruin", *Newcastle Chronicle*, 23 September 1926.
17. "New Bridge: Grim Work", *Shields Daily News*, 19 August 1925.
18. Ibid.
19. "North Country Notes", *Newcastle Journal*, 31 January 1928.
20. Ibid. Bottle Bank is thought to be named from the Anglo-Saxon word *botl*, meaning a place of residence. (Joseph Bosworth, "*botl*", Bosworth Toller's Anglo-Saxon Dictionary Online, https://bosworthtoller.com/40759).

21. "Old Goat Inn", *Shields Daily News*, 20 August 1925; "Gateshead, Bottle Bank, Goat Inn", TW Sitelines, www.twsitelines.info/SMR/7861

22. "Tyne Bridge Compensation", *Yorkshire Post*, 3 September 1925.

23. Ibid. Also demolished next door to Snowball's was the Moffatt Bros ironmongers and tool merchants shop, regarded as the oldest business of its type in the North.

24. "Best Shopping Street", *Newcastle Chronicle*, 7 December 1926.

25. "Symbol of Enterprise", *Newcastle Journal*, 22 October 1928.

26. "New Bridge Fatality", *Newcastle Chronicle*, 4 February 1926; "Fatal Blow on Head", *Newcastle Chronicle*, 16 February 1926. While reports from the inquiry give Frank's full name as Francis McCoy, death records show him as Franciscus McCoy. (Genealogical records).

27. "Strike's Effects", *Newcastle Chronicle*, 5 May 1926.

28. "Strikers Not Protected", *Newcastle Chronicle*, 11 May 1926.

29. "Many More Idle", *Newcastle Chronicle*, 18 May 1926.

30. "Fall From Train", *Yorkshire Post*, 10 December 1929.

31. "Durham Workman Injured", *Sunderland Echo*, 22 September 1926.

32. Anderson, "Anderson on the Tyne Bridge", 1930; "Discussion on Bridges", 1930.

33. "Sinking the Last Caisson", *Newcastle Chronicle*, 9 June 1926.

34. *Newcastle Chronicle (North Mail)*, 11 June 1926.

35. "Much-Bridged Tyne", *Newcastle Chronicle*, 11 June 1926.

36. "North's Great Exhibition", *Newcastle Chronicle*, 30 September 1926.

37. "Naming New Bridge", *Newcastle Chronicle*, 11 March 1927.

38. "Respite From Strain", *Newcastle Chronicle*, 19 November 1926.

39. Ibid.

7. BUILDING THE BRIDGE

1. "Hero Turned Thief", *Newcastle Journal*, 15 January 1927.

2. "Three Gallant Lads", *Shields Daily News*, 19 November 1925.

3. Newcastle Journal, 15 January 1927.

4. "Engineering Feat", *Shields Daily News*, 3 February 1927.

5. "New Bridge's Path", *Newcastle Chronicle*, 11 September 1926.

6. "Tyne Bridge", *Shields Daily News*, 27 April 1927.

7. "A Great Push", *Newcastle Journal*, 6 April 1927.

8. Robert's Golden Twist Tobacco ad, *Shields Daily News*, 18 May, 1927.

9. Average Weekly Wages, Hansard, 30 July 1925, https://api.parliament.uk/historic-hansard/written-answers/1925/jul/30/average-weekly-wages; National Minimum Wage, *Hansard*, 13 May 1925, https://api.parliament.uk/historic-hansard/commons/1925/may/13/national-minimum-wage; Measuring Worth, www.measuringworth.com/calculators/ppoweruk

10. Newcastle Breweries ad, *Newcastle Journal*, 25 April 1927.

11. Paul Joannou, Alan Candlish & Bill Swan, *Newcastle United: The Ultimate Record*, Newcastle: N Publishing, 2011. Hughie Gallacher was a Scottish international footballer who also played for Chelsea and Gateshead. After his football career ended, he settled in Gateshead where his life took a tragic turn. On 11 June 1957, he stepped from a footbridge over the London to Edinburgh mainline into the path of an oncoming express train. He was fifty-four years old.

12. *Newcastle Chronicle*, 24 January 1888.

13. *Newcastle Chronicle*, 8 March 1890. Bacon's studio remained at 81 Northumberland Street (at the present site of Marks & Spencer) until the area was redeveloped in the 1960s.

14. "Bond of Unity", *Newcastle Journal*, 27 February 1928.

15. "Super Bridge Builders", *Newcastle Journal*, 17 March 1927. Charles Mitchell had previously been involved in the construction of the Queen Alexandra Bridge over the River Wear. His family company, Messrs Mitchell Brothers of Glasgow, was the masonry contractor for that bridge, which was built between 1907 and 1909. ("Sunderland's High Level Bridge", *Newcastle Chronicle*, 5 July 1907).

16. "The New Tyne Bridge", *Shields Daily News*, 8 February 1927.

17. "Low-Rated City", *Newcastle Journal*, 28 May 1927.

18. Anderson, "Anderson on the Tyne Bridge", 1930. Some of the basements could have been around since the late medieval period. The oldest surviving merchant's house on Newcastle Quayside is The Cooperage, which was built in 1430. (Save the Cooperage, https://savethecooperage.com).

19. "New Tyne Bridge", *Newcastle Journal*, 22 July 1927.

20. William Edwin Wardill was a former piano teacher who was Mayor of Gateshead during five terms between 1914 and 1928.

21. "New Bridge's Opening", *Newcastle Journal*, 19 January 1928.

22. *Newcastle Journal*, 19 January 1928.

23. A section of erecting cable, manufactured by British Ropes Ltd and subsequently turned into a paperweight, can be viewed at Newcastle's Discovery Museum.

24. *Bridges: A Few Examples…*, Dorman, Long & Co Ltd, 1930.

25. "Tyne Bridge Progresses", *Newcastle Journal*, 12 January 1928.

26. "The Growth of the New Tyne Bridge", *Newcastle Journal*, 20 February 1928.

27. "Memories Span Years", *Newcastle Chronicle*, 11 October 1988.

28. "The Latest Bridge Stories", *Newcastle Journal*, 28 February 1928.

29. One former pitman was Charles Thompson, who was injured in a pit accident and unable to work. To make ends meet, he went to the bridge

and sold the workers hot tea and sandwiches. (via Thompson's grandson Edward Wealleans, online correspondence, 7 May 2022.)

30. "What Holds it Together: Fasteners & Fixings on Iconic Structures", WDS Group, https://issuu.com/wdsgroup/docs/what_holds_it_together_-_fasteners_

31. "Praise for Steel Bridge", Steve Luck Composer, https://steveluck.com/praise-for-steel-bridge

32. "Tyne Bridge Progress", *Newcastle Journal*, 12 January 1928; "Tyne Bridge Span Nearly Complete", *Newcastle Journal*, 24 February 1928.

33. "Good Times, Bad Times", BBC Press Office, www.bbc.co.uk/pressoffice/pressreleases/stories/2003/03_march/11/england_film_prog1.shtml

34. Unidentified clipping dated 12 February 1877, quoted in McCullough, *The Great Bridge*, 1972.

35. "Market Lane Hotel", Historic England, https://historicengland.org.uk/listing/the-list/list-entry/1106314

36. "monkey, n." OED Online, Oxford University Press, December 2020, (sourced from *Cassell's Encyclopaedic Dictionary*, 1885), www.oed.com/view/Entry/121265?rskey=5GcY1W

37. "Cullercoats Man Killed at Gateshead", *Newcastle Journal*, 26 October 1927.

38. *Newcastle Journal*, 12 September 1928. The George V Bridge opened on the Clyde in Glasgow in 1928, the same year as the Tyne Bridge.

39. "The New Tyne Bridge", *Newcastle Journal*, 9 December 1927.

40. "Tyne Bridge", *Shields Daily News*, 16 December, 1927.

8. CLOSING THE ARCH

1. "New Tyne Bridge", *Newcastle Journal*, 25 February 1928.

2. "Building Trades", *Newcastle Journal*, 27 February 1928.

3. *Newcastle Journal*, 5 March 1928.

4. *Newcastle Journal*, 15 February 1928.

5. "Tyne Bridge Progress", *Newcastle Journal*, 12 January 1928.

6. "Fatal Fall from New Bridge", *Newcastle Journal*, 22 February 1928.

7. "Fell 175 Feet", *Newcastle Chronicle*, 22 February 1928.

8. "Bridge Drama", *Newcastle Journal*, 20 February 1928.

9. "Fell 175 Feet", *Yorkshire Post*, 20 February 1928.

10. *Newcastle Journal*, 20 February 1928.

11. "Notes and Incidents", *Newcastle Journal*, 11 October 1928.

12. "The Tyne Bridge", *Britain's Greatest Bridges*, S1 E5, Channel 5, 18 November 2016.

13. *Newcastle Journal*, 22 February 1928.

14. *Daily Mirror*, 22 February 1928.

15. Ibid.; "Rescued 57 Persons", *Newcastle Chronicle*, 19 August 1939; *Newcastle Journal*, 20 February 1928. According to the latter source, three of the rescued persons died, not one.

16. *Newcastle Chronicle*, 19 August 1939.

17. *Newcastle Journal*, 20 February 1928.

18. *Brooklyn Daily Eagle*, 22 July 1869. John A. Roebling died of tetanus following an accident in which his foot was crushed against a dock by an arriving ferry.

19. "Second Tyne Bridge Fatality", *Newcastle Journal*, 26 June 1928.

20. "New Tyne Bridge", *Newcastle Journal*, 23 February 1928.

21. *Newcastle Journal*, 21 February 1928.

22. "Tyne Bridge Span Nearly Complete", *Newcastle Journal*, 24 February 1928.

23. "Bond of Unity", *Newcastle Journal*, 27 February 1928.

24. Ibid.

25. "New Tyne Bridge", *Newcastle Journal*, 25 February 1928.

26. *Newcastle Journal*, 27 February 1928.

27. Ibid.

28. "Origin of the Tyne Bridge", *Newcastle Journal*, 28 February 1928.

29. "To the Editor", *Newcastle Journal*, 3 March 1928.

30. T.H. Webster, *The New High-Level Bridge [at Newcastle-on-Tyne] and its Origin*, Newcastle: R. Ward and Sons, 1928 (published as a "Red Book", suggesting official significance, and available from "all newsagents" priced 6d); "Discussion on Bridges", 1930.

31. "The New Tyne Bridge and its Origins", *Newcastle Journal*, 3 March 1928. The book by Archibald Reed was *Bruce's School: with a Peep at Newcastle in the Fifties*, Walter Scott Publishing, 1903.

32. "The New Tyne Bridge", *Newcastle Journal*, 5 March 1928.

33. *Newcastle Journal*, 16 August 1928.

34. "Bridge Feat", *Newcastle Journal*, 5 March 1928.

35. Ibid.

36. "New Tyne Bridge", *Newcastle Journal*, 17 March 1928.

37. "200 Feet Above the Tyne", *Newcastle Journal*, 8 March 1928.

38. "The New Tyne Bridge", *Newcastle Journal*, 9 March, 1928.

39. *Newcastle Journal*, 10 March 1928. Full translation: "I've heard of a young girl going over the arch of the new Tyne Bridge." "Yes, girls now are doing everything. Sixty years ago they daren't have tried it." "How's that?" "The wind would have made parachutes of their clothes, and they'd have landed at Jarrow."

40. "Bridge to Health", *Newcastle Journal*, 30 March 1928.

41. "Collecting Quids for Kids", *Newcastle Journal*, 30 April 1928.

42. "Saturday's Joyous Rag Revels in Newcastle", *Newcastle Journal*, 30 April 1928. The robots were painted with swastikas—then a symbol of good-will or gratitude, and a marketing emblem for Newcastle's Lucky Cross Toffee. "Robot" had only recently entered the English language, and robots had yet to become familiar in sci-fi.

43. "Collecting Quids for Kids", *Newcastle Journal*, 30 April 1928.

44. "The King's Visit", *Newcastle Journal*, 12 May 1928.

45. *Newcastle Journal*, 30 April 1928.

46. *Northern Daily Mail*, 30 April 1928.

47. "North County Notes", *Newcastle Journal*, 12 May 1928.

48. "The Royal Visit", *Newcastle Journal*, 27 September 1928.

49. "Trinidad Lake Asphalt on New Bridge", *Newcastle Journal*, 9 October 1928. The asphalt was imported by the Limmer and Trinidad Lake Asphalt Co Ltd, which was the first company to use asphalt for road surfacing and had an office in Newcastle's Eldon Square.

50. "Strike on the New Tyne Bridge", *Newcastle Journal*, 4 October 1928.

51. Tyne Bridge Supplement, *Newcastle Journal*, 9 October 1928.

52. "Bridge Warehouse Interiors", *Newcastle Journal*, 25 April 1928.

53. "Lord Mayor and Tyne Bridge", *Newcastle Journal*, 26 April 1928.

54. Tyne Bridge Supplement, *Newcastle Journal*, 9 October 1928.

55. There are no known colour photographs of the construction of the bridge, but the different colours can be seen in an oil-on-canvas painting, "The Building of the Tyne Bridge" by Edward M. Dickey, which is held at Newcastle's Laing Art Gallery. (Art UK, https://artuk.org/discover/artworks/the-building-of-the-tyne-bridge-37039).

56. *Newcastle Journal*, 22 August 1928.

57. "Beauty and Strength", *Newcastle Journal*, 3 September 1928.

58. "Royal Visit", *Newcastle Journal*, 5 September 1928.

9. THE GRAND OPENING

1. "Impressions of the Visit", *Newcastle Journal*, 11 October 1928.

2. "Scene on Tyne Bridge", *Newcastle Journal*, 11 October 1928.

3. "Memorable Day for Tyneside", *Newcastle Journal*, 10 October 1928.

4. *Newcastle Journal*, 27 September, 8 October 1928.

5. Tyne Bridge Supplement, *Newcastle Journal*, 10 October 1928.

6. Gallaher's War Horse Tobacco ad, *Newcastle Journal*, 10 October 1928.

7. "Newcastle Business Man's Jubilee", *Newcastle Journal*, 4 January 1928; *Newcastle Journal*, 11 October 1928; *Newcastle Chronicle*, 22 April 1939.

8. Kitty Brightwell, "The Building of a Bridge", Remembering the Past, www.rememberingthepast.co.uk/memory/the-building-of-a-bridge

9. "Memories Span Years", *Newcastle Chronicle*, 11 October 1988.

10. "Features from 5NO", *Newcastle Journal*, 5 October 1928.
11. *Newcastle Journal*, 10 October 1928.
12. "The Queen's Day", *Newcastle Journal*, 11 October 1928.
13. Each child received a souvenir pamphlet from Newcastle City Council, personalised with their name, which contained the message: "To the boys and girls for whom these words are written, who have just begun their passage on the bridge of life, and who will go to and fro on the bridges of the Tyne, there is the lofty call to carry forward to future generations the progress which has brought them their own proud inheritance." (Chris Jackson, "Heaton Secondary Schools: The Beginning", Heaton History Group website, https://heatonhistorygroup.org/2018/09/04/heaton-secondary-schools-the-beginning/)
14. "King's Message of Hope", *Newcastle Journal*, 11 October 1928.
15. Kitty Brightwell, Remembering the Past, www.rememberingthepast.co.uk/memory/the-building-of-a-bridge. Newcastle United did play that afternoon, in a celebratory match against Scotland's Heart of Midlothian at St James' Park.
16. *Newcastle Journal*, 11 October 1928.
17. Ibid.
18. "King George V Makes Speech…", British Movietone YouTube channel, www.youtube.com/watch?v=DVwHaIVgDTk
19. Fiona Mackay, "Symbol in Steel", *Newcastle Journal*, 3 January 1981.
20. "Royal Visit to Tyneside", *Guardian*, 11 October 1928.
21. "Loyal Reception at Gateshead", *Newcastle Journal*, 11 October 1928.
22. "Royal Train Driven by Four Tired Men", *Reynolds Newspaper*, 21 October 1928.
23. "Wireless Notes", *Newcastle Journal*, 12 October 1928.
24. "Gramophone as Historian", *Yorkshire Post*, 22 February 1929; "Recording of the week: opening the Tyne Bridge", British Library Sound and Vision blog, 15 April 2019, https://blogs.bl.uk/sound-and-vision/2019/04/recording-of-the-week-opening-the-tyne-bridge.html
25. "The King on the Gramophone", *Daily Mirror*, 19 January 1929.
26. "The King: Historic Record", *Swanage Times*, 1 March 1929.
27. "Notes and Incidents", *Newcastle Journal*, 11 October 1928.
28. "Accident on New Tyne Bridge", *Newcastle Journal*, 11 October 1928.
29. "New Bridge", *Newcastle Journal*, 20 October 1928.
30. "The New Tyne Bridge", *Newcastle Journal*, 16 October 1928.
31. "The High Level", *Newcastle Journal*, 12 October 1928.
32. "View from Lofty Heights", *Newcastle Journal*, 15 October 1928.
33. *Newcastle Journal*, 12 October 1928.
34. "King Opens £1,250,000 Bridge", *Daily Mirror*, 11 October 1928.
35. "Cheering Thousands Line Royal Route", *Dundee Courier*, 11 October 1928.

36. "Courage of Tyneside", *Yorkshire Post*, 11 October 1928.
37. "Tyneside's Welcome to the King and Queen," *Newcastle Journal*, 11 October 1928.
38. "What the New Tyne Bridge Signifies", *Newcastle Journal*, 11 October 1928.
39. "Another Fine Model of the Tyne Bridge", *Meccano Magazine*, August 1929.
40. "Blaydon Engine Driver's Model of Tyne Bridge", *Consett Guardian*, 8 March 1929.
41. New Westgate advert, *Newcastle Journal*, 11 October 1928; "The New Tyne Bridge", Newcastle and District Amateur Cinematographers Association (ACA), BFI Player, https://player.bfi.org.uk/free/film/watch-new-tyne-bridge-1928-online
42. "His Majesty's First Talking Picture", *Newcastle Journal*, 11 October 1928.
43. "Symbol of Enterprise", *Newcastle Journal*, 22 October 1928. "Edward Cressy" was a pseudonym of former science teacher Clarence Creasey.
44. Warner Bros ad, *The Bioscope*, 1 March 1928. The first talkie, *The Jazz Singer* with Al Jolson, had premiered in the US in October 1927 but would not be seen in the UK until February 1929.
45. "Talking Film Protests", *London Daily News*, 24 November 1928; "Recent Speech of King George on Movietone Reel", *Hartford Courant* (Connecticut), 1 December 1928.
46. "The King's Speech", *Newcastle Journal*, 26 November 1928; New Oxford Theatre ad, *Guardian*, 8 December 1928.
47. "Anti-Mussolini Scene in Melbourne", *Guardian*, 4 February 1929.
48. "Tyne Bridge Lifts' Formal Opening", *Newcastle Journal*, 15 December 1928. Attendees at the lift-opening ceremony were presented with Dorman Long's silvered medals.
49. "Anderson on the Tyne Bridge", 1930; Measuring Worth, www.measuringworth.com/calculators/ukcompare
50. In his 1930 report, David Anderson provided itemised costs totalling £1,035,000. In a 1928 interview following the opening, he said the bridge cost £1,200,000. Local newspapers gave the total cost in 1928 as "nearly £1,250,000". ("Anderson on the Tyne Bridge", 1930; "A Great Scots Bridge Designer, *Dundee Courier*, 20 October 1928; "Six-Mile Route", *Newcastle Journal*, 10 October 1928).
51. "North's Loss", *Northern Daily Mail*, 12 February 1931; "North's Loss", *Northern Daily Mail*, 29 June 1929. Charles Parsons, another great North East industrialist, also died in 1931, on the day before Arthur Dorman.
52. "Dorman Long's Chairman", *Sheffield Independent*, 10 July, 1931.
53. "Responsible for Tyne Bridge", *Shields Daily News*, 8 September 1938.

54. The Wearmouth Bridge has no towers and its load is borne by rocker bearings rather than hinge pins.

55. "Harbour Bridge", *Sydney Morning Herald*, 25 February 1929.

56. "Harbour Bridge", *Sydney Morning Herald*, 25 March 1929; Sydney Harbour Bridge plaque, see blueplaques.net website, www.blueplaques.net/show_images.php?search_id=id!3393

57. "Harbour Bridge", *Sydney Morning Herald*, 13 March 1929.

58. "Commonwealth Arbitration Court", *Sydney Morning Herald*, 23 March 1929.

59. "Killed on Harbour Bridge", *Newcastle Morning Herald* (New South Wales), 27 March 1929.

60. "Higher Wages", *Sydney Morning Herald*, 28 March 1929.

61. "The Bridge Builders", *Sydney Daily Telegraph*, 26 March 1929.

62. "Gateshead Man Drowned", *Newcastle Journal*, 4 December 1928.

63. "Fall from Train", *Yorkshire Post*, 10 December 1929.

64. "Tyne Bridge No 2 From Mr Webster", *Newcastle Chronicle*, 27 April 1961.

65. "'Father' of the Tyne Bridge is Dead", *Newcastle Journal*, 17 October 1962.

10. CROSSING THE BRIDGE

1. John M. Mackennan, "Family's 600 Mile Trek to Tyneside," *Newcastle Sunday Sun*, 11 August 1935.

2. "Tyneside Unemployed", *Sunderland Echo*, 16 April 1929.

3. "Unearthing Newcastle", *Yorkshire Post*, 20 April 1929.

4. "Seven Wonders", *Yorkshire Post*, 6 February 1931.

5. "Wonderful New Tyne Bridge", Daily Herald (London), 6 October 1928.

6. *Excelsior* (Paris), 11 October 1928; *La Croix Du Nord* (Lille), 10 October 1928; *Los Angeles Times*, 20 May 1928.

7. "Harbour Bridge", *Sydney Morning Herald*, 19 January 1929.

8. "Scientific Principles of Bridge Building", *Western Mail*, 9 December 1932.

9. Around 200 Jarrow Marchers or Crusaders marched from Tyneside to London in October 1936 in a protest against poverty and unemployment.

10. J. Baker White, "New Trades For Old", *The Sphere*, 26 March 1932.

11. "Photographed Tyne Bridge, Fined £5", *Shields Daily News*, 14 November 1939.

12. "Salute Those Who Watched and Waited", *Newcastle Chronicle*, 23 May 1945. The Dornier Do 17 was a twin-engine bomber.

13. "We Saw Flour Mill Bombed", *Newcastle Chronicle*, 18 January 1988. The Old Spiller's Flour Mill on the Close was replaced by the better-known Spiller's Tyne Mill at Walker (once the tallest flour mill in the world), built in 1938 and demolished in 2011.

14. "Three Killed, Over 50 Hurt by Bomb in North-East", *Newcastle Journal*, 3 July 1940.

15. "Tyne Bridge Lights", *Shields Daily News*, 27 September 1941.

16. "Who Do You Think You Are Kidding Mr Hitler", *Newcastle Chronicle*, 9 September 1991.

17. "Symbol of Geordie Grit", *Newcastle Chronicle*, 12 July 1993.

18. "12 Tons of Paint!", *Sunderland Echo*, 21 June 1938.

19. *Shields Daily News*, 20 August 1938.

20. "Bowran's", *Newcastle Journal*, 19 January 1961.

21. "Splash of Colour for the Tyne Bridge", *Newcastle Chronicle*, 23 August 1960.

22. "Cold Grey Tyne Gets a Warm New Colour Scheme", *Newcastle Journal*, 16 August 1961.

23. "What's He Doing on the Tyne Bridge?" *Newcastle Chronicle*, 13 September 1961. The paint was again manufactured by Bowran's, and the workers were employed by Newcastle specialist painters William Latimer & Co. (This "spiderman" reference was a year before the first appearance of the "Spider-Man" comic book character, so neither the Tyne Bridge builders nor painters were being compared to the teenage webslinger.)

24. "Cold Grey Tyne Gets a Warm New Colour Scheme", *Newcastle Journal*, 16 August 1961.

25. "Tyne Bridge Brush-up Plan", *Newcastle Journal*, 4 January 1985.

26. Gateshead Council, Listed Building Consent Planning Application Ref No: 65/85, https://public.gateshead.gov.uk/online-applications/applicationDetails.do?activeTab=summary&keyVal=0006585

27. "Terry Gets Sacked for Bridge Stunt", *Newcastle Journal*, 31 October 1985.

28. "Lands on Car in 84ft Fall", *Daily Mirror*, 11 August 1939.

29. "Four Death Dives in 10 Days", *Gloucester Citizen*, 17 August 1939.

30. "Tyne Bridge Fatality", *Sunderland Echo*, 14 January 1929.

31. "Tyne Bridge Drama", *Northern Daily Mail*, 19 June 1929.

32. "Her Eyes Held Back Death", *Daily Herald*, 10 July 1957; "Girls Saw Man Leap to Death from the Tyne Bridge", *Northern Daily Mail*, 9 July 1957.

33. John Ritson, "The Fatal Fascination of the Coaly Tyne", *Newcastle Journal*, 12 August 1964.

34. Ibid.

35. "Icy Paint Saves Lives", *Newcastle Journal*, 24 November 1972.

36. Samaritans can be contacted at any time by calling 116 123 for free, by texting 07725 909090 or via email to jo@samaritans.org. For more information about contacting or supporting Samaritans go to www.samaritans.org.
37. In March 2022, off-duty PC Lisa Robertson stopped her car on the bridge to help a man in distress. The man was brought to safety. (Maria Cassidy, "Off-Duty Police Officer Hailed", *Newcastle Chronicle*, 9 March 2022).
38. "Boy Falls from Tyne Bridge", *Newcastle Journal*, 21 December 1964.
39. "Shoppers Chased by Bull", *Newcastle Chronicle*, 23 February 1968.
40. "Tyne Bridge Drama", *Newcastle Chronicle*, 26 February 1976.
41. "Lover's Leap Busker Sorry", *Newcastle Journal*, 4 March 1976.
42. Kathryn Riddell, "Tyne Bridge Protester Gives His Stay a Five-Star Review on TripAdvisor", *Newcastle Chronicle*, 29 June 2015, www.chroniclelive.co.uk/news/north-east-news/tyne-bridge-protester-gives-stay-9544394
43. Simon Phipps, *Brutal North: Post-War Modernist Architecture in the North of England*, Tewkesbury: September Publishing, 2020, p 15.
44. Stub sliproads that would have connected to the Bypass Bridge can be found on either side of the river. ("Central Motorway East Bypass", Pathetic Motorways, https://pathetic.org.uk/unbuilt/central_motorway_east_bypass, accessed 26 April 2022).
45. The A167 and A167(M) would have been part of the A1 before that road was also re-routed, initially via the Tyne Tunnel, which was opened in 1967, and later via the Western Bypass, which crosses the Tyne over the purpose-built Blaydon Bridge.
46. "Eddie's Ups and Downs", *Newcastle Chronicle*, 9 October 1978.
47. "We Built the Tyne Bridge", *Newcastle Chronicle*, 12 October 1978.
48. *Newcastle Chronicle*, 9 October 1978.
49. "Bridge of Memories", *Newcastle Chronicle*, 13 October 1978.
50. "I Was in the First Accident", *Newcastle Chronicle*, 19 October 1978.
51. "Thanks For the Spectacular Memories", *Newcastle Chronicle*, 26 October 1978.

11. A CULTURAL ICON

1. *Our Friends in the North*, BBC TV, 1996, BMG DVD released 2002.
2. *Building the New Tyne Bridge Between Newcastle and Gateshead*, Dorman, Long & Co, 1928/1929, via Yorkshire and North East Film Archive, www.yfanefa.com/record/16120. There was a screening at the Classic Picture House in Low Fell, Gateshead. ("Tyne Bridge Film", The Bioscope, 24 April 1929).
3. "Tyne and Wear (Unemployment)", Hansard, HC Deb 19 March 1984

vol 56 cc883–90, https://api.parliament.uk/historic-hansard/com-mons/1984/mar/19/tyne-and-wear-unemployment

4. "Mike Has Returned—With Cameras", *Newcastle Chronicle*, 9 July 1987.

5. Keith Emerson, "Remembering the Making of the Five Bridges Suite 40 Years On", Keith Emerson website, 6 October 2009, www.keithe-merson.com/MiscPages/2009/20091006-FiveBridges.html, accessed 25 April 2022.

6. "Queen of the Tyne", *Newcastle Chronicle*, 6 November 1981.

7. Grace McCombie, *Pevsner Architectural Guides: Newcastle and Gateshead*, New Haven and London: Yale University Press, 2009.

8. Nocturne by Nayan Kulkarni was one of the largest permanent art instal-lations in the country. As of 2022, the lights are not in operation.

9. "Driver Tells of Terror", *Newcastle Chronicle*, 3 December 1986.

10. Nick Loughlin, "Brendan Foster Looks Back at the Origins of the Great North Run", *Northern Echo*, 17 January 2020, www.thenorthernecho.co.uk/sport/18168262.brendan-foster-looks-back-origins-great-north-run

11. *Northern Echo*, 17 January 2020.

12. "Once Upon the Tyne", Great Run, www.greatrun.org/once-upon-the-tyne

13. George Caulkin, email correspondence, 25 April 2022. (Sir Bobby Robson Foundation, http://sirbobbyrobsonfoundation.org.uk).

14. *The Book of the Newcastle Breweries Ltd*, 1928–1929, courtesy of Michael Hewitt. The five points of the blue star represent five amalgamated breweries.

15. *Newcastle Chronicle*, 12 July 1993.

16. Rex Garratt, "Baby Born on Bridge", *Newcastle Chronicle*, 9 November 1984. While Arran was born in the middle of the bridge, his birth was recorded as occurring in Newcastle as his mother was on the way to a Newcastle hospital.

17. Julie Bradford, "Arran Back to his Berth-Place [sic]", *Newcastle Chronicle*, 19 July 1993.

18. McCombie, 2009.

19. This also reflected the fact that Brown Ale was no longer brewed in Newcastle, with production having moved in 2005 to the Federation Brewery in Gateshead. In 2010, production moved to Tadcaster in North Yorkshire, and then in 2017 to the Netherlands, so Newcastle Brown Ale is no longer brewed on Tyneside—although the label does still feature the blue star with the Millennium and Tyne bridges. (In the US, Newcastle Brown Ale has been reinvented as a Chicago-brewed craft ale, retaining a blue star but without the bridges).

20. "Laying Bare the Baltic", BBC Inside Out, 3 October 2005, www.bbc.

co.uk/insideout/northeast/series8/week5.shtml. Chris Burden went on to produce another work, "Tyne Bridge Kit", a dresser drawer unit containing components of a model bridge. In 2003, the Baltic displayed a model of the Tyne Bridge built by 3D Design students from Newcastle College out of pretzels. (Joanne Butcher, "85 Years of the Tyne Bridge: Landmark's a Star Attraction", *Newcastle Chronicle*, 27 February 2013, www.chroniclelive.co.uk/news/local-news/85-years-tyne-bridge-land-marks-1724388).

21. *Daily Telegraph*, 24 August 2002.

12. THE PRIDE OF TYNESIDE

 1. "The Tyne Bridge", Tripadvisor, www.tripadvisor.co.uk/ShowUser Reviews-g186394-d213822-r524314625-The_Tyne_Bridge-Newcastle_upon_Tyne_Tyne_and_Wear_England.html, accessed 21 April 2022.
 2. Jane Drinkard, "A Sunny Saturday at Brooklyn's Most Instagrammable Intersection", The Cut, April 2019, www.thecut.com/2019/04/the-most-instagrammable-street-corner-in-dumbo-brooklyn.html, accessed 27 April 2022.
 3. Space Invaders: Newcastle, www.space-invaders.com/world/newcas-tle, accessed 28 April 2022. Invader placed around 25 characters around Newcastle as part of his Space Invaders project.
 4. David Morton, "The Tyne Bridge: Recalling the One Worker Who Fell…", *Newcastle Chronicle*, 5 February 2016.
 5. Ray Marshall, "Marking Memory of Tyne Bridge Legends", *Newcastle Chronicle*, 3 October 2003, www.chroniclelive.co.uk/news/north-east-news/marking-memory-tyne-bridge-legends-1664151
 6. Karl Lattimer, online correspondence, 28 April 2022.
 7. Helen Rose, online correspondence, January to 28 April 2022.
 8. "Tyne Bridge—Kittiwake Colonies", Kittiwakes upon the Tyne, www.tynekittiwakes.org.uk/tyne-kittiwake-colonies/tyne-bridge-kittiwakes, accessed 27 April 2022.
 9. Paul Buskin, Kittiwakes upon Tyne (www.tynekittiwakes.org.uk), email correspondence, 3 May 2022.
10. "Security Tightened Following Illegal Tyne Bridge Rave", ITV News, 15 January 2017, www.itv.com/news/tyne-tees/2017–01–15/security-tightened-following-illegal-tyne-bridge-rave
11. Planning Application Summary, Newcastle City Council, https://publicaccessapplications.newcastle.gov.uk/online-applications/application-Details.do?activeTab=summary&keyVal=PG4V84BSIZ700, accessed 22 April 2022.
12. Unit44, "Hidden in Plain Sight", www.unit-44.com/exhibitions/hid-

den-in-plain-sight, accessed 3 May 2022. A decade earlier, in 2010 as part of the AV Festival, North Shields artist Will Schrimshaw created an audio installation, Space Against Itself, which manipulated sound-waves within the north tower to emphasise the building's acoustic energy.

13. "Eighth Iconic Bridge for River Tyne", *Newcastle Chronicle*, 16 July 2008, www.chroniclelive.co.uk/news/north-east-news/eighth-iconic-bridge-river-tyne-1472421

14. The arena will also be named the Sage, as the Tyneside-based account-ing software company has the naming rights for both venues.

15. Plans for a nearby 18-storey tower block development have also been opposed, partly because they will spoil another great view of the Tyne Bridge and its surrounds, from the lofty and much-cherished beer gar-den of the Free Trade Inn.

16. Jamie Brown, email correspondence, 25 April 2022.

17. Jamie Brown, *The Bonny Tyne Bridge*, 2021, lyrics reproduced with kind permission.

18. Chi Onwurah, email correspondence, 2 May 2022.

19. Planning Application Details, Gateshead Council, DC/22/00203/LBC, https://public.gateshead.gov.uk/online-applications/applicationDe-tails.do?activeTab=details&keyVal=R7R9DLHKL9T00; Newcastle City Council, 2022/0305/01/LBC, https://portal.newcastle.gov.uk/plan-ning/index.html?fa=getApplication&id=127619

20. Jack Brooke-Battersby, "Tyne Bridge Maintenance Bid Approved", Newcastle City Council, 3 June 2022, www.newcastle.gov.uk/citylife-news/council/tyne-bridge-maintenance-bid-approved

21. George Caulkin, email correspondence, 25 April 2022.

22. Steve Luck, email correspondence, 30 March 2022.

23. Ben Holland, email correspondence, 3 May 2022.

24. Dave Morton, email correspondence, 27 April 2022.

25. Andrew Hankinson, email correspondence, 29 April 2022.

26. Michael Chaplin, email correspondence, 25 April 2022.

27. Ian Hardie, online correspondence, 6 January 2022.

28. Christine Hutchinson, online correspondence, 5 April 2022.

29. David Simmons, online correspondence, 5 April 2022.

30. Mike Watson, online correspondence, 5 April 2022.

31. Emma Jane Stanley, online correspondence, 26 January 2022.

32. Derek Richardson, online correspondence, 6 January 2022.

33. Victoria Parkinson, email correspondence, 11 May 2022.

LIST OF IMAGES

Cover image adapted by Paul Brown, based on an illustration from *Meccano Magazine*, March 1931, Meccano Ltd, Liverpool, courtesy of Timothy Edwards, Meccano Index, (www.meccanoindex.co.uk)

01a Pons Aelius Roman altars, © Paul Brown.
Roman altars dedicated to Neptune and Oceanus (circa 122) found in the Tyne at the location of the Pons Aelius Roman bridge in 1875 and 1903. Held at the Great North Museum: Hancock and illuminated as part of the "Roman Britain in Colour" exhibition, 2022.

01b Old Tyne Bridge Blue Stone, © Paul Brown.
The Blue Stone (circa 1400) was set into the roadway of the Old Tyne Bridge and then the Georgian Tyne Bridge to mark the boundary between Newcastle and Durham. Held at the Castle Keep, Newcastle Castle.

02a The Old Tyne Bridge, 1739, Newcastle City Library Photographic Collection.
This image was dedicated to Mayor of Newcastle Cuthbert Fenwick by John Hilbert, probably in 1739. Gateshead is on the left, Newcastle on the right.

02b The ruins of the Old Tyne Bridge, 1771, Newcastle City Library Photographic Collection.
The remains of the Old Tyne Bridge following the Great Flood of 1771 in an image inscribed to Newcastle Mayor John Blackett by historian John Brand in 1772. Newcastle is on the left.

03a The Georgian Tyne Bridge, Newcastle City Library Photographic Collection, restored by Md Mazedul Islam.
The Georgian Tyne Bridge was built from 1774 to 1781 and demolished in 1868.

03b The Georgian Tyne Bridge and High Level Bridge, Newcastle City Library Photographic Collection, restored by Md Mazedul Islam.
The newly-built High Level (opened 1849) towers over the old Georgian Tyne Bridge in a photo from circa 1850s, taken from Gateshead.

04a The High Level Bridge and Georgian Tyne Bridge, circa 1865, Newcastle City Library Photographic Collection, restored by Md Mazedul Islam.
Boys play in a rowing boat in front of the High Level and the Georgian Tyne Bridge in a photo taken from the Gateshead riverbank.

04b The Temporary Tyne Bridge and High Level Bridge, Newcastle City Library Photographic Collection, restored by Md Mazedul Islam.
The Temporary Tyne Bridge was a wooden structure used during the demolition of the Georgian Tyne Bridge (1868) and the opening of the Swing Bridge (1876).

05a The Swing Bridge and High Level Bridge, 1887, Newcastle City Library Photographic Collection.
The Swing Bridge was built at the site of the Pons Aelius, Old Tyne Bridge and Georgian Tyne Bridge between 1873 and 1876.

05b The Swing Bridge, 1889, Newcastle City Library Photographic Collection.
Photographed with Newcastle and several still-surviving buildings in the background, including the Castle Keep, Cathedral of St Nicholas, Moot Hall, Fish Market (Neptune House) and Guildhall.

06a Tommy on the Bridge, Newcastle City Library Photographic Collection, restored by Md Mazedul Islam.
Tommy Ferens, known as Blind Tommy or Tommy on the Bridge, stood on the Georgian Tyne Bridge and then the Swing Bridge entertaining passers-by and asking for small change.

06b Tommy attracts a crowd, Newcastle City Library Photographic Collection, restored by Md Mazedul Islam.
Tommy attracts a crowd on the Swing Bridge in this photo taken circa 1905, two years before his death.

07a The Hell Gate Bridge, circa 1917, via Wikimedia Commons.
The Hell Gate Bridge under construction over the Hell Gate, a strait of the East River, in New York City. The bridge was designed by Gustav Lindenthal.

07b The Sydney Harbour Bridge, 1932, via Wikimedia Commons.
The Sydney Harbour Bridge under construction, New South Wales, Australia. Both the Sydney Harbour and Hell Gate Bridges share a very similar spandrel arch design. Designed by Ralph Freeman.

08a Tyne Bridge towers under construction, 19 Sept 1928, Tyne & Wear Archives & Museums.
A view of the Tyne Bridge under construction showing the distinctive crescent arch design that sets the Tyne apart from the Hell Gate and Sydney Harbour bridges. Designed by Ralph Freeman. Photo taken by James Bacon & Co for Dorman Long.

08b Ralph Freeman, via Wikimedia Commons.
Freeman was the consulting engineer for contractors Dorman Long on both the Sydney Harbour Bridge and the Tyne Bridge, and he produced the original designs for both.

09a Inside the first Tyne Bridge caisson, *North Mail Newcastle Daily Chronicle*, 8 March 1926.
Work supervisors and engineers photographed inside a pressurised caisson, used to sink the foundations for the Tyne Bridge. This was the first caisson to be sunk, on the Gateshead side in March 1926. Left to right: unknown, James Geddie (assistant contractor's agent for Dorman Long), James Ruck (contractor's agent for Dorman Long), Jack Hamilton (assistant chief resident engineer for Mott, Hay & Anderson), RF Hindmarsh (chief engineer for the Tyne Improvement Commission).

09b Inside the last Tyne Bridge caisson, *North Mail Newcastle Daily Chronicle*, 11 June 1926.
Inside the last of the four caissons, sunk in June 1926. Compressed air workers fill the working chamber with concrete from a skip.

10a Early work at Gateshead, Newcastle City Library Photographic Collection.
Work at the Gateshead approach for the bridge involved the building of an approach embankment with retaining walls, the erection

of support pillars, removal of part of St Mary's churchyard and the demolition of much of Bottle Bank, including the Steamboat Inn. Photo circa January 1927.

10b Work progresses at Gateshead, 10 Aug 1927, Tyne & Wear Archives & Museums.
The Gateshead embankment has been built and the steel approach span has been rolled out over its support columns. A temporary cradle has been built to support the first pieces of the Tyne Bridge's arch. Photo taken by James Bacon & Co for Dorman Long.

11a The Newcastle side of the arch, 2 Feb 1928, Tyne & Wear Archives & Museums.
A view captured during construction from the Gateshead side of the arch (note the shadow). Taken by James Bacon & Co.

11b The new bridge rises over the Tyne, 2 Feb 1928, Tyne & Wear Archives & Museums.
Viewed from Gateshead, the two halves of the arch are perhaps 150 feet apart, supported by huge cables and towers. Taken by James Bacon on the same day as the previous photo.

12a View of the Tyne Bridge from Gateshead, 9 Feb 1928, R Johnston & Sons postcard no 32.
The two halves of the arch grow closer. St Mary's Church is prominently shown. From Robert Johnston & Sons of Gateshead's "Monarch" series of postcards.

12b View from Newcastle Quayside, 9 Feb 1928, R Johnston & Sons postcard no 31.
The two halves of the arch, the support cables and the huge cranes on each arch-half are visible. Another Johnston postcard.

13a The arch nears completion, 23 Feb 1928, Tyne & Wear Archives & Museums.
The arch is almost complete as a final member is lowered into place above the Tyne. Photo by James Bacon.

13b The two halves of the arch almost meet, 23 Feb 1928, Tyne & Wear Archives & Museums.
The final member has been lowered into place, leaving a 9-inch gap. Two days later, the arch will be closed. Photo by James Bacon.

14a Tyne Bridge workers on a crane, 23 Feb 1928, Tyne & Wear Archives & Museums.
Workers gather on a crane near the apex of the Tyne Bridge. Near the middle of the bottom row in the light jacket is "spiderman" Kit Lattimer. Thomas McCullough, a plater, is second from the right in the second row. Photo by James Bacon.

14b Tyne Bridge construction staff, 2 March 1928, Tyne & Wear Archives & Museums.
Construction staff employed by Dorman Long & Co Ltd. Standing left to right: J Morgan (foreman mason), W Kingston (cashier), K Addison (general foreman), F Conaron (chief timekeeper), F Atkinson (chief storekeeper). Seated left to right: OTR Leishman (engineer no 2), James Geddie (chief assistant), James Ruck (contractor's agent), GIB Gowring (engineer no 1), EWC Symes (engineer no 3), W Pattison (foremen carpenter). Seated on ground: FDS Sandeman (junior).

15a Tyne Bridge workers on cables, 1928, author's collection, courtesy family members.
Workers balance on support cables at the Newcastle end of the Tyne Bridge, with the Side and mercantile buildings below. The worker in the white jacket with his cap on backwards is Kit Lattimer. Next to him is Sammie Cassidy. From the Dorman Long collection, likely taken by James Bacon in early 1928.

15b Tyne Bridge workers, circa 1928, author's collection, courtesy family members.
A team photo showing workers of various ages. John Webster is on the far right of the front row. John Morgan is at the far right of the back row.

16a View from the High Level Bridge, 6 March 1928, Tyne & Wear Archives & Museums.
A view of the Tyne Bridge taken by Bacon with Newcastle and the Cathedral on the left and Gateshead and St Mary's on the right. The support cables are now slack as the closed arch is bearing its own load.

16b Looking along the Tyne Bridge, 22 May 1928, Tyne & Wear Archives & Museums.

View along the Tyne Bridge towards Newcastle as work continues on its roadway, photo by Bacon.

17a Tyne Bridge towers under construction, 6 Sept 1928, Tyne & Wear Archives & Museums.
The towers under construction, shot from Newcastle by Bacon just over a month before the grand opening.

17b View from Newcastle Quayside, 6 Sept 1928, R Johnston & Sons postcard no 49.
The Tyne Bridge is almost complete, with the road deck installed and the support cables removed. The Gateshead tower is incomplete and the cranes have yet to be removed.

18a Tyne Bridge roadway nearing completion, 25 Sept 1928, James Bacon & Co no 250, Tyne & Wear Archives & Museums.
Taken from Gateshead by Bacon two weeks before the opening ceremony. Note the tram tracks and cables.

18b Opening of the Tyne Bridge by His Majesty the King, 10 Oct 1928, Johnston & Sons postcard.
The Royal Landau crosses the bridge towards Gateshead after the opening ceremony. Note the onlookers on St Mary's Church.

19a Herding sheep under the Tyne Bridge, Newcastle City Library Photographic Collection.
Taken at Sandhill, circa 1930s, photographer unknown.

19b Tyne Bridge from Gateshead, Newcastle City Library Photographic Collection.
Photo of the completed bridge, circa 1930s. Note the surviving buildings on Bottle Bank to the left, and the public convenience building at Number One Church Street on the right.

20a Aerial view of the Tyne Bridge, circa 1929, Newcastle City Library Photographic Collection.
This view from the Gateshead side of the Tyne shows the Newcastle approach to the bridge running straight up Pilgrim Street, before the creation of Swan House Roundabout.

20b Aerial view of the Tyne, Swing and High Level bridges, 1995, Newcastle City Library Photographic Collection.

A later view showing the Newcastle approach curving under Swan House Roundabout towards the Central Motorway. Note "the Boat" (*Tuxedo Royale*) under the Tyne Bridge.

21a The Tyne Bridge's alternative colour scheme, 1985, Newcastle City Library Photographic Collection.
Pictured shortly before a repaint restored it to green, the bridge was blue, grey and red from the 1960s through to 1985. Note the Boat and, in the background, the white Metro Bridge.

21b Quayside Sunday Market, 1986, Newcastle City Library Photographic Collection.
The centuries-old Quayside market has existed since the era of the Old Tyne Bridge. Pictured here beneath the newly-painted Tyne Bridge.

22a *Payroll*, 1961 (dir Sidney Hayers).
The gang's truck makes a U-turn on the Tyne Bridge.

22b *The Likely Lads*, 1976 (dir Michael Tuchner).
Rodney Bewes as Bob Ferris under the blue Tyne Bridge.

23a *Stormy Monday*, 1988 (dir Mike Figgis).
Tommy Lee Jones and Sting face off on the High Level Bridge.

23b *Our Friends in the North*, 1996 (dir Simon Cellan Jones).
Daniel Craig as Geordie Peacock crosses the Tyne Bridge.

24a1 Newcastle Brown Ale, photo by Sam Cavenagh, licensed under CC BY 2.0, www.flickr.com/photos/cavenagh/8016873768
The Tyne Bridge features on the Newcastle Breweries Blue Star.

24a2 Newcastle v Liverpool programme, 1984, © Paul Brown.
Kevin Keegan wears the Tyne Bridge on the Blue Star on the black and white stripes.

24b Runners on the Tyne Bridge, photo by Jon Hill, licensed under CC BY 2.0, www.flickr.com/photos/padsbrother/5008615898
Taken during the 30th Great North Run, 19 September 2010.

25a Angel of the North, © Paul Brown.
Another icon of the North-East, Gateshead's Anthony Gormley sculpture was erected in 1998.

side of the carriageway is another plaque dedicated to the designers and builders.

31a Tyne Bridge at night, photo by Chris Robson, licensed under CC BY 2.0, www.flickr.com/photos/silverfox1969/3920046894
The bridge illuminated at night in a photo taken in 2009.

31b Tyne Bridge in reduced circumstances, 2022, © Paul Brown.
Rusty and in need of refurbishment in early 2022.

32a View from the High Level Bridge, © Paul Brown.
The Tyne Bridge and the Swing Bridge (and the Millennium Bridge) from the High Level.

32b View from the Castle Keep, © Paul Brown.
The Tyne Bridge from the battlement roof of the Castle Keep at Newcastle Castle.

SELECT BIBLIOGRAPHY

Books and Reports

Ammann, O.H., "The Hell Gate Arch Bridge and Approaches...", *Transactions of the American Society of Civil Engineers*, vol. 82, no. 1, 1918.

Anderson, David, "Anderson on the Tyne Bridge, Newcastle", *Minutes of the Proceedings of the Institution of Civil Engineers*, vol. 230, 1930.

Bourne, Henry, *The History of Newcastle upon Tyne*, Newcastle: John White, 1736.

Bruce, J. Collingwood, *The Roman Wall*, 2nd ed., London: John Russell Smith, 1853.

——————, "The Three Bridges Over the Tyne at Newcastle", *Archaeologia Aeliana*, vol. 10, 1885.

Clephan, James, "Old Tyne Bridge and its Story", *Archaeologia Aeliana*, vol. 12, 1887.

Ellwood, Steve, *River Tyne*, Stroud: Amberley Publishing, 2015.

Freeman, Ralph, "The Design of a Two-hinged Spandrel-braced Steel Arch", *Minutes of the Proceedings of the Institution of Civil Engineers*, vol. 167, 1907.

Graham, Frank, *The Bridges of Northumberland and Durham*, Newcastle: Frank Graham, 1975.

Jackson, Dan, *The Northumbrians: North-East England and Its People*, London: C. Hurst & Co., 2019.

Linsley, Stafford M., *Spanning the Tyne*, Newcastle Libraries & Information Service, 1998.

Mackenzie, Eneas, *A Descriptive and Historical Account of the Town and County of Newcastle upon Tyne*, Newcastle: Mackenzie and Dent, 1827.

Manders, Frank & Potts, Richard, *Crossing the Tyne*, Newcastle: Tyne Bridge Publishing, 2001.

McCombie, Grace, *Pevsner Architectural Guides: Gateshead and Newcastle*, New Haven & London: Yale University Press, 2009.

SELECT BIBLIOGRAPHY

McCullough, David, *The Great Bridge*, New York: Touchstone, 1972.

Oliphant, James, *The Case of Mr James Oliphant, Surgeon...*, Newcastle: B. Fleming, 1768.

Rennison, R.W., *Civil Engineering Heritage: Northern England*, London: Thomas Telford, 1996.

Smeaton, John & Wooler, John, *A Report Relative to the Tyne Bridge*, Newcastle: Thomas Saint, 1772.

An Account of the Great Floods in 1771 and 1815..., Newcastle: Emerson Charnley, 1818.

Bridges: A Few Examples of the Work of a Pioneer Firm in the Manufacture of Steel and Steelwork, Dorman, Long & Co Ltd, 1930.

"Discussion on Bridges", *Minutes of the Proceedings of the Institution of Civil Engineers*, vol. 230, 1930.

"Discussion on Sydney Harbour Bridge", *Minutes of the Proceedings of the Institution of Civil Engineers*, vol. 238, 1934.

Newspapers and Periodicals

Tyneside: *The Chronicle / Daily Chronicle / Evening Chronicle / North Mail* ("Newcastle Chronicle"); *The Journal* ("Newcastle Journal"); *Gateshead Observer*; *Newcastle Courant*; *Shields Daily News*; *Shields Gazette*; *Sunday Sun*.

Also: *Daily News*; *Guardian*; *Illustrated London News*; *Journal of the Institution of Civil Engineers*; *Meccano Magazine*; *Monthly Chronicle of North County Lore and Legend*; *New Civil Engineer*; *Northern Echo*; *Sydney Morning Herald*; *Sydney Sun*.

Websites

Historic England, https://historicengland.org.uk

ICE (Institution of Civil Engineers) Virtual Library, www.icevirtualli-brary.com

Kittiwakes upon the Tyne, www.tynekittiwakes.org.uk

Measuring Worth, www.measuringworth.com

Meccano Index, www.meccanoindex.co.uk

Ordnance Survey maps, National Library of Scotland, https://maps.nls.uk/os

Oxford Dictionary of National Biography, www.oxforddnb.com

Society of Antiquaries, Newcastle upon Tyne, www.newcastle-antiquar-ies.org.uk

SELECT BIBLIOGRAPHY

Structurae, https://structurae.net

Vision of Britain Through Time, www.visionofbritain.org.uk

Genealogy sources: Ancestry (library edition), www.ancestrylibraryedition.co.uk; Family Search, www.familysearch.org; Find My Past, www.findmypast.co.uk

Newspaper archives: British Newspaper Archive, www.britishnewspaper-archive.co.uk, Newspapers.com, www.newspapers.com, Trove, https://trove.nla.gov.au/newspaper

Audio/Visual

"Building the New Tyne Bridge Between Newcastle and Gateshead", Dorman, Long & Co, 1928/1929, Yorkshire and North East Film Archive, www.yfanefa.com/record/16120

"King George V Makes Speech...", 1928, British Movietone YouTube channel, www.youtube.com/watch?v=DVwHaIVgDTk

"New Tyne Bridge", Pathé, 1928, British Pathé, www.britishpathe.com/video/new-tyne-bridge

"Recording of the Week: Opening the Tyne Bridge", British Library Sound and Vision blog, 15 April 2019, https://blogs.bl.uk/sound-and-vision/2019/04/recording-of-the-week-opening-the-tyne-bridge.html

"The New Tyne Bridge", Newcastle and District Amateur Cinemato-graphers Association (ACA), BFI Player, https://player.bfi.org.uk/free/film/watch-new-tyne-bridge-1928-online

ACKNOWLEDGEMENTS

Much like the Tyne Bridge, this book was built with the assistance and support of an army of grafters—friends, family, editors, artists—who helped punch its rivets into place.

Many thanks to Sebastian Ballard, Jamie Brown, Paul Buskin, George Caulkin, Michael Chaplin, Michael Dwyer and all at Hurst, Timothy Edwards, Andrew Hankinson, Ian Hardie, Michael Hewitt, Ben Holland, Christine Hutchinson, Mohammad Mazedul Islam, Steve Kennedy, Karl Lattimer, Hazel Lambert, Steve Luck, Dave Morton, Sarah Mulligan, Chi Onwurah, Victoria Parkinson, Richard Pike, Max Regan, Helen Rose, David Silk, David Simmons, Emma Jane Stanley, Mike Watson, Edward Wealleans, John Webster and everyone else who shared their thoughts and memories of the Tyne Bridge, told me the stories of their ancestors, assisted with research and images, and helped publish, promote and place this book into your hands.

I'm grateful for our invaluable libraries, particularly Newcastle Libraries, Edinburgh Libraries, and the British Library at Boston Spa, plus fine institutions the Great North Museum: Hancock, the Discovery Museum, Newcastle Castle and Tyne & Wear Archives & Museums. Thanks to all of their staff.

Much of this book was written during the Great Unpleasantness and resulting lockdowns, during which online archives were a vital resource. I should acknowledge in particular the British Newspaper Archive, Newspapers.com, Ancestry, and Family Search, and their staff and scanning machines.

Genuine thanks to readers, reviewers and booksellers who have supported this book and my previous efforts. Every page turn is appreciated. Every tweet, email and recommendation, too.

Lastly, some personal love and thanks. To my mam and dad, Carol and Geoff, my most eager readers. And finally, to Louise for

ACKNOWLEDGEMENTS

accompanying me on this journey, from the Brooklyn Bridge to the Tyne Bridge, this book could not have been written without you.

Paul Brown, 2022
A Faithful Son of Father Tyne

INDEX

INDEX

INDEX

INDEX

INDEX

Morgan, John, 191

Morpeth, Northumberland, 1

Morral, Harry, 112

Morton, Dave, 188

Motherwell Bridge Co, 70

motor cars, 53, 54–5

Mott MacDonald, 145

Mott, Basil, 61, 65, 77–9, 114, 121, 122, 136

Mott, Hay & Anderson, 3, 61, 65, 71, 77–80, 86, 88, 143, 145, 171, 190

Mott, Mark, 79

Movietone, 142, 145, 167

Muller, Norman, 119

Muller, Norman, 190

Murtha, Patricia 'Tish', 193

music, 169–70, 187–8

Mussolini, Benito, 142

Mylne, Robert, 37

Nail, Jimmy, 169, 192

National Health Service (NHS), 125

National Wages and Conditions Council, 59

Nazi Germany (1933–45), 153–6

Nelson's Column, London, 2

Nepos, Aulus Platorius, 10

Neptune altar, 14–15

Neville, Mike, 192

New Bridge Committee, 60, 61

New High-Level Bridge and its Origin, The (Webster), 122

New Westgate cinema, Newcastle, 141

New Year's Eve, 184

New York, United States

Brooklyn Bridge, 6, 42, 84, 110–11, 119

Hell Gate Bridge, 3, 67–70, 73, 75, 79, 86, 177

Manhattan Bridge, 181

Queensboro Bridge, 67, 86

Newcastle, Tyne and Wear, 1, 2, 3

All Saints Church, 8, 89, 102, 115, 131, 140, 190

Black Gate, 21, 60

Blue Stone demarcation, 25, 30, 34, 35, 37, 45, 48, 50

Castle Keep, 1, 8, 13, 17, 21, 43, 60, 115, 140, 174, 179

Central Library, 193

Central Station, 193

Chamber of Commerce, 54, 58, 81, 122

chares, 185–6

Civil War Siege (1644), 23, 26

Council, 55, 58, 61, 62, 71, 190

Coxlodge, 105

Eagles, 193

Exhibition Park, 34

Eye Hospital, 141

Moot Hall, 131

Pilgrim Street, 54, 56, 58, 61, 88–9, 104–5, 145, 149, 162

river crossing, purpose as, 3

Royal Arcade, 163

Royal Victoria Infirmary, 85, 112, 125, 138, 139, 158

St Nicholas' Cathedral, 1, 8, 13, 43, 60, 115, 140, 152, 174

Theatre Royal, 40

INDEX

INDEX